LANGUAGE, MEDIA AND CULTURE

Language, Media and Culture: The Key Concepts is an authoritative and indispensable guide to the essential terminology of the overlapping fields of Language, Media and Culture. Designed to give students and researchers 'tools for thinking with' in addressing major issues of communicative change in the 21st century, the book covers over 500 concepts as well as containing an extensive bibliography to aid further study. Subjects covered include:

- Authenticity
- Truthiness
- Structures of feeling
- Turn-taking
- Transitivity
- Validity claims

With cross referencing and further reading provided throughout, this book provides an inclusive map of the discipline, and is an essential reference work for students in communication, media, journalism and cultural studies, as well as for students of language and linguistics.

Martin Montgomery is Emeritus Professor of Literary Linguistics at the University of Macau, China, where he was formerly Dean of the Faculty of Arts and Humanities and Head of the Departments of English and of Communication. He is also Visiting Professor at the University of Strathclyde, UK, where he served as Head of the Department of English Studies and Director of the Scottish Centre for Journalism Studies.

LANGUAGE, MEDIA AND CULTURE

The Key Concepts

Martin Montgomery

LONDON AND NEW YORK

First published 2019
by Routledge
2 Park Square, Milton Park, Abingdon, Oxon OX14 4RN

and by Routledge
711 Third Avenue, New York, NY 10017

Routledge is an imprint of the Taylor & Francis Group, an informa business

© 2019 Martin Montgomery

The right of Martin Montgomery to be identified as author of this work has been asserted by him in accordance with sections 77 and 78 of the Copyright, Designs and Patents Act 1988.

All rights reserved. No part of this book may be reprinted or reproduced or utilised in any form or by any electronic, mechanical, or other means, now known or hereafter invented, including photocopying and recording, or in any information storage or retrieval system, without permission in writing from the publishers.

Trademark notice: Product or corporate names may be trademarks or registered trademarks, and are used only for identification and explanation without intent to infringe.

British Library Cataloguing-in-Publication Data
A catalogue record for this book is available from the British Library

Library of Congress Cataloging-in-Publication Data
Names: Montgomery, Martin, author.
Title: Language, media and culture : the key concepts / Martin Montgomery.
Description: Abingdon, Oxon ; New York : Routledge, 2018. | Series: Routledge key guides | Includes bibliographical references and index.
Identifiers: LCCN 2018003937| ISBN 9781138047051 (hardback) | ISBN 9781138047075 (pbk.) | ISBN 9781351018821 (e-book)
Subjects: LCSH: Language and culture. | Mass media and language. | Communication and culture.
Classification: LCC P35 .M66 2018 | DDC 306.44—dc23
LC record available at https://lccn.loc.gov/2018003937

ISBN: 978-1-138-04705-1 (hbk)
ISBN: 978-1-138-04707-5 (pbk)
ISBN: 978-1-351-01882-1 (ebk)

Typeset in Bembo
by Apex CoVantage, LLC

CONTENTS

Introduction vi
Acknowledgements ix
How to use this book x
List of key concepts xi

THE KEY CONCEPTS 1

Bibliography 142
Index 154

INTRODUCTION

It is widely accepted that there has been a revolution over the last two or three decades in media of communication. The World Wide Web was implemented and the internet came online as the last century gave way to the present. Terrestrial broadcasting was replaced by digital, and the use of social media became widespread. Clearly, technological developments in the media – such as the computerisation, digitalisation and miniaturisation of communicative devices – have played an enormous role in these changes. In less than three decades the capacity for sending and receiving messages in many different ways across enormous distances almost instantaneously has changed radically, effectively ending the tyranny of distance.

While the capacity to communicate has changed, so also has its character. In the long history of communicative change, we can distinguish at least three important phases: print (preceded crucially by writing); broadcasting; and the new, digital media. Each phase, of course, overlaps with previous phases and incorporates qualities from the past; but the phases remain distinct from each, defined in part, at least, by virtue of their different technologies: the mechanical technologies of print; the electrical technologies of broadcasting; and the electronic, digital technologies of the new media.

The characteristic kinds of technology at stake in these three phases, however, are intimately bound up with different kinds of cultural and social arrangements that constitute in each case the contexts of communication. Thus, around print a publishing industry evolved to bring print communication to its audiences, who in turn tend to read it in isolated, privatised fashion. Broadcasting, on the other hand, required significant investment in analogue equipment and technical expertise along with an infrastructure of wireless transmitters to reach mass audiences, who often experienced output in domestic settings. This in turn is very different from new media where communication takes place in pairs or in networks, as well as to larger audiences, in which actors produce as well as receive, often with no more than a hand-held device. Very crudely, in the evolution of these phases of communication the movement has been from one-or-few-to-many to a situation of many-communicating-to-many.

These transitions cannot but be accompanied by profound changes, not only in the cultural context of communication, but also in the nature of the acts of communication that take place in these settings. If, for instance, the characteristic modes of broadcasting rested on showing and telling, then the characteristic modes of the new, social media tend to be reaction and argument. To begin, however, to capture what is different and characteristic about one phase of communication over another we cannot afford to ignore what lies at the centre of nearly every act of communication: it is founded on the word, whether it be spoken or written, with images or without. For language – either in itself or by implication – forms the basis of all communication whatever the medium, whatever the technology.

It is for this reason that this book tries to bring together concepts related to language, to media and to culture in the belief that only by thinking through the relations between them will we be able to understand the enormous changes in communication taking place presently at an unprecedented pace. For if communication is at the core this book's concerns, there is also, I believe, a growing recognition that only when language, media and culture can be understood in an integrated way can we satisfactorily address the major communicative issues of our time.

At present, there is no precisely unified field of study or single discipline to do this. Instead, increasing numbers of scholars, students and researchers find themselves working along the interfaces between cultural and communication studies, linguistics and sociolinguistics, and media and internet studies. This book, then, is devised as a guide to help those, perhaps already acquainted with one field of study as student or researcher, to engage with another. Thus, it draws necessarily on several fields, from sociology to linguistics, from cultural and media studies to journalism studies, sometimes simply to provide a quick definition, sometimes with the aim of providing tools for thinking with. Sometimes terms are clearly technical but with a well-established use within a field or discipline – such as *scopophilia* or *habitus*. Sometimes, however, they are concepts which face two ways, with wide currency in everyday discourse on the one hand, and with an emerging, more specialised sense in the study of communication on the other – concepts such as *sincerity* or *authenticity*.

Most entries – almost all – try to provide for the disciplinary provenance of a term. This is followed immediately by a very brief definition, subsequently expanded. The entry then offers pointers to related concepts and, finally, suggestions for further reading.

In this way it is hoped that the book will provide a field guide to the uninitiated who wants to steer a course through the fields of language, media and culture, but equally that it might provide bridges between fields for those who want to increase their range of conceptual tools for addressing significant aspects of our changing world of communication.

Martin Montgomery
November 2016,
Glasgow

ACKNOWLEDGEMENTS

I would like to thank many people.

Thank you to Professor John Laver, eminent scientist and wise and erudite scholar, whose persistent invitations got me started.

Thanks to many students on the MA in English at the University of Macau whose freshness of vision led me to concepts I would not otherwise have encountered.

Thank you to my recent Ph.D. students, Daniel, Hongqiang, Tong, Susie and Alice, who taught me so much – more than they will ever guess.

Thank you to my then post-doc, Sharanya Jayawickrama, who in the early stages of the book wrote such elegant and succinct entries. She provided me a model that I never managed to live up to. Her entries included in this final draft are designated with the initials *SJ*.

Thank you to the University of Macau, not least for my sabbatical period in 2015, but for much else as well, and especially to my colleagues in the Department of English and the Department of Communication for providing always such a congenial and intellectually stimulating academic environment.

Thank you to the University of Strathclyde in Glasgow for providing me a second academic home during 2015 as Visiting Professor, and especially to Dr Michael Higgins and to Mo who graciously arranged it and looked after me.

And, last of all, but by no means least, thank you to Nadia Seemungal-Owen and Elizabeth Cox for getting me to the finishing line.

HOW TO USE THIS BOOK

The layout of entries and the accompanying notations are illustrated below.

                grammatical form   disciplinary origins of term

                                       preliminary short definition

context of situation (*np*) (LINGUISTICS) the extra-linguistic context of an utterance. The term derives from the work of the British functional linguist. M.A. K. Halliday, which rested on the claim that the selection of linguistic form for an utterance is partially determined by features of its context of situation. Relevant features of context typically amount to more than the physical environment or setting of the utterance, but include more especially factors such as the type of social relationship involved, the nature of the medium adopted, the kind of activity in which the utterance is embedded, and the topic being conveyed. Halliday believes that, as users of the language we are constantly making and recognizing adjustments in the linguistic selection of form, depending upon the context of situation. Thus, an utterance such as 'I observed the suspect proceeding east along Sauchiehall Street' is unlikely to occur outside courtroom testimony: in less formal contexts of situation the same idea is likely to be rendered as '1 saw 'im goin' towards town'. Contexts of situation vary from those that are relatively open and negotiable in character (such as family or peer group conversation) to those of a more institutionalized and closed nature (such as court room proceedings, media interviews, classroom lessons, and so on). Any society or social formation will feature a number of common, recurring but salient contexts of situation, which Halliday termed *typical* contexts of situation. The totality of these comprise that society's *context of culture*. In this way the term context of situation confirms the sociological and anthropological orientation of Halliday's work, with context of situation providing a crucial mediating concept between the linguistic order and the social order. Indeed, in developing the concept, Halliday himself acknowledges a debt through the British linguist Firth (1890 - 1960) to the Anglo-Polish anthropologist Bronislaw Malinowski (1884 - 1942). As a concept its explanatory power is limited by the difficulties of capturing the dialectical relationship of (*language*) to situation. On the one hand language is sensitive to its context of situation. On the other hand it is active in defining and constituting that very context of situation. It is difficult to hold both insights simultaneously without some sense of circularity => MEANING POTENTIAL, REGISTER, SPEECH EVENT. *Further reading* Halliday, M.A.K. (1978), Montgomery, M. (2008)

items in italics are defined   related concepts defined
elsewhere in the book   elsewhere in the book

LIST OF KEY CONCEPTS

accent 3
access 4
accessed voices 4
accountability/accountability interview 4
active audience 5
actuality 5
adaptation 5
address 5
adjacency pair 5
aesthetics 5
affiliation 6
affordance/affordances 6
agenda setting 7
agent 8
ambient affiliation 8
ambient sound 8
anchor 8
animator 8
anti-language 8
Article 19 9
asynchronous communication 9
audience 9
Auteur Theory 10
authentic, authenticity 10
authentic talk 11
author/authorship 11
autocue 11

back channel behaviour 11
bias 12
bricolage 12
broadcasting 12
broadsheet 13

celebrity 14
censorship 14
chat room 14
chat show 14
cinematic apparatus 15
citizen journalism 15
closed text 15
closure 15
codes 16
coherence 16
cohesion 16
cold media 17
collocation 18
commissioning editor 18
communication 18
communication science 19
communicative ethos 19
communicative functions 20
community 20
competence 20
concordance 21
congruence theory 22

LIST OF KEY CONCEPTS

consensus 22
consent 22
content analysis 22
context of situation 22
continuity 23
control 23
conversation 24
conversation analysis (CA) 24
conversational styles 24
conversationalisation 25
copy editor 25
copywriter 25
corpus linguistics 25
counter culture 25
creative and cultural industries 25
creativity 26
critical discourse analysis (CDA) 26
crossing 27
cultivation theory 27
cultural capital 27
cultural imperialism 28
cultural industries 28
culture 28
cyberculture 28
cyberspace 29

data mining 29
dead air 29
decode 29
decoding 29
deconstruction 30
defamation 30
deixis 30
demographics 31
deviance 31
diachronic 31
dialect 32
dialogue 34
diegesis 34
diegetic sound 34
diffusion 35

digital/digitalisation 35
digital divide 35
digital media 35
digital platform 36
digital storytelling 36
diglossia 36
discourse 37
discourse act 38
discourse historical approach 38
discursive amplification 38
discursive gap 39
disinformation 40
documentary 40
dominant ideology 40
domination 40
doxing 40
dumbing down 40

editorial 41
electronic commons 41
electronic democracy 41
electronic publishing 41
emergent culture 41
encoding 42
establishment 42
ethnography 43

face 43
face-threatening act (FTA) 44
face-to-face communication 44
Facial Action Coding System (FACS) 44
Facial Affect Scoring Technique (FAST) 45
fake news 45
FAST 45
feminism 45
fifth estate 45
film language 46
film noir 46
film theory 47
fisking 47

LIST OF KEY CONCEPTS

flaming 47
flashback 47
focalisation 48
folk culture 48
folk devils 48
footing 48
fourth estate 49
frame/framing 49
free press 49
freedom of information 49
Freedom of Information Act 49

gatekeeper 50
genderlects 50
genre 50
geodemographics 51
gesture 52
ghost writer 52
glasnost 52
global media 52
global village 52
globalisation 53
gossip 53
grammar 54
groups 55

habitus 55
hard news 55
harijans 56
hegemony 56
hermeneutics 56
high culture 56
hot media 57
hybridity 57

iconic 57
identification process 57
ideological state apparatus (ISA) 58
ideology 58
imagined community 58
immediacy 58
impartiality 59

implicature 59
improvisation 61
individualisation 61
influence 61
informalisation 61
information and communications technology (ICT) 62
information commons 62
information rich 62
information society 62
information technology 62
infotainment 62
inoculation effect 62
instant messaging 63
integration 63
intellectual property 63
interaction 63
interactive media 63
intercultural communication 64
internet 64
interpellation 64
interpersonal communication 65
interpretive community 65
intersubjectivity 66
intertextuality 66
interview 66
intonation 66
intrapersonal communication 67
irony 67

Jakobson's model of communication 67
jouissance 67
journalese 68
journalism 68

kernel (of narrative) 68
knowledge society 68

labeling process 68
language pollution 69
langue 69

LIST OF KEY CONCEPTS

leak 70
legitimation 70
libel 70
linguistic determinism 70
linguistic relativity 70
literary agent 71
live/liveness 71
localisation 72

magazine 72
mainstream media 72
manufacture of consent 73
marketing 73
marketisation of discourse 73
market research 73
mass audience 73
mass communication 74
mass media 74
mass production 74
McLuhanism 74
meaning 74
meaning potential 75
media events 75
media of communication 76
mediasphere 76
mediate/mediated 76
mediated communication 77
mediation 77
mediatisation 77
melodrama 78
membership categorisation
  device 78
message 79
meta-communication 79
metadiscourse 79
modernism 79
modes of address 79
montage 80
moral panic 81
multi-accentuality 81
multi-modality 82
myth 81

narration 83
narrative 83
narrative codes 84
narrative kernel 84
narrative satellite 84
negotiated reading 84
netizen (digital native) 84
network 84
network society 84
neutralism 85
new media 85
news 84
news anchor 85
newscaster/newsreader 86
newspaper 86
news presentation 86
news values 87

op-ed 88
open text 88
objectivity 89
opinion poll 89
oppositional reading 89
oral culture 89
orality 89
other 89

para-social
  interaction 90
parody 91
parole 91
participation
  framework 92
pastiche 92
persistence of vision 93
persona 93
personal influence 93
personalisation 93
personality 94
personal media 94
personal space 94
persuasion 94

platform 94
point of view 94
popular culture 94
postmodernism 95
post-structuralism 95
power 96
pragmatics 96
preferred reading 98
press officer 98
primary orality 98
projection 98
propaganda 98
protocols of use 98
proxemics 99
public opinion 99
public relations (PR) 100
public service broadcasting 100
public sphere 101
publishing industry 101

questionnaire 102

rapport-talk 102
readership 102
reading public 102
real-time communication 102
reality television 102
reciprocity of perspectives 104
redundancy 104
reflexivity 104
register 104
reinforcement 105
report-talk 105
representation 106
resemiotisation 106
residual culture 106
resistive reading 106
response token 107
rhetoric 107
royalties 107
rumour 107

salience 107
salutation display 107
satellite (of narrative) 107
satire 107
scopophilia 108
script 108
secondary orality 108
self-concept 108
self-disclosure 109
self-identity 109
selfie 109
self-image 109
self-monitoring 109
self-presentation 110
semantic prosody 110
semantics 111
semiosis 114
sexism 115
Shannon and Weaver's model of communication 115
signification 115
signifying practice 115
silence 115
sincerity 115
slander 116
soap opera 116
sociability 116
social media 117
social network 118
socialisation 118
soft news 118
sound bite 118
source 119
speech 119
speech act 120
speech balloon 121
speech (/language) community 121
sphere of consensus 122
spin 123
spin-doctor 123
standard language 123

LIST OF KEY CONCEPTS

strategic silence 123
striptitle 123
structuralism 124
structures of feeling 124
style 125
sub-culture 125
subject position 125
subjectivity 125
subliminal 125
suture 126
synchronous communication 126
synthetic personalisation 126

tabloid 126
tabloidisation 126
talk 127
talk-in-interaction 127
talk show 127
taste 128
technological determinism 128
technology 128
telex 129
text 129
thought balloon 130
time-space compression/ distantiation 130
transculturation 131
transformation 131
transgression 131

transitivity 131
troll, to troll, trolling 133
truth 134
truthiness 134
turn 134
turn-taking 134
two-way 135

universality 135

validity claims 135
verbal devices 137
viral 137
virtual community 137
virtual reality 137
virus 138
visual culture 138
voice-over 138
vox pop 138

white space 138
Wikipedia 138
wired society 139
wired world 139
World Wide Web 139
writing 139

youth culture 140

zoetrope 141

LANGUAGE, MEDIA AND CULTURE

The Key Concepts

accent *n. SOCIOLINGUISTICS.* Distinctive ways of pronouncing the sounds of a language associated with membership of a particular social *group* defined by reference to region and/or social *class*. Most *languages* are subject to some kind of regional variation in pronunciation, and the more widely dispersed the language the greater is the likelihood of accent variation. Thus, the French of Quebec sounds to a native speaker quite different from the French of Paris; and Portuguese as spoken in Brazil sounds quite different to a native speaker of Portuguese as spoken in Portugal. English is something of an extreme example in this respect since it has a range of different accents which are associated with a distinctive national *affiliation*: hence, for example, Irish, Indian, American, Nigerian and Australian accents of English. But accent variation does not, of course, stop at this level of differentiation. In the case of British English, for example, there is a whole spectrum of internal variation ranging from regionally marked rural and urban accents (such as Somerset, Scouse or Geordie), through to that pattern referred to as Received Pronunciation (RP), commonly heard on the BBC's World Service, amongst the judiciary, in public schools and so on. In this sense, all speakers have 'an accent', including habitual users of Received Pronunciation. And although this latter accent is now primarily a class-based accent, it is important to note that historically it once had strong regional affiliations with the area south-east of the English Midlands. Its specific promotion through, for example, the English public schools in the 19th century, and the BBC in the early phases of sound *broadcasting* helps to explain its social ascendancy today in the UK, where it now seems to be the neutral or unmarked accent of English to such an extent that it becomes identified with the 'natural' and 'right' way of speaking the language. It is probably now the most widely understood and spoken accent within the UK and until recently was an accent commonly adopted for teaching English as a foreign language. This does not, however, make RP more correct as an accent of English than other patterns of pronunciation. It may command more prestige, but it is worth remembering that all accents attract social stigma and approval in varying measure from varying quarters. And, whilst experimental studies of reactions to accents within the UK have shown that RP speakers are rated more highly than regionally accented speakers in terms of general *competence*, these same studies have also shown that RP speakers emerge less favourably than regionally accented speakers on scales of personal integrity and social attractiveness. Such judgements ultimately have a social rather than a linguistic basis. Judgements of the correctness and aesthetic appeal of particular patterns of pronunciation are similarly difficult to justify by reference to intrinsic properties of the sounds themselves. They are strongly motivated – if unconsciously – by social factors. => ACCESSED VOICES, DIALECT. *Further reading* Foulkes, P. and Docherty, G (Eds.) (1999) Urban Voices: Accent Studies in the British Isles. London: Arnold.

access *n. JOURNALISM & MEDIA STUDIES.* The degree to which channels of *mass communication* are open to an individual or a *group*. The vast majority of the world's population have either very limited access, or none at all. The powerful and the official, the celebrated and the connected, especially in the Western world, have privileged access to agents such as newspaper and television journalists to help to disseminate their personal views, most often in the support of the status quo. Their entrée to mass communication has been characterised as having *accessed voices*. => ACCESSED VOICES, MASS COMMUNICATION.

accessed voices *np. pl. JOURNALISM STUDIES, MEDIA STUDIES, MASS COMMUNICATION.* Those people in a society who are given easy *access* to *mainstream media*, especially members of the *power* elite – experts, politicians, celebrities – who are not necessarily representative of society as a whole. => ACCESS, MASS COMMUNICATION.

accountability/accountability interview *n./np. BROADCAST TALK, CONVERSATION ANALYSIS, DISCOURSE STUDIES, JOURNALISM STUDIES.* Quality of being held liable or responsible for the accuracy, rightness or appropriateness of one's actions and/or words. Inasmuch as the press, *broadcasting* and the media constitute a sphere through which and in which the public can scrutinise the actions or performance of government – or the powerful more generally – they constitute an important means of holding elite figures to account. This is the basic premise of the work by Habermas on the *public sphere*, notions of the *Fourth Estate* or the idea behind the commonly used phrase 'speaking truth to power'. In practice, it has led to the development of specific *genres* of *discourse* in the media that rehearse precisely the aim of holding public figures to account, one of these being the widely adopted use of the current affairs *interview* to interrogate the actions, words or motives of establishment figures. Well-known interviewers become celebrated for their ability to put difficult questions to interviewees, acting in this way like 'tribunes of the people'. In current affairs interviews of this type public figures are made accountable in relation to a relevant *news* event or topic of the moment for their own words or deeds or for the actions /statements of the institution with which they are associated. => ALIGNMENT, FIFTH ESTATE, FOURTH ESTATE, INTERVIEW, PUBLIC SPHERE. *Further reading* Clayman, S. and Heritage (2002); Montgomery (2007)

active audience *np. MEDIA & CULTURAL STUDIES*. Emphasises the role of the audience in responding to the media. The *meanings* of media *texts* do not lie totally within the texts themselves. Instead, audiences make sense of and use the media within social and personal contexts and are not passive recipients of media *messages*. => ENCODING/DECODING, INTERPRETIVE COMMUNITIES, OPEN TEXT. *Further reading* Fiske, J. (1987) Ch. 5.

actuality *n. FILM STUDIES, JOURNALISM STUDIES*. Film footage of real events, places, persons or things which can provide the raw material for *documentary* films or news reports. => DOCUMENTARY, NEWS.

adaptation *n. FILM STUDIES, LITERARY AND CULTURAL STUDIES*. A screen version – usually film or television – of a work previously published as prose fiction – usually a novel or short-story. From the earliest days of cinema it has been common to use novels as story material for film, with Dickens being a particularly popular author for screen adaptation. Well over half of Hollywood films are based on previously published prose fiction that has been adapted for screen. Critical attention, however, tends to focus on adaptation of classic fiction by authors such as Shakespeare, Jane Austen and Dickens, rather than, for example, J.K. Rowling or Ian Fleming. => FILM LANGUAGE, NARRATIVE. *Further reading* Hutcheon, L. (with Siobhan O'Flynn) (2012)

address *n. DISCOURSE STUDIES; MEDIA STUDIES*. => MODES OF ADDRESS.

adjacency pair *np. CONVERSATION ANALYSIS, LINGUISTICS, SOCIOLOGY*. Conversational exchange between speakers consisting of two parts (thus, a 'pair' of utterances) in which the occurrence of the first part of the pair predicts or requires the production of an appropriate second part of the pair. Typical adjacency pairs are 'question' followed by 'answer', or a 'greeting' followed by a 'greeting'. The concept of adjacency pair, originally formulated by the U.S. sociologist, Harvey Sacks (1935-1975), was the first step to describing some of the structural and sequential constraints that underpin coherent *talk*. The term is widely used in the study of *conversation* and, more generally, in the analysis of *talk-in-interaction*. => COHERENCE, CONVERSATION, TALK-IN-INTERACTION, SPEECH ACTS. *Further reading* Hutchby, I. and Woofit (2008); Levinson, S. (1983)

aesthetics *n. pl. FILM STUDIES, LITERARY & CULTURAL STUDIES, PHILOSOPHY*. Branch of philosophy devoted to elucidating the nature of beauty, especially in literature and the arts. In the 18th and early 19th centuries the emphasis within this field lay on describing how beauty was perceived and appreciated. Later the emphasis began to fall on how the qualities of a beautiful object could be defined in such a way as to distinguish what is beautiful from what is not; and this in turn led to an attempt to articulate the grounds of good *taste*, thereby making strong connections with the criticism, especially, of fine art, but also literature and music. In its later guises aesthetics could thus be seen as underpinning questions of value and judgment as these were deployed by different critical and artistic schools. As such, aesthetics often attempted to ground definitions of beauty ahistorically in relation to other transcendental terms such as goodness, *truth*, pleasure and complexity (or simplicity). Questions of aesthetic taste still attract significant interest; but judgements of this kind are increasingly considered to be socio-culturally determined and/or simple matters of personal preference, and therefore relative rather than absolute. Despite this, questions of aesthetic judgement refuse to disappear, remain interesting (e.g. in the form of 'lists of the best') and consequently provoke continuing reflection, not just in literature and the arts but also and increasingly within the domain of *popular culture*. => TASTE, VALUE. *Further reading* Eco, U. (2010)

affiliation *n.* JOURNALISM, SOCIOLOGY. Official relationship with an association or organisation, carrying special status or rights and obligations. The bearer of affiliated status is empowered to speak or act in some way for the organisation or association. In *broadcast media*, especially in the context of *news* and current affairs, speakers are selected on the basis of some kind of warrant, as witness, as expert, as public figure, as spokesperson, as correspondent. Many of these roles are based on an affiliated status which will be stated in their introduction or with an accompanying graphic, e.g. 'Member of Parliament for Croydon East'. => ACCESS, ACCESSED VOICES. *Further reading* Thornborrow, J. (2015)

affordance/affordances *n./n. pl.* CULTURAL AND COMMUNICATION STUDIES, MEDIA, PSYCHOLOGY. A term derived from the work of the American psychologist, James J. Gibson (1904-1979). Gibson's main interest was in visual perception, and he adopted the term in order to emphasise how our approach to the recognition or perception of material in the environment operates less in terms of an engagement with abstracted features such as size, shape or colour, and more in terms of utility: in other words, it is as if we approach the environment considering 'what can this (particular thing) be used for?' rather than 'what is this?' Some media scholars (Hutchby, 2001; Juris, 2012) have adopted the term to highlight qualitative differences between different technologies in terms of their differing potentialities for *communication*. The communicative affordances of a phone, for instance, are not the same as a VHF two-way radio (such as 'walkie-talkie', as used by established radio taxi cabs, emergency services and so-on.) The communicative technologies of *writing*, for example, consist of much more than techniques of committing agreed sets of symbols to a semi-durable medium. Considered in terms of their affordances, writing technologies (as compared, for example, with *speech*) allow for various kinds of *time-space distantiation*; they 'afford', or allow, writer and reader to be separated in time and space. They allow, for instance, for a uniform *message* to reach many readers, distributed across different contexts. They afford opportunities for interrupted and repetitive reception (the written *text* does not need to be read in its entirety on one occasion), and for working and re-working a message before, or even after, publication or transmission. The affordances of writing are, in this way, quite different than speech, at least in the pre-digital, pre-electronic era. Latterly, of course, analogue and digital recording allows some of the communicative affordances of writing to be applied to speech itself, or more generally to *live* performance. One of the many affordances of *digital* recording, for instance, especially in the arena of sports and entertainment, is the capacity for deliberate view and review, as 'action-replay', of an episode immediately succeeding the moment of initial *broadcasting*, even as part of the live moment itself (see Marriott, 1996, 2007). It is important to recognise that these affordances are not in any crude or simple way 'determined' by the properties inherent to the *technology* itself. They may be shaped by the technology, partly because of its designed nature. But the affordances of a particular technology may well be further enlarged and discovered in the process of its use. 'Messaging', or texting, as an affordance of the mobile phone, to the degree that messages now exceed voice calls, could hardly have been predicted when the mobile phone was first introduced. Affordances, then, often constitute a discovery or extension of the unanticipated possibilities of existing *technologies*. => SPEECH, TECHNOLOGY, TECHNOLOGICAL DETERMINISM, TIME-SPACE DISTANTIATION, WRITING. *Further reading* Hutchby, I. (2001); Gibson, J.J. (1979); Juris, J.S. (2012)

agenda setting *np. JOURNALISM STUDIES.* A way of referring to how the news media set the topics and the terms of public debate. Agenda setting is partly a matter of how topics get selected but also a question of the degree of *salience* which is accorded to them. By setting the agenda, news media not only *frame* issues for public attention and debate but by implication help shape the contours of *public opinion*. => FRAMING, NEWS, NEWS VALUES, PUBLIC OPINION. *Further reading* McCombs, M. (2005)

agent *n. PUBLISHING.* A professional intermediary who advises an author on the prospective salability of publishing projects, sometimes also on matters of *audience*, content and *style*, and represents their interests in financial and other negotiations with publishers and media organisations. Agents are increasingly providing management of the author as a client, for example in ensuring that the agreed date for delivery of a contracted *text* is honored, thus easing what can be a problematic load on publishers and media organisations. Equally, in placing book projects with suitable publishers, the agent is acting in part on behalf of the publisher, as well as of the author.

ambient affiliation *np. COMMUNICATION STUDIES, INTERNET STUDIES, SOCIAL MEDIA.* The loose relationship in micro-blogging between those who post *messages*, those who may read them, may follow them, may respond to them and so on. The term was coined by Zappavigna (2011) to capture the creation of virtual *audiences* and *networks* in the larger multicasting environment of *social media* such as Twitter or Sina Weibo. Here participants in the multifarious flow of *communication* must find those whose interests and concerns they may share and with whom they may satisfactorily 'affiliate'. According to Zappavigna (2011), they do so by taking advantage of various kinds of metadata and searchable forms such as hashtags as well as finding common linguistic ground in shared idioms, slang and other verbal forms. In this way the notion of *ambient affiliation* suggests how "virtual groupings afforded by features of electronic text, such as metadata, create alignments between people who have not necessarily directly interacted online" (2011, p. 1). => AUDIENCE, PARTICIPATION FRAMEWORK, VIRTUAL COMMUNITY. *Further reading* Zappavigna (2011); (2013)

ambient sound *np. FILM, RADIO, TELEVISION.* The presence of naturally occurring background sound in a recorded or *live* scene, such as traffic noise in a street scene, the clatter of dishes and background chatter in a café scene, or jet engine noise in an airport scene. It may function as an important supporting sign of the realism or *authenticity* of a scene so is sometimes added or modified in post-production. => ACTUALITY, DIEGETIC SOUND.

anchor => NEWS ANCHOR.

animator => PARTICIPATION FRAMEWORK.

anti-language *n. SOCIOLINGUISTICS.* The specialised language of a *sub-culture* or *group* that occupies a marginal or precarious position in society, especially where central activities of the group place them outside the law. Anti-languages may be understood as extreme versions of social *dialects*. Often the subculture or group (the 'anti-society') has an antagonistic relationship with society at large, and their natural suspicion of outsiders makes it difficult to study their language; but some examples have been documented – notably the language of Polish prison life (*grypserka*) and that of the Calcutta underworld. In addition to these relatively contemporary cases, some historical records survive of a variety known as 'pelting speech' – an argot employed by roving bands of vagabonds in Elizabethan England. Linguistically, such languages are marked by re-lexicalisation (i.e. coining new words for old) and over-lexicalisation (proliferation of vocabulary items in fields of special interest to the group). Both processes enhance secrecy and can also involve playful and sometimes aesthetic uses of the resulting vocabulary (e.g. in rapping). => DIALECT, SUB-CULTURE. *Further reading* Halliday (1978); Montgomery (2008a)

Article 19 *n.* HUMAN RIGHTS. An article in the Universal Declaration of Human Rights that declares the following: "Everyone has the right to freedom of opinion and expression; the right includes freedom to hold opinions without hindrance and to seek, receive and impart information and ideas through any media regardless of frontiers." => ACCESS, ACCESSED VOICES, CENSORSHIP.

asynchronous communication *np.* COMMUNICATION STUDIES, INTERNET STUDIES, SOCIAL MEDIA. Occurs when *communication technology* allows or requires gaps in the temporal flow of *mediated communication* so that it does not take place in 'real time' – unlike, for instance, most forms of *face-to-face communication*. It is a feature of many forms of messaging in *new media* that responses may overlap, be delayed, or otherwise interrupted, thereby undermining the sense of continuous temporal sequence and flow. The concept is important for distinguishing between different kinds of communication, such as *conversation* and *instant messaging* => FACE-TO-FACE COMMUNICATION, REAL-TIME COMMUNICATION, SYNCHRONOUS COMMUNICATION.

audience *n.* COMMUNICATION & MEDIA STUDIES. Those for whom a public mode of *communication* is designed. Traditionally the term would apply most easily to those present at and addressed by speeches, theatrical performances and various kinds of public entertainment. The term, has a special resonance in media studies where it denotes the multiple and collective addressee particularly of print and broadcast communication. Indeed, the notion of the audience has become a special object of study with competing notions of active and passive audience. => ACTIVE AUDIENCE, OVERHEARING AUDIENCE, PARTICIPATION FRAMEWORK.

Auteur Theory *np.* FILM STUDIES, FILM THEORY. An approach to film criticism that emphasises the role of the individual director (from the French word *auteur* for author) in giving particular aesthetic shape to a film, or to a body of film work, in terms of its visual *style*, thematic concerns, scripting and acting, so that it becomes an expression of their personal vision. The approach was associated with French New Wave film criticism, and – in its emphasis on the individual director – accentuated the role of the autonomous artist over the constraints of Hollywood's studio production-line approach and its associated commercial pressures. => AUTHOR. *Further reading* Caughie, J. (Ed.) (1981); Jeong, S. and Jeremi Szaniawski (Eds.) (2017)

authentic, authenticity *adj., n.* COMMUNICATION STUDIES, DISCOURSE ETHICS, DISCOURSE STUDIES genuine, trustworthy, original. Individuals, especially in the *public sphere*, appear to be authentic partly on the basis of the kinds of statement they make. And a sense of authenticity has become one kind of claim to validity that may be applied to utterances. However, utterances may make different kinds of claim to validity. Indeed, the most obvious *validity claim* is the claim to *truth*, by virtue of which we might ask: does this statement offer a faithful description of objects, events, or states of affairs in the world? Thus, assertions about climate change, for instance, are routinely inspected for their truth value and evidence can be adduced in their support. However, statements are considered valid (or invalid) in a variety of other ways, including also in terms of their *sincerity* and/or their authenticity. In the latter case an assertion may lack validity in terms of its correspondence to the world of objects and events but may gain an alternative validity as a statement of the speaker's beliefs: in other words, it may not exactly be *true*, but it may still come across, to some hearers, as a *truthful* – or authentic – statement of the speaker's beliefs. In the case of Donald Trump, for example, many assertions made by him are considered questionable – invalid – in terms of their truth value, but they appeal to certain sections of his *audience* as authentic statements of who he is and what he stands for. To one kind of audience they are invalid because untrue; but to another kind of audience they achieve validity despite this because they seem authentic – genuine, trustworthy, original. In the case of authenticity, the judgement about validity of utterances is not so much by reference to the real world of objects and events but by reference to the qualities of the person who utters them. The *mediation* and the *mediatisation* of the public sphere has been accompanied by an increasing *personalisation* of politics; and as part of these processes it seems that the validity of claims in the public sphere has come to rest as much upon their presumed authenticity as on their truth. => PUBLIC SPHERE, SINCERITY, TRUTH, TRUTHINESS, VALIDITY CLAIMS. *Further reading* Dynel, M (2016); Montgomery, M. (2017); Scannell, P. (1996)

authentic talk *np. DISCOURSE ETHICS, DISCOURSE STUDIES*. A way of talking that seems to project the *authenticity* of the speaker. Authentic talk in the *public sphere* is a condition to which some kinds of broadcast *talk* aspire, in which traces of scriptedness or rehearsal for performance are avoided, effaced or suppressed. Any loss in precision or fluency is compensated for by a sense of directness, informality and participatoriness. => AUTHENTICITY, SINCERITY, VALIDITY CLAIMS. *Further reading* Montgomery, M. (2001)

author/authorship *n. LITERARY STUDIES*. The occupation or activity of creating texts or works. The idea of an author as the originating source of a text has assumed increasing importance from the Romantic period onwards. Previously, attributing authorship by name to a text was considered less important than knowing its type (e.g 'elegy', 'obituary') and function. However, from at least the 19th Century, the identity of the author becomes a way of establishing the value, authenticity, and singularity of a text, especially within minority or high culture – less so within folk or popular culture. Fine art would be a case in point, where establishing the authorship of a painting can significantly alter its value, both culturally and financially. => AUTEUR THEORY, PARTICIPATION FRAMEWORK. *Further reading* Barthes, R. (1977)

autocue *n. BROADCAST TALK*. A device that allows presenters to read a *script* while looking directly to camera (or to the *audience*). It is used most commonly in studio-based television work, typically in *news* reading. It was developed in the second half of the 1950s in both the UK and the US (where the device is known as the 'teleprompter', sometimes shortened to 'prompter') and was first adopted for *news presentation* in the early 1960s. Early versions used a paper scroll alongside and close to the camera, but this been superseded by digital running script reflected by mirrors onto a glass screen between the presenter and the camera. In this way a news reader, for instance, is able to adopt direct visual *address* to the audience, regarded as television's characteristic *mode of address*. => MODES OF ADDRESS, PARA-SOCIAL INTERACTION.

★★

back channel behaviour *np. CONVERSATION ANALYSIS, SOCIOLINGUISTICS, SOCIAL INTERACTION*. Vocal or visible feedback given by a hearer to a speaker in the course of *talk-in-interaction*. It may include smiles, laughter, head-nodding and vocal but non-verbal expressions such as 'mmhum', 'mm', 'wow', etc., as a supportive accompaniment to the speaker's *turn*. Inasmuch as they do not interrupt or impede the speaker's turn, they are said to occupy not the main channel of *communication* between speaker and hearer but the back channel. In broadcast *talk*, however, vocal back channel behaviour may be reduced to avoid signaling alignment with the speaker (for instance, by the interviewer towards the interviewee in political *interviewing*), or simply to avoid distraction for the broadcast or overhearing *audience*. => CONVERSATION, SPEECH, TALK-IN-INTERACTION. *Further reading* Gardner, R. (2001)

bias *n.* CULTURAL AND COMMUNICATION STUDIES, JOURNALISM AND MEDIA STUDIES. In *news* coverage, refers to a systematic tendency on the part of a news provider to depict events from a particular political or ideological standpoint. Allegations of bias in the US or UK context are more usually made against broadcasters than *newspapers*, on the grounds that the latter are more restricted in their *audience* and have traditionally been recognised as partisan, whereas the former make more explicit claims to *impartiality*, and indeed, in the case of public service broadcasters, may be required to be so. Much academic research has accumulated around the question of proving or disproving bias in the case of supposedly non-partisan broadcasters, whether in terms of trends or individual cases. It has rarely been conclusive, though periodic high-profile interventions keep issues of bias alive. From the Falklands War (1982) onwards, governments of the day have accused the BBC of anti-war *bias*. => IDEOLOGY, IMPARTIALITY, OBJECTIVITY. *Further reading* Anderson and Sharrock (1979); McNair (2009); Philo, G. et. al. (2013).

bricolage *n.* (*Fr.*) CULTURAL STUDIES. A way of using everyday objects for new, unintended symbolic purposes; a form of symbolic re-cycling. In classic cases of cultural bricolage, an everyday object such as a safety pin is taken from its primary field in first aid or child care and re-cast symbolically as a brooch or other form of ornamentation. Bricolage is often a symbolic tactic of particular sub-cultural *groups* and is a resource for defining their distinctive *style*. The re-appropriation of the safety pin for ornamentation, for instance, was a common symbolic motif in the dress of punks. => PASTICHE, POSTMODERNISM.

broadcasting *n.* MEDIA & COMMUNICATION STUDIES. Transmission of *messages* from a single source simultaneously to multiple receivers. Television and radio are prototypical examples of broadcasting. The defining characteristic of broadcasting was that large *audiences* shared in the reception of a single event transmitted via a public medium of *communication* from a fixed source to multiple receivers which in turn had limited portability. Early radio receivers and televisions typically occupied domestic space, and both viewing and listening were organised around schedules. The classic age of broadcasting covers the last half of the 20th century. Since then, the digitisation of communication and the growth of the *internet* has seen a relative decline in broadcasting, narrowly defined. The typical content of broadcasting is available on a variety of *digital platforms* including, for instance, the tablet and laptop, and its availability is no longer restricted to scheduled transmission times and particular kinds of space. Instead there has been a growth of multicasting and narrowcasting, where smaller audiences are targeted via media with interactive *affordances*. Indeed, with the development of *new media*, *personal media* and *social media* (such as Facebook, WeChat, Instagram and Twitter) reciprocal and multi-directional communication flows have begun to supplant the one-to-many arrangements of broadcasting. => DIGITAL MEDIA, MASS COMMUNICATION, MASS MEDIA, SOCIAL MEDIA. *Further reading* Crisell, A. (2002) Scannell, P. and Cardiff (1991); Scannell, P. (2000)

broadsheet *n. JOURNALISM AND COMMUNICATION STUDIES.* A kind of *newspaper*. Broadsheet newspapers use a large format, usually 750 x 600 mm (29.5" x 23.5"), which was gradually adopted as an industry standard after the British government placed a tax on the number of pages in a newspaper in 1712. The large format of broadsheet newspapers contrasts with smaller sized newspapers often referred to as *tabloids*, which measure 430 x 280 mm (16.9" x 11.0"), almost half the size of a broadsheet. However, the differences between broadsheet and tabloid newspapers go beyond questions of size. Tabloid newspapers have tended to reach larger *readerships* than broadsheet newspapers and have drawn on a different mix of *news values*, emphasising particularly *popular culture*, *personalisation* and human interest. Broadsheet newspapers by contrast have tended to target a minority readership associated with the holders of economic, educational and *cultural capital*, and their news values have correspondingly given more space to politics, government, diplomacy, the economy and foreign news. More recently, however, many established and quality newspapers have changed from their previous large-format broadsheet size to a more compact format closer to, or identical with, the tabloid format while insisting that there has been no erosion of or change in their established news values. => HARD NEWS, NEWS VALUES, TABLOID, TABLOIDISATION. *Further reading* Conboy, M. (2004); Williams, K. (2010)

★★

celebrity *n.* CULTURAL STUDIES. Person who achieves special status within *popular culture* primarily on the grounds of fame and/or notoriety deriving from the amount of media coverage that they attract rather than their intrinsic qualities, achievements or attributes. => PERSONALISATION. *Further reading* Marshall, P.D. (2006)

censorship *n.* JOURNALISM AND COMMUNICATION STUDIES, POLITICAL COMMUNICATION. Controlling the public dissemination of information by suppressing or deleting anything found to be objectionable. Censorship is not new: the Catholic church, for instance, published a list of prohibited books in 1559, partly in response to the introduction of the printing press a century or so earlier. And censorship applies to many forms of public *communication*: for instance, books, plays and theatrical performance, films, *newspapers*, *broadcasting* and the *internet*. When practised by governments, enforced by formal administrative bodies and sanctioned by legal *codes*, it can serve to shape and perpetuate an official version of the *truth*. But not all censorship is official and governmental: it can work implicitly by means of social pressure and established practice to favour certain topics and versions of the truth over others. Even in societies with no official censorship, journalists will admit to various forms of self-censorship. The rise of the internet has posed particular challenges to censorship, principally because the sources and the routes of communication are so de-centralised they are difficult to regulate. Nonetheless, governments with a major investment in the *power* of the state are prepared to commit large resources to trying to censor internet communication. => POWER. *Further reading* Billiani, F. (2007); Simon, J. (2014)

chat room *np.* CONVERSATION ANALYSIS, INTERNET STUDIES. An internet or *cyberspace* facility that allows several users to communicate in real time but in virtual space, often with assumed identities, in a form of synchronous conferencing. => DIGITAL MEDIA, SYNCHRONOUS COMMUNICATION. *Further reading* Hutchby, I. (2000).

chat show *np.* BROADCAST TALK, MEDIA & COMMUNICATION STUDIES. A *genre* of radio or television programme where the prime emphasis falls on *talk* between a host and guests who are selected on the basis of having something to say on the (usually light-hearted) topics at hand, or who have some kind of *celebrity* or semi-celebrity status. It tends to be used primarily in the context of British *broadcasting* and is often associated there with comedy or with comedian hosts. The equivalent or similar generic label in the US, now more widely established, is *talk show*. => CELEBRITY, TALK SHOW. *Further reading* Tolson, A. (1991)

cinematic apparatus *np. FILM & CINEMA STUDIES.* The mode of *representation* adopted by mainstream cinema which constructs a particular viewing position for the spectator that embodies within it the *dominant ideology* of society. The term reflected the particular concerns of *film theory* in the 1970s influenced by Althusserian Marxism and Lacanian psychoanalysis. => CONTINUITY EDITING, SCOPOPHILIA. *Further reading* De Lauretis, T. & S. Heath (Eds.) (1985)

citizen journalism *np. JOURNALISM & MEDIA STUDIES.* Contributions made voluntarily by ordinary citizens, often as unpaid bystanders or witnesses, to gathering and disseminating the *news*. Citizen journalism has a long history, particularly in societies where mainstream *journalism* was felt to be comprised through *censorship*, *bias* or extreme partisanship, of providing an alternative to existing news outlets. More recently, however, the rise of new *digital media* has vastly extended the scope of ordinary people to capture unfolding events in situations where *mainstream media* are not on the scene, perhaps through difficulties of *access* (e.g. in conflict zones), or before sufficient time has elapsed for them to reach the event. In some respects, this amounts to a form of *user-generated content* but particularly in the area of news and current affairs. The term became particularly active in the first decade of this century and overlapped with concerns about the threat to traditional print and broadcast news media from the rise more generally of *new media* with their ability to cut costs and undermine the traditional economics of the mainstream news industries. => NEW MEDIA, NEWS, USER-GENERATED CONTENT. *Further reading* Allan, S. & Einar Thorsen (2009)

closed text *np. LITERARY LINGUISTICS, SEMIOLOGY/SEMIOTICS.* A *text* whose meaning is not open to interpretation can be described as a closed text. The term is associated with the work of the Italian semiotician and literary theorist, Umberto Eco (1932-2016), in which special emphasis is given to the role of the reader in completing the meaning of the work (which may, for instance, be a novel, poem, piece of music, legal text or scientific report). Some works – closed texts – limit by design the kinds of meaning that the reader may discern in them. Examples might be legal or scientific texts. Eco, however, had a particular interest in the work of art as an 'open work', which he described as a dynamic 'work in movement', effectively open to an unlimited range of interpretations and possible readings. => HERMENEUTICS, OPEN TEXT. *Further reading* Eco, U. (1981)

closure *n. CULTURAL STUDIES.* A satisfactory conclusion, particularly to a *narrative*. => NARRATIVE.

codes *n. pl.* COMMUNICATION STUDIES, SOCIOLINGUISTICS. Systems that organise the transfer of meaning or information by articulating together various kinds of signal (for instance, sounds, signs, written characters, symbols or words) and specifying the rules that convert one signal into another form or *representation*. In sociolinguistics they may designate particular fashions of speaking associated with specific *groups* or *contexts of situation*. Codes, additionally and separately, may consist simply of rules or guidance for conduct or behaviour: the chivalric code regulated the conduct of medieval knights; the 'Hays code' defined the boundary between acceptable and unacceptable behaviour in motion pictures produced for a public *audience* in the United States from 1934 to 1968. => COMMUNICATION THEORY, PROTOCOLS OF USE.

coherence *n.* CRITICAL DISCOURSE ANALYSIS, DISCOURSE STUDIES, LINGUISTICS. The underlying intelligibility of connected *discourse*, especially when it consists of several utterances (or sentences) strung together. Early students of discourse analysis from a linguistic perspective faced a fundamental problem of trying to explain for any given instance of language in use "how one utterance followed another in a rational, rule-governed manner" (Labov 1972a: 299). Within a sentence the rules of *grammar* or syntax specified how the elements of a sentence hung together – how, for instance, a subject agreed with a verb. Beyond the individual sentence, however, in connected discourse, it was more difficult to spell out the underlying relationships between one utterance and another. On the one hand the difference between coherent and incoherent discourse was intuitively apparent (rather like the difference between a grammatical and an ungrammatical sentence). But the actual mechanisms that made discourse coherent were less easy to specify. One approach to the problem examined cohesive ties between utterances, such as lexical repetition or the use of pronominal reference. But while it was clear that a lengthy *text* would often display many cohesive ties, some texts could still be coherent as discourse while lacking obvious signs of *cohesion*. Searching for an answer to the problem of coherence required linguists to begin to explore aspects of contextual meaning, and this in turn gave rise to the subfield of linguistic *pragmatics*. Here the connectedness of discourse was explored in terms of devices such as conversational *implicature*, presupposition and *speech* (or discourse) act. => COHESION, CONVERSATION ANALYSIS, DISCOURSE, MEANING, PRAGMATICS, TEXT. *Further reading* Eggins, S. & Slade (1997); Labov, W. & Fanshel (1977); Levinson (1983); Widdowson, H. G. (2004)

cohesion *n.* DISCOURSE STUDIES, LINGUISTICS. A property of *texts* whereby their status as a meaningful semantic entity is realised and sustained by ties or devices that link one sentence with another. These ties operate across sentence boundaries, transcending the structural limits of the sentence, and are of various kinds, partly grammatical and partly lexical. Grammatical cohesion is carried by, for instance, conjunction, using items such as *then, moreover, consequently*, or *nevertheless* to bind one sentence to another; or it may be carried by devices such as reference or substitution. In the case of reference, pronouns are used to refer back to entities mentioned previously in the text: thus, in the following example, the second sentence is tied to the first by the pronouns *his* and *him*. "John is living alone. *His* partner left *him* 9 years ago." In the case of substitution, items such as *do* or *did* are substituted for those occurring earlier, as in the following: "Joan had been told not to kneel during the national anthem. But she **did so** anyway." In all these cases of cohesion a closed class of grammatical items (conjunctions, for instance, or pronouns) is used to effect cohesion between one part of a text and another. The other major type of cohesion – lexical cohesion – is perhaps more significant than all other kinds of cohesion and relates to the patterning of open class lexical (or vocabulary) items in a text through repetition, reiteration and *collocation*. The following example is rich in lexical cohesion, some of which has been italicised: "In rivers and *landlocked* venues we need to look at the *land forecast* and *modify* it for over the *water*. In coastal *waters*, however, we can use the sea *forecast* and *modify* it for the influence of the *land*." Any text, therefore, hangs together cohesively by means of an intricate network of ties between one part of the text and another, and the operation of these devices of repetition, substitution, reference and so on is testament to the resources inherent in the language system for building texts as semantically unified wholes. These resources, however, will be utilised differently depending upon the context of the text, and in this way these variations contribute significantly to the characteristic 'textures' of different *styles* and *genres*. => COHERENCE, COLLOCATION, DISCOURSE, GENRE, MEANING, STYLE, TEXT. *Further reading* Halliday, M.A.K. and Hasan (1976); Hoey, M. (1991)

cold media *np*. MEDIA & CULTURAL STUDIES. A term suggested by the Canadian cultural and media theorist Marshal McLuhan (1911–1980) and used in opposition to *hot media* to distinguish between types of medium by their degree of high or low definition. A cold or 'cool' medium is low definition and requires more involvement by the user in its *decoding*. A hot medium is high definition and therefore requires less decoding effort. Typical examples of cold media are cartoons and television (in the latter case before the advent of the high definition flat screen). Film and radio by contrast are, for McLuhan, examples of hot media because their sensory qualities depend on a well-defined perceptual stimulus. The binary opposition of hot and cold has attracted some criticism but is derived from McLuhan's central claim that "the medium is the message" – in other words, that the sensory properties of the medium itself rather than whatever content it carries should be the primary focus of study. => HOT MEDIA. *Further reading* McLuhan, M. (2001)

collocation *n.* DISCOURSE STUDIES, LINGUISTICS. The tendency of individual words to co-occur with other particular words of a language in everyday *discourse*. Thus, *dark* collocates strongly with *night*, insofar as they tend to co-occur. The same could be said of the relationship of *deadly* to *nightshade* or *nuclear* to *weapon*. The study of meaning, using this approach, investigates the meaning of a word in terms of its patterns of collocation, on the principle (enunciated by J.R. Firth, 1890-1960, a British linguist who first formulated the notion of collocation) that 'you shall know a word by the company it keeps'. (Compare Wittgenstein: 'the meaning of a word is its use in the language'.) Collocation does, however, imply statistical profiles of patterns of co-occurrence. These have proved notoriously difficult to produce until recently when it has become possible to apply sophisticated computational techniques to very large corpora of data, sometimes showing unexpected co-dependencies – for instance, the word *cause* with *trouble* or *disaster*. Recent dictionaries – for instance, the *Collins Cobuild English Language Dictionary* – have been developed using such techniques. => MEANING, SEMANTICS, SEMANTIC PROSODY. *Further reading* Sinclair, J. (1991); Sinclair, J. (2004)

commissioning editor *np.* PUBLISHING. One who identifies and acquires material for publication. Traditionally the term applied to book publishing, and the commissioning editor played an important role in building up a publisher's list. More recently the term has been applied to *magazine* articles and other forms of media publication including television documentaries, comedy programmes and drama.

communication *n.* COMMUNICATION STUDIES. The sharing of thoughts, ideas, attitudes, feelings and values by means of words, signs or symbols. The concept implies some degree of matching or correspondence between the act of symbolising and any reciprocal act of interpretation. Nearly all accounts of communication, however, recognise that it rarely takes place without some kind of gap between symbolisation and interpretation, which may involve distortions, misunderstandings, deceptions and other kinds of imperfection.

Human communication is rarely perfect. Indeed, the human capacity for language from its outset entails the possibility that we fail to make our meanings clear – accidentally or deliberately. Indeed, the difficulties of communication are the salient problems of modernity and postmodernity: linguistic philosophy sought to eliminate many problems in traditional philosophy by returning as closely as possible to what can be formulated in ordinary language; political sociology sees crises of *legitimation* in terms of distorted communication; some gender theorists see the incompatibilities between men and women as problems of communication and mutual misunderstanding. Accordingly, it may make better sense to describe communication as the negotiation and exchange of meanings, thus shifting the emphasis to the process of communication rather than the result. The study of communication has unfortunately been compartmentalised (especially in the US) in sub-fields such as *mass communication* and *interpersonal communication* (thereby overlooking important interrelationships between the two and the development of concepts germane to both, for example, *community*). A striking exception to this compartmentalisation is the concept of the 'two step flow' in communication originated in work by Katz and Lazarsfeld (1955) => COMMUNITY, DISCURSIVE GAP INFLUENCE, INTERPERSONAL COMMUNICATION, MASS COMMUNICATION. *Further reading* Cherry, C. (1978); Scannell, P. (2007); Williams, R. (1962/2016)

communication science *np.* COMMUNICATION STUDIES. Adopts empirical methods, most often associated with quantitative social science, to study the effects of the *mass media* on large populations. It has tended to focus on *public opinion* research, *political communication*, and advertising. It is more popular in the US than in Europe, where the latter has traditionally emphasised the contextualised study of communicative form and has been more concerned with questions of *signification*, *representation*, meaning and *ideology*. => MASS MEDIA, POLITICAL COMMUNICATION, PUBLIC OPINION. *Further reading* Hayes, A.F. (2015)

communicative ethos *np.* CULTURAL & COMMUNICATION STUDIES. The kind of repertoire of attitude and value that makes up the distinctive dominant key or tone of *communication* associated with major revolutions in the technologies of communication. The communicative ethos of *oral cultures*, for instance, is thought to be different from that of print cultures. Likewise, the communicative ethos of digital *social media* is considered to be different in character than that of *terrestrial broadcasting*. => AUTHENTICITY, FISKING, SINCERITY, SOCIABILITY, TROLLING. *Further reading* Ong, W.J. (1982/2002); Tannen, D. (2002); Scannell, P. (1996)

communicative functions *np.* LITERARY LINGUISTICS, MEDIA. A way of understanding *communication* in terms of its uses. Various schemes have been proposed to describe the functions or uses of communication, most of which identify functions such as the following: communication for the formation or projection of self and identity; communication to influence or change the behaviour of others; communication to convey facts, information or ideas; communication for the purpose of play or pleasure; and communication to express feelings, emotions or intuitions. => JAKOBSON'S MODEL OF COMMUNICATION, SPEECH ACT *Further reading* Jakobson, R. (1960)

community *n.* CULTURAL STUDIES, SOCIOLOGY. A *group* of persons bound in any particular instance by a selective combination of shared values, common purpose, ties of kinship, shared goods, shared rituals and/or locale. In many cases, members of a community will know each other by name or recognise each other by appearance. In this way, the sense of mutual recognition by members of each other implies that most communities are not large but restricted in number to tens or hundreds (though note – of course – predecessors of the European Union (EU), known as the European Economic Community (EEC), later the European Community (EC)). The term is often – though not exclusively – used of religious communities, and certainly the notion of a shared purpose applies most easily in such cases. It is noticeable that the term is rarely used negatively: it nearly always carries positive connotations. Increasingly, however, it has come in the digital age to be pre-modified by terms such as 'virtual', 'online' and 'imagined', in this way extending its application to forms of association that transcend ties of locale, co-presence and mutual recognition. => IMAGINED COMMUNITY, INTERPRETIVE COMMUNITY, VIRTUAL COMMUNITY. *Further reading* Anderson, B. (2006); Silverstone, R., Ch.11; Williams, R. (1963a); (1983)

competence *n.* LINGUISTICS. The native speaker's tacit and intuitive knowledge of their language. The U.S. linguist Noam Chomsky developed this technical sense of the term as a challenge to what were current trends in American linguistics of the 1950s which declared that language could be studied as a purely behavioural phenomenon independently of meaning and of its underlying mental structure. Through the notion of competence, Chomsky shifted the focus of linguistic study away from verbal behaviour to our intuitions about language – particularly those that enable any native speaker to distinguish between grammatical and ungrammatical sentences in his or her native language. With these intuitions as its focus, the goal of linguistics became that of describing or *modelling* the rules that go into making up the native speaker's *grammar*. These rules are descriptive, but ultimately amount to a formal, explicit model of the native speaker's competence. Chomsky declared that these rules – the grammar – amount to a statement of knowledge and must be clearly distinguished from what actual people do when speaking the language. This he described as *performance* and argued that since speakers of the language make numerous slips while talking, leaving sentences unfinished, making false-starts and other mistakes, then mere performance could provide no reliable guide to underlying competence. It was thus no use studying what people did if you wanted to find out what they knew. This knowledge, or competence, however, was a necessary precondition for performance. Chomsky's isolation of competence as the descriptive goal of linguistics involved him in deliberate idealisations. Competence was that of 'the ideal speaker hearer in the homogeneous speech community'. It was thus not socio-culturally determined in any way but comprised a basic mental faculty, belonging to all, which formed an essential part of our genetic inheritance. In this way Chomsky's work emphasise the unity of humankind in language – what is for him our common *access* to the *power* of *speech*. But by deliberately overlooking variation in language from situation to situation, he laid himself open to criticism for separating language off from its social context and avoiding issues of institutionalised inequalities in the social valuation of differing fashions of speaking. At the same time, his emphasis on competence also led him to overlook important regularities in the apparent disfluencies of performance, which later work in *conversation analysis*, for instance, suggests are part of the social purposes of speech. Ultimately, however, his emphasis on competence, tacit knowledge and mental structures laid the foundation for the burgeoning interest in cognition, cognitive linguistics and cognitive science more generally, which has marked the opening decades of this century. => CONVERSATION ANALYSIS, LANGUE, PAROLE, PERFORMANCE. *Further reading* Chomsky, N. (2008); Pinker, S. (2015)

concordance *n. CORPUS LINGUISTICS.* A list of all the key words of a *text* in alphabetical order, sometimes with information about their context. Invented originally to enrich the study of biblical text, *corpus linguistics* has much refined and extended its use with the advent of digital technologies. Concordances can, for instance, help to reveal relative frequencies and assist with the comparison of the verbal contexts of individual items. => COLLOCATION, CORPUS LINGUISTICS. *Further reading* Sinclair, J. (1991)

congruence theory *np.* POLITICS. Proposes that forms of government achieve stability as long as the patterns of authority inherent in them are widely dispersed through other institutions in society such as those of family, school and work. A stable democracy, for instance, is likely to be accompanied in civil society by patterns of authority in which permissiveness, lack of hierarchy and the importance of written *codes* are thematised.

consensus *n.* POLITICS. The solidarity of belief or sentiment or a general agreement that involves the *consent* of all participants. A decision reached through consensus may not be the most favoured of all participants, but it functions as the most acceptable decision or resolution of an issue. *SJ*

consent *n.* CULTURAL STUDIES, POLITICS. An important concept in the thinking of the Italian Marxist, Antonio Gramsci (1891–1937), where it is counter-posed to coercion. For Gramsci, dominance and subordination in a class society is achieved as much through consent as coercion; and consent is manufactured through the widespread circulation of key ideas that are congruent or at least compatible with everyday, commonsensical ways of thinking. Dominant *groups* or classes maintain their *control* (or *hegemony*) over subordinate groups to the degree that they can recruit generally dispersed, symbolic elements of *popular culture* to their cause. => CONTROL, HEGEMONY, IDEOLOGY, POWER, POPULAR CULTURE. *Further reading* Gramsci, A. (1971)

content analysis *np.* MEDIA STUDIES. A social science methodology designed to quantify the recurrence of categories of content in a body of data such as *news* or other forms of *mediated communication*. *Further reading* Pettey, G. et al (2018)

context of situation *np.* LINGUISTICS. The extra-linguistic context of an utterance. The term derives from the work of the British functional linguist M.A. K. Halliday (1925–2018), which rested on the claim that the selection of linguistic form for an utterance is partially determined by features of its context of situation. Relevant features of context typically amount to more than the physical environment or setting of the utterance but include more especially factors such as the type of social relationship involved, the nature of the medium adopted, the kind of activity in which the utterance is embedded and the topic being conveyed. Halliday believes that, as users of the language, we are constantly making and recognising adjustments in the linguistic selection of form, depending upon the context of situation. Thus, an utterance such as 'I observed the suspect proceeding east along Sauchiehall Street' is unlikely to occur outside courtroom testimony; in less formal contexts of situation the same idea is likely to be rendered as 'I saw 'im goin' towards town'. Contexts of situation vary from those that are relatively open and negotiable in character (such as family or peer *group* conversation) to those of a more institutionalised and closed nature (such as court room proceedings, media *interviews*, classroom lessons and so on). Any society or social formation will feature a number of common, recurring but salient contexts of situation, which Halliday termed *typical* contexts of situation. The totality of these comprise that society's *context of culture*. In this way the term context of situation confirms the sociological and anthropological orientation of Halliday's work, with context of situation providing a crucial mediating concept between the linguistic order and the social order. Indeed, in developing the concept, Halliday himself acknowledges a debt through the British linguist J. R. Firth (1890–1960) to the Anglo-Polish anthropologist Bronislaw Malinowski (1884–1942). As a concept its explanatory power is limited by the difficulties of capturing the dialectical relationship of language to situation. On the one hand language is sensitive to its context of situation. On the other hand it is active in defining and constituting that very context of situation. It is difficult to hold both insights simultaneously without some sense of circularity. => MEANING POTENTIAL, REGISTER, SPEECH EVENT. *Further reading* Halliday, M.A.K. (1978); Montgomery, M. (2008a)

continuity *n.* FILM & MEDIA STUDIES. Refers in its simplest sense to the task of ensuring that details (for example, of clothing and appearance) in succeeding film shots match each other, even after a lapse of time in the production process. In a more elaborate way it refers to the conventions of shooting and editing film so that the *narrative* unfolds in an easily intelligible fashion. The conventions of *continuity* editing are mostly associated with commercial (Hollywood) film-making and are sometimes challenged by avant-garde or 'art-house' movies. => FILM LANGUAGE.

control *n.* COMMUNICATION & CULTURAL STUDIES, CRITICAL DISCOURSE ANALYSIS. Exercising *influence* over the behaviour, thoughts and attitudes of others. Social control is a crucial component in how a society maintains order; and social control theory has typically distinguished between informal and formal social controls. Informal mechanisms of control depend upon the internalisation of norms through the processes of *socialisation*, the breach of which is sanctioned through various kinds of social pressure, including shame, ridicule, stigma and ostracisation or exclusion. Formal mechanisms of control depend more on the application of explicit force by state agencies, including the police, the prison service and the armed forces, with formally defined networks of sanctions applied by the courts and the judiciary. The control of populations by the state depends increasingly on sophisticated use of the modern media including *marketing*, advertising, *social media*, and *public relations*, criticised by some scholars as purveyors of *propaganda*. => HEGEMONY, PROPAGANDA, IDEOLOGY, POWER. *Further reading* Fairclough, N. (1992), (2015); Thornborrow, J. (2002)

conversation *n.* ETHNOMETHODOLOGY, SOCIOLOGY. Spontaneous, unscripted, spoken interchange between two or more people, usually face-to-face, where the roles and topics are not pre-determined and the *style* tends to informality. Often considered as the prototypical case of naturally occurring *talk* and as a baseline for comparison with status-marked and institutionalised *genres* of verbal behaviour. => TALK-IN-INTERACTION.

conversation analysis (CA) *np.* ETHNOMETHODOLOGY, SOCIOLOGY. A research tradition deriving from a branch of sociology known as ethnomethodology devoted to the detailed analysis of conversation as an instance of the situated social order. CA treats *conversation* as the outcome of participants' methods of practical reasoning with the task of analysis being to show how this is accomplished. Thus, CA seeks to display by the close analysis of transcribed conversational data the methods adopted by participants in achieving orderliness – the conversational structures to which participants attend and the interpretive work which they undertake. A major and early, but enduring, focus of attention within CA has been on the conversational *turn-taking* machinery – how participants know when to take a *turn*, for instance, and how different types of turn cohere with each other. The origins of CA may be traced back to a set of transcribed lectures given by the American sociologist Harvey Sacks (1935–1975) over an eight-year period from 1964 to 1972 and subsequently published in two volumes in 1994 as *Lectures on Conversation*. However, the initial emphasis on conversation *per se* as the object of analysis has gradually been replaced by a broader interest in *talk-in-interaction*. This has enabled CA to engage with a wider corpus of data than naturally occurring conversation, and elements of the CA approach have enjoyed wide currency in fields such as education, applied linguistics, health communication, media studies and social psychology. => ADJACENCY PAIR, COHERENCE, DISCOURSE ANALYSIS, MEMBERSHIP CATEGORISATION ANALYSIS, TALK IN INTERACTION, TURN TAKING. *Further reading* Hutchby, I. and Woofit, R. (2008); Schegloff (2007)

conversational styles *np. pl.* SOCIOLINGUISTICS. Adjustments made by conversationalists to their manner of speaking depending upon contextual factors, particularly those relating to the nature of the social relationship between interlocutors. => CONVERSATION, REGISTER, STYLE.

conversationalisation *n.* CRITICAL DISCOURSE ANALYSIS, SOCIOLINGUISTICS. The adoption of conversational *modes of address* in public *discourse*, using colloquial forms closer to *speech* than *writing*, as a way of emphasising an informal, even pseudo-intimate, relationship with the *audience*. It is particularly evident in certain *genres* of public discourse such as advertising, political speech-making and occasionally the *news*, where it is underpinned by techniques of direct *address* and the use of the *autocue* (sometimes described as 'the sincerity machine') to emphasise or facilitate extempore, unscripted *styles* of delivery. => INFORMALISATION, PARA-SOCIAL INTERACTION, SOCIABILITY. *Further reading* Fairclough, N. (1992), (1994)

copy editor *np.* PUBLISHING. One who improves or corrects the format, layout, spelling, punctuation and *grammar* of a *text* prior to printing and publication.

copywriter *n.* ADVERTISING, PUBLIC RELATIONS. One who supplies *text* ('copy') for the purpose of advertising goods or services. Copywriters usually work for advertising agencies as members of a team including the art director. The copywriter supplies the words, the art director the images. Advertising copywriters officially designate themselves as 'creative' and can be understood as part of the *creative and cultural industries*.

corpus linguistics *np.* LINGUISTICS. The use of large databases of continuous *text* to reveal patterns in word usage. These may range from statistical information about the co-occurrence of particular words to more qualitative accounts of the habitual meanings associated with them. => COLLOCATION, CONCORDANCE. *Further reading* Sinclair, J. (1991)

counter culture *n.* MEDIA. A social movement whose belief systems and norms are defined in opposition to those of mainstream society. The term is attributed to the U.S. historian Theodore Roszak (1933–2011), author of *The Making of a Counter Culture* (1969), and is most often used in relation to the protest movements of the 1960s (for instance, against the Vietnam War) which were seen as much more than solely political demonstrations but as rooted in a generational shift in ideas, beliefs and values reflecting a counter *culture*. => CULTURE, SUB-CULTURE, YOUTH CULTURE.

creative and cultural industries *np. pl.* MEDIA & CULTURAL STUDIES. Associated with individual (or *group*) *creativity* where ideas, and the *texts*, artefacts, programmes and techniques in which they are embodied, are developed and exchanged for financial gain. Core examples of creative industries are *broadcasting*, publishing, film production, drama and music. However, the term is broad enough to include other areas such as advertising, fashion and architecture, as well as research and design. The term has gained particular currency in policy circles as a response to the decline of older, 'rust-belt' industries; the outsourcing of many industrial processes to the emerging economies of China, Brazil and India; and the desire by the mature and stagnating economies of the West to try and capitalise on their remaining advantages in the areas of *intellectual property* rights, including those of knowledge-generation, transfer and innovation. => CREATIVITY, CULTURE, INTELLECTUAL PROPERTY, POPULAR CULTURE. *Further reading* Hartley, J. (2005); Hesmondhalgh, D. (2013)

creativity *n.* MEDIA & CULTURAL STUDIES. The capacity to produce (or create) works which are original, novel and innovative. Associated, at least since the Romantic period, with the composition of poetry, music, painting and sculpture (and other works of the imagination), it is increasingly used to underpin and valorise developments in the *creative and cultural industries* such as advertising and fashion. => CREATIVE AND CULTURAL INDUSTRIES. *Further reading* Hartley, J. (2005)

critical discourse analysis (CDA) *np.* LINGUISTICS, SOCIOLINGUISTICS, SOCIOLOGY. A research tradition within the social sciences that seeks to blend approaches deriving from *discourse analysis* with insights from critical social theory. The early work in this tradition grew out of linguistics and was indeed called initially 'critical linguistics'. The relevant models of linguistics for this approach were functional rather than formal, Hallidayan rather than Chomskyan, and particularly interested in showing how patterns of grammatical choice could embody a world view or how patterns of sentence-type or pronoun could be an instrument of *control*. Later work, associated with the British specialist in linguistics Norman Fairclough (1941–), places more emphasis on the analysis of connected discourse and seeks to integrate this with a social theory that takes a critical stance (usually neo-Marxist) towards contemporary social change. This has led to broad accounts of discursive change understood in terms of tendencies such as the democratisation, *marketisation*, *informalisation* and *conversationalisation* of discourse. More recently CDA has itself taken on a new guise as the *Discourse Historical Approach*, whose analyses are often committed to combating racism and *sexism*, as well as charting the historical evolution of oppressive discourse. => CONTROL, CONVERSATIONALISATION, IDEOLOGY, INFORMALISATION, MARKETISATION, POWER. *Further reading* Fairclough, N. (1992); Wodak, R. (2015); Wodak, R. & Meyer, M. (2009)

crossing *n.* SOCIOLINGUISTICS. Originally used to describe the adoption amongst U.K. teenagers of ethnically marked fashions of speaking borrowed from another *group* than the one to which the speaker primarily belongs. Such borrowing implies a degree of positive evaluation of other ethnic groups at a sub-cultural level. => ETHNICITY, STYLE, SUBCULTURE. *Further reading* Rampton, B. (2017)

cultivation theory *np.* MASS COMMUNICATION & MEDIA STUDIES. Examines how people respond over time to the social realities depicted on television and how television as a medium of *mass communication* shapes perceptions of reality. It was initially developed by the Hungarian-American communication theorist George Gerbner (1919–2005), who studied the 'cultivated', or long-term cumulative effects, of television on viewers. Gerbner specifically focused on the representation of violence on American television and investigated the ways in which television produces a shared symbolic environment for viewers that contributes towards the creation of normative social roles and behaviour. *Further reading* Gerbner, G. (2002)

cultural capital *np.* CULTURAL STUDIES, SOCIOLOGY OF CULTURE. The *power* that accrues to individuals and *groups* on the basis of the knowledge they hold and the cultural resources they are able to access by virtue of their position within society. According to this view, social advantages are not merely based on material resources but on a variety of valued social practices that can include favoured ways of speaking and writing, *access* to key knowledge *networks* and understanding of prestigious art forms and how to express the canons of *taste* that go with them. Perhaps the simplest and most direct form of cultural capital is level of education as expressed in the attainment of particular qualifications, but the most sustained treatment of cultural capital may be found in the work of the French sociologist Pierre Bourdieu (1930–2002), especially his extended study of the social basis of aesthetic judgement (or taste) in *Distinction*. Here he shows how ways of articulating taste are closely related to class position; and the performance of judgment provides ways of distinguishing one group from another ("taste classifies", says Bourdieu, "and it classifies the classifier"). The term, of course, is a metaphorical extension from its original use in political economy to designate how those who own the means of production can extract additional (or surplus) value from the process of production. The notion of cultural capital suggests that those who hold it have gained access to other forms of value over and beyond the financial. Studies of cultural capital usually suggest that the mechanisms that convert cultural into financial capital (and vice versa) are indirect and complex. Recent debates about the value of a university degree, however, display a tendency to calculate exactly the financial return on what might formerly have been understood intuitively as simply cultural capital. => AESTHETICS, POWER, TASTE. *Further reading* Bourdieu, P. (1984)

cultural imperialism *np.* CULTURAL STUDIES. Refers to the process or practice of extending the *power* of one country over another through formal policy or informal processes that shape ideas, customs and social behaviour. Cultural imperialism is usually supported by strategies of diplomacy and economic sanction, rather than by the direct application of military force, conquest and settlement. SJ

cultural industries *np.* CULTURAL STUDIES => CREATIVE AND CULTURAL INDUSTRIES.

culture *n.* CULTURAL STUDIES. A much-contested term ("one of the two or three most complex words in the English language", said the Welsh critic and progenitor of cultural studies Raymond Williams (1921–88) in *Keywords*, 1976, p. 87), 'culture' is used differently in different fields of enquiry. In the social sciences, particularly in anthropology, it means the whole way of life of a people, taken to include not only material artefacts, whether for ornament or practical use, but also *myths*, rituals, kinship systems and culinary practices. What binds these diverse practices together is their role as symbolic systems, giving meaning and structure to everyday life. As the U.S. anthropologist Clifford James Geertz (1926–2006) put it: culture is "a system of inherited conceptions expressed in symbolic forms by means of which men communicate, perpetuate, and develop their knowledge about and attitudes toward life". But 'culture' has a narrower sense that can be summed up in the words of the Victorian poet and intellectual, Matthew Arnold (1822–88): "culture [is the] pursuit of our total perfection by means of getting to know, on all the matters which most concern us, the best which has been thought and said in the world, and, through this knowledge, turning a stream of fresh and free thought upon our stock notions and habits". This sense of intellectual and artistic culture (and self-cultivation) is the one still active in debates around the fault-lines between mass culture and minority culture, *popular culture* and *high culture*, where notions of popular and mass culture often carry implicitly less value than minority or high culture. => CULTURAL CAPITAL, CULTURAL IMPERIALISM, CULTURAL INDUSTRIES, CYBERCULTURE. *Further reading* Eagleton, T. (2000); Williams, R. (1986)

cyberculture *n.* INTERNET & CULTURAL STUDIES. A multivalent term used to refer to the *culture* evolving from the widespread use of the *internet* and which often refers to information and knowledge exchange. Cyberculture includes a wide variety of human *interactions* that are *mediated* by computer *networks*, including online gaming, blogging and other *social media*, peer-to-peer file sharing and e-commerce. It can also refer to intellectual and cultural issues and movements such as cybernetics and cyberpunk. => CULTURE, CULTURAL CAPITAL, CYBERSPACE, SUBCULTURE. *Further reading* Kennedy, B.M. and Bell, D. (Eds.) (2007) SJ

cyberspace *n.* INTERNET & MEDIA STUDIES. A term first attributed to the American-Canadian science fiction author William Gibson (b. 1948) and which in common usage refers to the global *network* of computer processing systems, *information technology* infrastructures and telecommunications networks through which online *communication* takes place. Cyberspace can also be understood as a social rather than a technical space, in which people share information and ideas, engage in business and entertainment activities and initiate social and political discussions. => CYBERCULTURE.

★★

data mining *np.* INTERNET AND COMMUNICATION STUDIES. A field of computer science that involves the process of analyzing large data sets to extract information and discover patterns. It is also known as Knowledge Discovery in Databases, a term coined by Gregory Piatetsky-Shapiro in 1989. Data mining is an interdisciplinary field that utilises methodologies from applied statistics, artificial intelligence and database management. It can involve cluster analysis of *groups* of data records, anomaly detection of unusual records, and association rule mining of dependencies in records. SJ

dead air *np.* RADIO, TELEVISION. A period during which a television or radio broadcast is unintentionally interrupted, so that there is a gap in the transmission of material, either through operator error or for technical reasons. It is also used in cases where an individual broadcaster has lost his or her train of thought. Among professional broadcasters, dead air is considered one of the worst things that can happen. => BROADCASTING.

decode *v.* COMMUNICATION & CULTURAL STUDIES. => DECODING.

decoding *pppl.* COMMUNICATION & CULTURAL STUDIES. The process of making sense of a *message* and interpreting it according to its relevant *codes* of interpretation. The term gained a particular currency in television studies following the work of the British-Jamaican cultural theorist and sociologist Stuart Hall (1932–2014) in which he adopted a semiotic approach to highlight the role of the *active* *audience* in relation to the media. => ACTIVE AUDIENCE, ENCODING. *Further reading* Hall, S. (2007)

deconstruction *n.* PHILOSOPHY AND LITERARY STUDIES. An approach to the interpretation of *texts* which emphasises the problematic nature of meaning, especially when interpretation seems to rest upon viewing the text in terms of binary oppositions. A deconstructive approach will seek to expose the underlying hierarchy on which these oppositions are based. => POST-STRUCTURALISM, STRUCTURALISM. *Further reading* Norris, C. (2002)

defamation *n.* JOURNALISM AND LAW. Causing injury to a person's reputation and standing in society by making false statements or claims about them. Just as causing bodily harm to someone by physical action is subject to legal redress, so is making statements that harm an individual's reputation. In legal circles a distinction is usually made between *libel*, where the defamatory statement is published in recorded form, and *slander*, where the defamation is spoken. To be actionable a defamatory statement must be false and deemed capable of lowering the standing of the plaintiff in the estimation of right-thinking members of society. => CENSORSHIP, FREE PRESS.

deixis *n.* LINGUISTICS, PRAGMATICS. Words or expressions whose precise meaning always depends upon the particular context of their situation. Deictic items in effect point outwards (*deixis* is derived from the Greek, 'to show') from the *text* to the extra-linguistic context. They include words such as 'this', 'that', 'here', 'there', 'us', 'you', etc. Deictic items may be seen as falling into three major categories: *person* (or *social*) *deixis* such as 'I', 'you', 'he/she/it', 'we', 'they', 'me', 'mine', 'us', 'ours', 'them', 'theirs'; *temporal deixis* such as 'now', 'then', 'yesterday', 'today', 'tomorrow'; and *place deixis* such as 'here', 'there', 'away', 'this', 'that'. These words shift their referential meaning from context to context by 'pointing' to different entities: thus 'I' refers to whoever is speaking at the moment of utterance. Deixis thus raises crucially important issues about language and meaning. Consideration of deictic terms helps to show how the meaning of many utterances does not reside purely in the words themselves but depends also upon the context in which the words are uttered. For it is only by reference to context that we can recover the particular meaning of particular deictic expressions. The shifting character of deictics can be used for rhetorical effect in political speeches. In the closing section of Obama's speech to supporters in New Hampshire during his 2008 presidential campaign, note the way in which the scope of the first person plural pronoun, 'we', changes as he draws towards the close.

and so tomorrow (.) as we take the campaign South and West (.) as we learn
that the struggles (.) of the textile workers in Spartanburg (.)
are not so different than the plight of the dishwasher in Las Vegas (.)
. . .
we will remember that there is something happening in America (.)
that we are not as divided as our politics suggests (.)
that we are one people (.)
we are one nation (.)
and together (.) we will begin the next great chapter. . .

In the beginning of this extract, *we* encompasses campaign supporters ("as *we* take the campaign.."). Then *we* seems to encompass not only supporters but those following the campaign ("as *we* learn that the struggles (.) of the textile workers.."). In the last few lines, however, the meaning of *we* stretches wider again, to encompass *we* the people and *we* the nation. Indeed, Obama's words tend to reach outwards to include the widest possible *audience* for his utterance, and this in part is built on his use of the *verbal device* of the deictic *we*. => COHESION, DISCOURSE, MEANING, PRAGMATICS, RHETORIC, VERBAL DEVICE. *Further reading* Charteris-Black, J. (2013); Levinson, S.C. (1983)

demographics *n. pl.* GEOGRAPHY, SOCIOLOGY. The data resulting from the scientific study of the characteristics of a population as practised within *demography*. Such data has become of increasing interest in the *cultural industries* of *broadcasting*, *marketing* and *social media* in efforts to identify precise types of *audience*, consumer or voter for particular products, parties or programmes. In this context, a *demographic* is shorthand for a demographic profile of particular interest to an advertiser, broadcaster, political party or film-maker.

deviance *n.* SOCIOLOGY. Violation of social norms to a degree that can be perceived as a threat to the social order. What counts as deviance will, of course, vary over time and from place to place. For some sociologists, therefore, deviance is not considered to be a quality of the act that a person commits, but rather a consequence of the application by others of rules and sanctions to the deviant. In this account deviance is an outcome of a *labeling process*: the deviant is one to whom the label has successfully been applied; and deviant behaviour is behaviour that people label as such. => FOLK DEVILS, MEMBERSHIP CATEGORISATION DEVICE.

diachronic *adj.* HISTORICAL LINGUISTICS. To study something diachronically is to study it as an integrated system changing over time. The term diachronic is particularly associated with the work of the Swiss linguist Ferdinand de Saussure (1857–1913), who set up a distinction in linguistic study between studying language as a system of meanings at one moment in time *(synchronic linguistics)* and studying changes in the system of meanings from one temporal point to another *(diachronic linguistics)*. When he formulated this distinction (first made public in his 1911 lectures), the linguistics of his day was still primarily concerned with historical analysis. It was thus concerned with the origins of language and families of languages; with changes in pronunciation from one period to another; and with tracing changes in the meaning of individual words from their origin in a source language. Saussure regarded these endeavours as fundamentally flawed because they were atomistic and neglected the interrelated components of the system by focusing on isolated elements. The proper historical study of language depended, for Saussure, on initially describing the overall shape of the language, synchronically, before proceeding to the description of its change over time. Synchronic study thus became, in Saussure's view, logically prior to diachronic study; and the latter became – in effect – the comparison of temporally discrete synchronic states. In this sense, Saussure was not, as has sometimes been claimed, against the historical study of language. On the contrary, he was concerned to establish the historical study of language *(diachrony)* on a sounder footing. However, one effect of his *Course in General Linguistics* was to re-orientate the whole direction of linguistic research away from the study of historical change and on to the current state of the language, so that historical linguistics has, until recently, suffered a period of relative neglect. => LANGUE, PAROLE, SYNCHRONIC. *Further reading* Culler (1976); Saussure (1974)

dialect *n.* SOCIOLINGUISTICS. A socially or regionally marked version of a language made up of distinctive patterns of sentence construction, vocabulary and pronunciation. The use of one dialect rather than another depends basically upon the social class and regional origins of the speaker. Examples of dialect differences in English cover a wide range of phenomena and include matters such as: the use of multiple negation ('I hadn't got nothing to fall back on'), which is common in some English dialects but not in others; variation in vocabulary (the same entity – a young person in cheap fashionable clothes and jewelry, for instance, may be designated differently, as 'chav', 'ned', 'charva', and 'pikey', etc., in different dialects in different parts of the UK); and distinctive patterns of pronunciation (for instance, using a glottal stop, '/?/', instead of '/t/', in words such as 'bitter', 'Luton', 'letter', 'bottle', 'butter', a feature which is common in parts of London and has been spreading in SE England and further north). The latter kind of variation, purely in terms of sound, is also known as *accent*. Accent, however, refers *only* to pronunciation, and is thus not as inclusive a term as dialect, which embraces a wider range of linguistic variation. Indeed, in the UK it is possible to find the standard dialect being spoken in a range of regional accents. Everyone speaks a dialect, whether it be a non-standard regional dialect or the standard dialect. The standard UK dialect itself evolved out of a particular regional dialect of the south-east English Midlands and gained pre-eminence not because of any intrinsic linguistic superiority, but simply because it was the dialect spoken in that part of the country that was particularly influential in the emergence of the modern UK nation-state. It was the dialect spoken at the universities of Oxford and Cambridge and by important sections of the mercantile class. Thus, its growing adoption from the 15th century onwards as the preferred dialect in education, in certain key professions such as the law, and indeed for written *communication* in general, is more a question of historical contingency than of any special linguistic qualities. Its adoption as a standard dialect, particularly for written communication, leads to normative pressure on other less socially prestigious dialects. This in turn gives rise to the mistaken view that the norms of the standard are inherently more correct then those of other dialects — a judgement which is unconsciously based on social factors rather than linguistic considerations. From a linguistic viewpoint all dialects are equal in their ability to communicate the intentions of their users, although a particular dialect can become identified with a particular communicative role. *Broadcasting* provides a sounding board for these changes in the everyday evaluation of accents and dialects. Around the middle of the 20th century it would have been rare to hear regionally marked accents in broadcast *news presentation* and *continuity* announcements — although the BBC did use a well-known radio *personality* with a marked Yorkshire accent to read the *news* during wartime, on the grounds that the domestic *audience* could be sure of his *authenticity*. More recently, however, regional accents have become common. BBC Radio 4, for instance, features speakers with recognisable Jamaican, Northern Irish, and Scottish accents in UK-wide news and continuity. Scottish women are well represented: the Radio 4 announcer Arlene Fleming, for instance, describes her own accent for professional purposes as follows: "Natural mild versatile Scottish accent. Warm, informative, funny or serious can tone up the Scots or neutralise it." => ACCENT, NEWS PRESENTATION, NEWSCASTER. *Further reading* Hodson, J. (2014); Thøgersen et al. (Eds.) (2016)

dialogue *n.* LITERARY LINGUISTICS. A literary or, more specifically, a dramatic form that represents the exchange of speaking *turns* between two or more characters or persons. Theatre *scripts* take the form of dialogue. The *speech* of characters in a film is referred to as film dialogue. More broadly, however, the term refers to a foundational property of language as rooted in the exchange between one speaker and another. => CONVERSATION, DISCOURSE, SCRIPT. *Further reading* Hodson, J. (2014) Quaglio, P. (2009); Richardson, K. (2010).

diegesis *n.* FILM STUDIES, MEDIA STUDIES, NARRATIVE THEORY. Used in narrative theory (particularly *film theory*) to refer to the fictional world established in and by the *narrative*, i.e. to refer to the world in which the events of the narrative are held to be taking place. In film analysis the concept is useful for distinguishing between different sources in the sound track. Most film music, for instance, is extra-diegetic: while it may add colour and intensity to the depiction of action, it cannot be traced to a source in the scene. In a war movie, however, the sound of tank tracks audible over an image of a moving tank would be an obvious example of intra-*diegetic sound*. This perception of a sound being intra-diegetic, emerging from within the narrative world, is – it must be noted – an achieved effect of the film-maker, requiring complicity from the *audience*. As viewers, we are primed to see correspondences of some kind between sound and image so that what we hear in film matches in some way what we can see. The distinction between extra-diegesis and intra-diegesis has other applications, such as – for instance – distinguishing between different kinds of narrator. An intra-diegetic narrator is one who plays a role, major or minor, in the world of the narrative's events as opposed to an extra-diegetic narrator who exists autonomously outside the world of the narrative. => AMBIENT SOUND, DIEGETIC SOUND, FOCALISATION. *Further Reading* Bordwell, D. and Thompson (2004); Rimmon-Kenan, S. (2003)

diegetic sound *n.* FILM, MEDIA, TELEVISION. Elements of sound, such as *voice*, traffic noise, and waves breaking, that can be traced to a recognisable source within a recorded or *live* scene. For example, film *dialogue* is commonly regarded as diegetic sound, whereas *voice-over narration* is not. Music as part of a film sound track and used as an accompaniment to unfolding action within the film would normally not be considered diegetic, unless the scene actually features a source such as a band or orchestra visibly playing the music. => ACTUALITY, AMBIENT SOUND, DIEGESIS, DOCUMENTARY, FILM LANGUAGE, *Further reading* Bordwell, D. and Thompson (2004).

diffusion *n.* The spread, transmission or circulation of elements, ideas and substances. As a concept, diffusion is used in a wide range of disciplines including biology, chemistry, economics, physics and sociology. It can be applied to any subject area to explain the phenomenon of movement and spread, for example, to explain how ideas, *styles*, *technologies* and languages spread through *cultures*. SJ

digital/digitalisation *adj./n.* COMMUNICATION & CULTURAL STUDIES, INTERNET STUDIES. The use of binary coding to represent information by converting it to sequences of one or another digit, 0 or 1. Digital coding is universally used in computing and computer programming from where it has spread – partly through the development of micro-processing – to innumerable kinds of information or data transfer, including visual and oral/aural forms such as pictures, *speech* and music. Previously such forms would have been represented and stored by copying and transferring them in the form of an analogue or continuously varying signal (for example, marks on paper, traces on parchment or vinyl disk). Digital processing, by contrast, allows huge variation in methods of data storage and transfer. Most modern *communication* devices such as phones, radios, televisions and of course computers no longer transfer information in the form of analogue signals but have become digitised and are hence referred to as *digital media*, which has now become a loose cover term for hand-held communication device and the communication *platforms* associated with them. => ANALOGUE, DIGITAL MEDIA, NEW MEDIA, SOCIAL MEDIA. *Further reading* Jones, R.H. et al (Eds.) (2015)

digital divide *np.* COMMUNICATION & CULTURAL STUDIES, INTERNET STUDIES. Recognises that *access* to digitised information via *information and communications technology (ICT)* and the *World Wide Web* is unequal on various grounds related to variations in the availability of the required technological infrastructure interacting with other social factors such as age, class, gender and level of education. => INFORMATION AND COMMUNICATIONS TECHNOLOGY. *Further reading* Compaine, B.M. (2001)

digital media *np.* INTERNET & MEDIA STUDIES. Electronic media where information is stored, manipulated and transferred in digital (rather than analogue) form. Computer-based *communication* relies upon digital rather than analogue signals to transfer information; and the conversion of analog information into digital form has enhanced greatly the potential for communicating sounds, images, characters and words in a multi-modal signal or *message* by both old and *new media*. By extension the term also refers to common forms that freely circulate by virtue of digitisation, including video games, music files, digital photographs, etc. => DIGITALISATION, INFORMATION AND COMMUNICATIONS TECHNOLOGY, NEW MEDIA, SOCIAL MEDIA. *Further reading* Jones, R.H. et al (Eds.) (2015)

digital platform *np. INTERNET & MEDIA STUDIES.* A digital platform provides content and/or services through a variable blend of hardware and software. In this sense, a smartphone or a laptop constitutes a digital platform by allowing users to access content online on the *World Wide Web.* At the same time, organisations that maintain a digital presence, such as *news* providers or *social media* sites, can also be considered as digital platforms. Thus, Facebook or Buzzfeed may be regarded as digital platforms for social networking or news, respectively. In the latter sense, digital platforms tend to have a named and durable online presence with a defined architecture which delivers a distinctive kind of experience. Traditional media organisations, based formerly on print or *broadcasting*, have been at pains to build digital platforms to maintain their presence. => AFFORDANCE, DIGITALISATION, DIGITAL MEDIA, NEW MEDIA, SOCIAL MEDIA. *Further reading* Jones, R.H. et al (Eds.) (2015)

digital storytelling *np. INTERNET & MEDIA STUDIES.* A workshop-based practice in which people are taught to use a variety of digital tools and media (e.g., video and stills cameras, audio recording, etc., along with associated editing software) to tell short audio-video stories, usually about their own lives, in forms that combine still imagery, moving imagery, *voice*, music and *text*. It brings together *narrative*, memoir and autobiography using accessible digital techniques in such a way as to make stories that are easy to upload to the *internet* or otherwise disseminate electronically. Digital storytelling, in the words of Hartley and McWilliam (2009, 3), can "give voice to the myriad tales of everyday life as experienced by ordinary people in their own terms." => DIGITALISATION, NEW MEDIA, SOCIAL MEDIA. *Further reading* Couldry, N. (2008a); Hartley, J. and McWilliam (2009); Lambert, J. (2013); Page, R. (2018)

diglossia *n. SOCIOLINGUISTICS.* Contrasting linguistic varieties within a *speech community* – one of which is high status, the other low status – which are used in complementary contexts. Thus, the high variety will most likely be used for *news* broadcasts, religious services, newspaper *editorials* and traditional poetry, whereas the low variety will be used for everyday *conversation*, sports commentary, *soap opera* and other informal contexts. Clear examples of diglossia are to be found in the Arabic-speaking world. In most, if not all, Arab countries two varieties of Arabic exist side by side – Colloquial Arabic learnt informally at home as the first language, and Classical Arabic acquired by explicit instruction at school. The *grammar*, pronunciation and some of the vocabulary of the two forms of Arabic are different. The language of the Qur'ān – the sacred *text* of Islam – is in Classical Arabic, and partly for this reason the high variety is fairly uniform throughout the Arabic-speaking world, despite strong regional variations in the local variety of Colloquial Arabic. Indeed, the availability throughout the Arab world of Classical Arabic helps to guarantee a degree of mutual intelligibility when speakers of quite divergent forms of Colloquial Arabic meet. Other diglossic situations may be found in Greece (between Classical Greek and Demotic Greek) and in Switzerland (between High German and Swiss German). While English-speaking communities do not seem to display such strong internal division into two contrasting varieties, it is still possible to recognise a cline or scale of competing varieties which are accorded differing degrees of prestige. => ACCENT, DIALECT. *Further reading* Thøgersen et al. (Eds.) (2016); Ferguson, C.A. (1959)

discourse *n. LINGUISTICS, CRITICAL DISCOURSE ANALYSIS SOCIOLINGUISTICS.* The organisation and patterning of language beyond and between sentences (or utterances). From a linguistic perspective, discourse is a level of linguistic organisation similar to sound patterning (phonology) or sentence structure (syntax). Indeed, some approaches to discourse analysis extrapolate analytic methods from the description of other levels of linguistic organisation and extend them upwards to the domain of inter-sentential patterning. A fundamental premise of linguistic discourse analysis is that linguistic organisation does not stop with the sentence but underpins the way sentences are composed into a discourse. However, the exact nature of linguistic patterning and organisation beyond the sentence remains in dispute. As the American sociolinguist, William Labov, put it: "The fundamental problem of discourse analysis is to show how one utterance follows another in a rational, rule-governed manner – in other words, how we understand coherent discourse" (Labov, W., Sociolinguistic Patterns, Philadelphia 1972, 252). Indeed, from the beginnings of work on the linguistic organisation of discourse most researchers have been at pains to point out that formal linguistic links between one sentence or utterance and another are rarely sufficient to account for the *coherence* of discourse and that ultimately at this level of inquiry it is impossible to disentangle the social from the linguistic. And since the coherence of discourse is only partly linguistic, it depends ultimately on social and ideological knowledges. This, indeed, provides the starting point for *critical discourse analysis*, which takes as its focus precisely the unstated assumptions, presuppositions and *implicatures* that are routinely woven into any discourse but which the methods of critical discourse analysis can help explicate. Inasmuch as *CDA* draws on critical social theory it aligns itself with other major traditions of work in contemporary social science associated with scholars such as the French post-structuralist thinker Michel Foucault (1926–1984) or the political philosophers Laclau and Mouffe, where discourse is a more general term for the whole (often contradictory) social process of making sense. => COHERENCE, COHESION, CONVERSATION ANALYSIS, CRITICAL DISCOURSE ANALYSIS, POST STRUCTURAL ANALYSIS, PRAGMATICS, TEXT. *Further reading* Gee, J.P. (2014); Mills, S. (2004)

discourse act *np*. CRITICAL DISCOURSE ANALYSIS, DISCOURSE STUDIES, LINGUISTICS. Language as a form of action in context, a way of doing things with words. As well as a vehicle for informing, or for representing and depicting reality, language provides the means to compliment, thank, joke, promise, insult, greet, boast, declare war and so on. These are actions that we perform in *discourse*, sometimes – as in the case of greeting – with little propositional content or reference to objective reality. In these cases, language *is* the action, and it is difficult to conceive how actions such as promising or apologising or insulting could else be done except in words. But while such actions have an essential linguistic basis, they also have a social content and dimension. For one thing the performance of an action through linguistic means is dependent on features of context in which the utterance takes place: the same utterance may realise different actions in different contexts. In addition, the actions have a social impetus, shape and *influence* and in themselves constitute the building blocks of social *interaction*. When discourse is seen from the perspective of action, as well as – or including – *representation*, it is seen as constitutive of social relationships. It is interpersonal in its function as much as ideational. => COHERENCE, CONVERSATION ANALYSIS, CRITICAL DISCOURSE ANALYSIS, PRAGMATICS, SPEECH ACT. *Further reading* Gee, J.P. (2014)

discourse historical approach => CRITICAL DISCOURSE ANALYSIS.

discursive amplification *np*. DISCOURSE STUDIES, MEDIA, NEWS AND JOURNALISM, PRAGMATICS. A discursive practice designed to ensure the *salience* of statements in the *public sphere*. Any claim made in the digitised public sphere must compete for attention with an almost infinite array of other statements circulating for public consumption at the same time. Salience, indeed, has always been an issue in the public sphere; and since the 19th century, at the very least, the *news* industry (long before the advent of 'new' media) recognised this by identifying and singling out for attention reportable events in terms of their *news value*. But the news industry tended to do this – certainly in the days when print or *broadcasting* was dominant – in incremental ways. In effect, the life cycle of a story would be extended as long as new details topped, in some ways, the previous ones, and subsequent statements could strengthen the impact of previous ones. For instance, initial news of Kennedy's assassination was developed in successive statements like the following:

- *Three shots were fired at Kennedy's motorcade*
- *An unknown sniper fired three shots at President Kennedy*
- *President Kennedy seriously wounded in downtown Dallas*

Each statement amplifies the impact of the developing story by moving upwards through a scale, from 'shots fired at . . . a motorcade', to 'seriously wounded'. Naturally, there are important reasons why news organisations would not want to overshoot the facts in the first place. There is, for instance, the general pragmatic maxim not to say what might turn out to be untrue. But, as a story develops in the public sphere, a general rule of discursive amplification requires those who report it not to simply reiterate what has already been said. They must seek to provide not only 'the latest' (and we could say 'the strongest'), but also 'the exclusive' version of it, thereby distinguishing their report from others in the information market. In doing so they operate under the pressure of what could be reformulated for the public sphere, as the principle of discursive amplification: *Do not simply reiterate what has been said before: make a stronger statement rather than a weaker one if the audience is interested in the extra information that could be conveyed by the stronger.* While this may be a significant rule of news *discourse* and may apply more generally in the public sphere, there are exceptions. Donald Trump's use of Twitter is an interesting case of the almost continuous use of maximum discursive amplification with scant regard for truth. => NEWS VALUES, PRAGMATICS, PUBLIC SPHERE.

discursive gap *np*. COMMUNICATION STUDIES, DISCOURSE STUDIES. A gap in language (and understanding) that can arise between senders (such as television *newscasters* or doctors) and receivers (such as *audiences* or patients). On such occasions, there is a difference between the languages used by the two *groups*: the public institution uses a formal language, while the domestic audience adopts a less formal, more personal language. The popular *tabloid* press - at least in the U.K. - has attempted to close this gap by using its own version of the language of its *readership* – laced with colloquialisms and specialised slang – to engage their readers or audiences => DIGLOSSIA, READERSHIP, TABLOID.

disinformation *n.* JOURNALISM STUDIES, NEWS MANAGEMENT. A mode of discursive manipulation wherein deliberately inaccurate or false information or partial *truths* are spread to *audiences* to convince them of false conclusions. => FAKE NEWS, PROPAGANDA, SPIN DOCTOR. *Further reading* Miller, D. (ed.) (2004)

documentary *n./adj.* FILM & MEDIA STUDIES. Non-fiction filmmaking for cinema (and later for television) which is designed to document or disclose some aspect of reality. Often shaped by didactic purposes or made for the historical record, documentary filmmaking exploits cinema's potential for observing and interpreting life. An early theorist of documentary, the Scottish film-maker John Grierson (1898–1972), described it as "the creative treatment of actuality". The emergence of *reality television* as a popular television *genre* has prompted critical debate about the relationship between it and documentary, but documentary is regarded as distinct on the basis of its seriousness of purpose. => ACTUALITY, CONTINUITY, FILM LANGUAGE, REALISM, REALITY TV. *Further reading* Nichols, B. (2010)

dominant ideology *np.* MEDIA & CULTURAL STUDIES. The commonsense values, beliefs and mores of the ruling *group* in society which become the key defining elements in the common stock of everyday knowledge held by most social groups irrespective of whether these ideas serve the interests of the majority or not. => HEGEMONY, IDEOLOGY, INTERPELLATION, PROPAGANDA. *Further reading* Abercrombie, N. and Bryan S. Turner (1978); Eagleton, T. (2007); Thompson, J.B. (1990); Van Dijk, T.A. (1998)

domination *n.* MEDIA & CULTURAL STUDIES. The capacity of one *group* to exert *control* over others in such a way that compliance is achieved not so much by force as by voluntary compliance or assent. The *power* relationship of dominance and subordination is thus a structured relationship that remains 'in place' and active over a set of contingent and varying circumstances. => CONTROL, IDEOLOGY, POWER.

doxing *ppl.* INTERNET STUDIES. Slang term (derived from the abbreviation of 'docs' for documents) for releasing or publicising on the *internet* records of an individual or organisation, which were previously private or difficult to obtain. => COMMUNICATIVE ETHOS, FISKING, FLAMING, TROLLING.

dumbing down *phr v.* MEDIA & CULTURAL STUDIES. The attempt to make artistic or cultural material accessible and appealing for a *mass audience* either by simplifying it or by introducing elements intended to enhance its popularity. The term is pejorative and is based on the assumption that the original material has been changed in ways that undermine its *authentic* qualities as information, art or cultural product. Both *infotainment* and *tabloidisation*, for instance, may be seen as instances of dumbing down. => TABLOIDISATION.

★★

editorial *n.* JOURNALISM STUDIES, NEWSPAPERS AND THE PRESS. The part of a *newspaper* devoted to expressing the opinion or viewpoint of the publication on a topic of current interest. It occupies a highlighted position, usually near the centre pages in the case of a traditional newspaper format, and appears under a heading to indicate its nature. Editorials are not attributed to an individual named author but are conventionally understood to be the (anonymous) work of the newspaper's editorial board. The term can also be used to distinguish journalistic content in the newspaper from paid advertising content or 'advertorial'. Editorials may be understood, therefore, as a *genre* of journalistic *writing* in which judgements are made about current events in an impersonal but authoritative manner as the considered view of the newspaper and are generically quite distinct from reporting, reportage and *op-ed* pieces. => GENRE, NEWSPAPER, OP-ED, WRITING.

electronic commons *np.* INTERNET STUDIES => INFORMATION COMMONS. SJ

electronic democracy *np.* INTERNET STUDIES, POLITICAL COMMUNICATION. The use of communications and information *platforms* and technologies for political purposes in democratic sectors of local communities, regions or states, nations or global political processes. Citizens, the media, political organisations, elected representatives and governments may engage in e-democracy strategies and processes. It can involve the use of the *internet* as a campaigning tool, the issue of transparent *access* to information online and open social forums that connect policy-makers and citizens. SJ

electronic publishing *np.* INTERNET STUDIES, PUBLISHING. Using digital means to disseminate online what was formerly published in printed form. Thus, *newspapers*, journals and books are all now published electronically and are available online for access by laptop computer, tablet and smart-phone but are also available in other digital formats such as CD and DVD.

emergent culture *np.* CULTURAL STUDIES. The way in which new values, beliefs, meanings and forms of social practice are continually being created within the cultural field. The term derives from the Welsh cultural theorist Raymond Williams (1921–1988) and was part of his attempt to see the cultural field in its totality as a constant negotiation or struggle between tendencies in which the emergent, dominant and *residual cultures* are crystallised and defined by the processes of selective tradition and incorporation => COUNTER CULTURE, CULTURE, DOMINANT IDEOLOGY, RESIDUAL CULTURE. *Further reading* Williams, R. (2003) (pp. 121–128)

encoding *n. MEDIA AND CULTURAL STUDIES.* The process whereby information from a source is transformed into signs, characters, symbols or other forms of *representation* for the purposes of *communication*. The reverse process, whereby signs or symbols are transformed into meanings or information interpretable by a receiver, is known as *decoding*. Initial accounts of encoding and decoding assumed that the two processes of encoding and decoding were broadly congruent and complementary. However, beginning in the early 1970s, the Jamaican and British sociologist and cultural theorist Stuart Hall (1932–2014) proposed a model of encoding/decoding that stressed the situated and contextualised character of the two processes, emphasising that the output from the *code* could be quite different from the input under the real, historical circumstances of use. Hall suggested, indeed, that decoding was an active process in which *audiences* may interpret in three quite different ways. In the first, they may share the *dominant* code adopted in encoding and *decode* the *message* or *text* within the terms set by that code. In the second way, however, they may decode within the terms of the dominant code while simultaneously 'negotiating' and integrating discrepant elements into the decoding process. In the third way, audiences may reject the terms of the dominant code and decode the message or text in a globally oppositional fashion, finding in it a meaning radically counter to what was intended. These three ways of decoding underpin respectively what came to be described as the *dominant* or *preferred reading*, the *negotiated reading*, and the *oppositional* or *resistive reading*. Hall's model has been highly influential and has been considered one of the key conceptual frameworks of the field of cultural studies. => ACTIVE AUDIENCE, DECODING. *Further reading* Hall, S. (2007)

establishment *n. MEDIA AND CULTURAL STUDIES, POLITICS.* A *network* or *group* that operates as an informal centre of *power* and *influence* in society. The term has particular currency in Britain, where it is taken to include those who occupy key positions in major political parties, banking, finance, industry and the media, as well as in the top echelons of the civil service, non-governmental organisations (*NGO*)s and the ancient universities. A 'revolving door' is often said to operate between these institutions so that it is not uncommon for establishment figures to move between influential positions in different institutions – between the civil service and the universities, for instance, or between politics and commerce. => IDEOLOGY, POWER. *Further reading* Sampson, A. (2005)

ethnography *n. ANTHROPOLOGY, CULTURAL STUDIES, SOCIOLOGY, SOCIOLINGUISTICS.* Initially a branch of anthropology devoted to recording, analysing and interpreting the daily life, customs and social practices of pre-literate *groups*. The approach was founded by the London-based, Polish anthropologist Bronislaw Malinowski (1884–1942), who stressed the importance, in trying to understand societies very different from one's own, of establishing close daily contact with local informants and of situating their reports of daily life and customs in their actual social context. Malinowski's influence on social anthropology was immense, but he also had far-reaching effects on J.R. Firth (1880–1960) and the London School of Linguistics, as well as subsequently on M.A.K. Halliday's functional linguistics, both of which displayed strong commitment to the analysis of utterances in their *context of situation*. Malinowski's approach also underpins the sub-branch of sociolinguistics known as the ethnography of speaking (or communication) founded by the U.S. scholar Dell Hymes (1927–2009). More recently the study of media production and consumption was enriched by the application of ethnographic methods which have been applied more generally as one of the leading qualitative methods in educational, sociolinguistics and cultural studies research. => AUDIENCE, CONTEXT OF SITUATION, REGISTER. *Further reading* Morley, D. (1992); Saville-Troike, M. (2008)

★★

face *n. ANTHROPOLOGY, LINGUISTIC PRAGMATICS, SOCIOLOGY.* The relative social standing that a person claims for him/herself in the course of performing his or her chosen image or identity in situated social *interaction*; hence *facework*, the actions taken by individuals to make their behaviour appear consistent with their social image. As a sociological term it was developed by the U.S-Canadian sociologist, Erving Goffman (1922–1982), who drew on studies of Chinese *culture*, where concepts of face are widely understood and applied in everyday life. (Chinese has an extensive lexicon of more than 100 terms to cover different aspects of *face*, many of them difficult to translate into English.) The term was co-opted for linguistic anthropology and linguistic *pragmatics* by the British researchers Penelope Brown and

Stephen Levinson in their influential theory of linguistic politeness (1987). Here the notion of *facework* is elucidated by reference to the idea of *face-threatening acts (FTAs)* which can either undermine the interlocutor's positive image, made manifest by their adopted line in interaction, or restrict their freedom of action. Politeness strategies, for Brown and Levinson, are designed to mitigate and attenuate *FTAs* and are considered by them to be universal, though their precise form will vary from language to language. Media linguistics and the study of broadcast *talk* has a long-standing interest in face and politeness partly as a source of data for studying politeness itself but also because of the special conditions that may underlie the performance of politeness (and impoliteness) in public. => POLITENESS. *Further reading* Brown and Levinson (1987); Goffman (2005)

face-threatening act (FTA) => FACE.

face-to-face communication *np.* COMMUNICATION STUDIES, SOCIOLOGY OF INTERACTION. Takes place without the benefit of technologies of *mediation* in conditions where the parties to *communication* are mutually present to each other and able to monitor and respond to a range of bodily signals, including *intonation*, facial expression and bodily movement. Thus, face-to-face communication can rely on a range of contextual cues not necessarily available in *mediated communication*. It also tends to take place in *real-time* with more immediate recourse to a reciprocity of perspectives which allows for the activation of repair strategies if communication for some reason falters. The boundaries between face-to-face communication and mediated communication have become less clear with the advent of *digitalisation* and the increasing possibilities for communication to take place without parties being physically co-present to each other, relying instead on various kinds of virtual co-presence. Whereas, formerly, mediated communication was the antithesis of face-to-face communication, there is increasingly less contradiction between the two. Nonetheless, in the development of communication in the life of an individual, face-to-face communication is still regarded as the basic, prior precondition for communicative development. => DIGITALISATION, MEDIATION, SYNCHRONOUS COMMUNICATION. *Further reading* Boxer, D. (2002)

Facial Action Coding System (FACS) *n.* PARALINGUISTICS. The system was invented in 1978 by the U.S. psychologists Paul Ekman (1934–) and Wallace V. Friesen and psychologist, psychiatrist and neuroscientist Richard J. Davidson (1951–). It has an accompanying FACS Manual and an associated Investigator's Guide and was updated in 2002 by the first two authors and the behavioural scientist Joseph C. Hager. It was designed to investigate and measure the way in which the movement of facial muscles contributes to the expression of key emotions such as happiness and sadness, surprise and disgust.

Facial Affect Scoring Technique (FAST) *n.* PSYCHOLOGY. => FACIAL ACTION CODING SYSTEM TECHNIQUE.

fake news *np.* JOURNALISM STUDIES, POLITICS, SOCIOLOGY. Expression that rose to prominence during the 2016 U.S. presidential campaign and was used frequently thereafter to describe *news* that was either factually inaccurate or following an inappropriate news agenda, thereby distracting from or subverting the 'real' news stories of the moment. President Trump, for instance, has described stories of collusion between his campaign team and Russian state actors, designed to gain electoral advantage for him, as 'fake news', distracting from what he asserted to be the 'real news' which was the propensity of unnamed U.S. government *sources* to *leak* information embarrassing to his administration. The rise of *social media* and the proliferation of websites devoted to news has undoubtedly increased the prevalence of stories that circulate on the *internet* propagating spurious accounts of current events. Items purporting to be news on social media *platforms* such as Facebook or Twitter (e.g. the notorious 'Pizzagate' story) are thought by some to have adversely influenced the outcome of the 2016 U.S. presidential election to the degree that in the future, some argue, social media platforms should bear responsibility for withdrawing items that purport to be news but which are false. Debates of this kind inevitably touch on sensitive questions regarding the validity of claims in the *public sphere, censorship* and the credibility and limits of *journalism*. 'Fake news' was named word of the year in 2017 by Collins Dictionary. => CENSORSHIP, CITIZEN JOURNALISM, PUBLIC SPHERE, TRUTH, TRUTHINESS, VALIDITY CLAIMS.

FAST *abbrev.* => FACIAL AFFECT SCORING TECHNIQUE.

feminism *n.* MEDIA. A set of social and political movements and principles that advocate and support equal rights for women. It may take various forms depending upon the nature of the inequality it seeks to redress but broadly seeks to establish equal rights and opportunities for women in areas including education, employment and democratic systems and to challenge discrimination against women in areas such as law and the media. In the words of the American feminist and social activist, bell hooks (2015): "Simply put, feminism is a movement to end sexism, sexist exploitation, and oppression." *SJ*

fifth estate *np.* INTERNET STUDIES, JOURNALISM STUDIES. An extension of the notion of the *Fourth Estate*, a well-established term, which has been used to refer to the role of the press in pursuing and developing forms of democratic and public *accountability*. The Fifth Estate refers to the growing use of the *internet* and related digital technologies in enhancing these processes by creating a space for networking individuals to provide an additional source of accountability in government, politics and many other sectors of networked societies in such a way as to challenge the *influence* of other established bases of institutional authority. The use of the term suggests an implicit distinction between the established institutional bases of the press and *broadcasting*, as highly capitalised *mainstream media* with corporate identities, and the more fluid, informal and networked nature of digital online *social media*. => CITIZEN JOURNALISM, FOURTH ESTATE. *Further reading* Dutton, W. (2012)

film language *np*. FILM STUDIES, SEMIOTICS. Rules or *codes* of visual composition routinely followed in film-making. The notion of film language was developed from a semiotic perspective by the French critic, Christian Metz (1931–1993), who applied concepts drawn from the linguist Ferdinand de Saussure (1857–1913) to the analysis of film, treating it as the product of a code of *communication* as if it was structured like language. Just as language is based on units of structure in which elements such as words combine to form larger units such as sentences, so with film: the smallest unit, the shot, combines into structures such as the episode. The task for Metz was to set out the rules of combination for composing these structures in the same way as a linguist might specify the rules that make up the *grammar* of a language. The paradox of Metz's approach was that it had very little to say about film *dialogue*, treating film ultimately as if it were a purely visual medium with no oral-aural component. Nonetheless it inspired a significant body of analytical work considering in detail how one film shot followed another in a rule-governed way and contributes significantly to our understanding of film as a visual artefact. => CONTINUITY EDITING, FILM THEORY, MONTAGE. *Further reading* Monaco, J. (2009)

film noir *np*. (*Fr*: literally, 'black film') FILM AND MEDIA STUDIES. A type of film-making, distinguished by *style* and subject matter, associated with a strand of Hollywood cinema in the 1940s and 1950s. Originally 'noir' tended to be shot in black and white, using low key lighting which plunged elements of a scene (including facial features) into dark shadow, 'night-for-night' shooting, a fondness for oblique lines and unsettling camera angles. In terms of content, there was an emphasis on corruption and despair, violence and crime, and they often revolved in plot terms around a *femme fatale*. Although film noir was dominant in the 1940s and 1950s, there are later examples, such as *Klute* (1971) and *Body Heat* (1981), which re-work the theme and style of noir in colour in the 1970s and 1980s. More recently, 'Nordic Noir' has served as a term to describe television crime series, mostly from Sweden and Norway, emphasising similar themes of corruption, despair, violence and crime but sometimes with a strong female lead character playing the detective, as in *The Bridge*. *Further reading* Silver, A. (ed) (2004)

film theory *np.* FILM & MEDIA STUDIES. The study of film from an academic perspective with particular attention to its relationship to reality, to its *audiences*, to its modes of production, to its *genres* and to its formal characteristics. => CONTINUITY EDITING, FILM LANGUAGE, GENRE, MONTAGE, SCOPOPHILIA. *Further reading* Elsaesser, T. (2015)

fisking *prpl.* INTERNET STUDIES. A slang term and neologism for a certain kind of contribution to the blogosphere in which one writer takes another to task for a prejudicial, biased or inaccurate comment by subjecting them to a process of forensic rebuttal. It is reputed to have been inspired by the journalist Robert Fisk, a long-time commentator on Middle Eastern affairs. Some believe that Fisk's *journalism* was unreliable, and so fisking became modelled on the activity of taking Fisk to account. Others believe that Fisk's own journalism was an example of the forensic exposure of the lies and deceits in western accounts of the Middle East so that he himself was the exemplar for how to do fisking. Either way the interest of the term lies in how it coins a name for a certain kind of verbal performance considered distinctive and peculiar to the blogosphere. => COMMUNICATIVE ETHOS, FLAMING, TROLLING.

flaming *prppl.* COMMUNICATION STUDIES, CULTURAL STUDIES, INTERNET STUDIES. Slang term for the use of aggressive, abusive or inflammatory comments in the blogosphere which have the potential for provoking heated online exchanges. Related terms would be *trolling* and *fisking*. It is noteworthy that slang words for modes of verbal performance regarded as distinctive and peculiar to the *internet* tend to feature forms of aggression rather than solidarity. Some commentators speculate that online anonymity, as well as operating in an underspecified social context without normal cues from face-to-face *interaction*, favours forms of social disinhibition in which flaming, trolling and fisking is encouraged so that these have become the defining characteristics of the *communicative ethos* of the blogosphere. => COMMUNICATIVE ETHOS, FISKING, TROLLING. *Further reading* Higgins, M. and Angela Smith (2017)

flashback *n.* FILM & LITERARY STUDIES. An interjected scene or sequence that takes a *narrative* back to a point prior in time to that which it has currently been reached. Most commonly used to refer to film but also applicable to other forms of narrative such as drama, the comic strip and the novel. => NARRATION, NARRATIVE, NARRATIVE CODES.

focalisation *n.* LITERARY LINGUISTICS, NARRATOLOGY. Refers to the choice of perspective through which a *narrative* is presented. The term was coined by the French narrative theorist Gérard Genette 1930–2018, who adopted it in preference to the widely used term *point of view* in literary criticism. While it is clear that every story is told from a specific perspective, Genette's recourse to the term focalisation emphasises how the process of telling a story typically involves more than shifts in visual perspective but also shifts in the kind of experience and knowledge available to a narrator in addition to their position within or outside the narrative. Indeed, Genette develops a typology of different kinds of focaliser and focalisation beginning with a distinction between external focalisers and character focalisers. Although Genette was primarily concerned with avowedly literary narratives (many of his examples are drawn from the French modernist writer Marcel Proust) his terminology has been widely adopted in studies of narrative, especially by other narratologists such as Mieke Bal. => ALIGNMENT, STANCE. *Further reading* Bal, M. (2009); Genette, G. (1980).

folk culture *np.* CULTURAL STUDIES. The traditional *culture* of a settled, mostly rural *community* usually kept alive by word of mouth, personal example and informal apprenticeship in its ways. => ORAL CULTURE, COMMUNITY.

folk devils *nppl.* CULTURAL STUDIES, SOCIOLOGY. Members of a social *group* regarded by mainstream society as both deviant and as a threat to the general social order. Typically folk devils are discovered among the less advantaged members of society, and it is usually difficult to find statistical support for the scale and incidence of their undesirable behaviour. In other words, the threat that they pose is as much imagined as real. For this reason, folk devils need particular properties to resonate as such with the general population, and it is common for some negative characteristics of the group to be highlighted and exaggerated. The identification of a folk devil is usually matched by a degree of shared moral outrage at their behaviour. 'Football hooligans', for instance, have more potential to be folk devils than 'bankers'. => DEVIANCE, MORAL PANICS, NEWS VALUES, TABLOIDISATION. *Further reading* Critcher, C. (2003); Critcher, C. et. al. (2013)

footing *n.* SOCIOLOGY, SOCIAL INTERACTION. The stance or alignment taken up by a participant on a moment-by-moment basis in the course of an *interaction* in relation to the communicative events at hand. The term derives from the work of American sociologist, Erving Goffman (1922–1982). => PARTICIPATION FRAMEWORK.

fourth estate *np. JOURNALISM STUDIES.* A term used by Thomas Carlyle (1795–1881), the Scottish historian, essayist and social commentator, reporting Edmund Burke (1730–97), the Irish statesman, political thinker and philosopher, as saying that, while the Westminster Parliament consisted of 'Three Estates', the Lords Spiritual (the Church), the Lords Temporal (the Peerage) and the Commons (members of the House of Commons), there was 'a Fourth Estate more important than they all' – namely the press. Burke was not necessarily wrong to imply that the press of the day, communicating the discussions and decisions of Parliament to the general public but also adding their own sometimes scathing commentary, wielded more *influence* than all Three Estates combined. The term is still used to refer to the press, and *journalism* in general, and its responsibilities to hold the powerful to account. => ACCOUNTABILITY, ACCOUNTABILITY INTERVIEW, ESTABLISHMENT, FIFTH ESTATE, PUBLIC SPHERE. *Further reading* Conboy, M. (2004), Ch. 9

frame/framing *n./prepl JOURNALISM & MEDIA STUDIES.* In the composition of the *news*, material is framed: it is selected, focused and presented according to tacit theories about what exists, what happens and what matters. The term derives from the work of American sociologist Todd Gitlin (b. 1943), though it bears useful comparison with work in artificial intelligence and cognitive linguistics. => AGENDA SETTING, NEWS VALUES. *Further reading* Mcleod, D. (2014)

free press *np. JOURNALISM & MEDIA STUDIES.* A term used to describe *journalism* that is free from *control* by the state, political parties or commercial interests, with the implication that it can thereby be considered honest and truthful.

freedom of information *np. JOURNALISM & MEDIA STUDIES.* A widely held principle that citizens have a right to know information of public interest held by their government. Prototypical instances of information in the public interest would be expert advice commissioned or data collected by governments on scientific, health, safety, legal, commercial or financial matters, especially where this is intended to shape or determine policy. At least 70 governments worldwide have enshrined the principle in legislation.

Freedom of Information Act *np. JOURNALISM & MEDIA STUDIES.* A federal law passed in the United States in 1966 that allows for the full or partial disclosure of information held by the U.S. government. The Act defines the kind of information subject to disclosure, outlines the procedures for disclosure and specifies exemptions. The same name is used for two similar pieces of legislation later passed by Acts of Parliament in the UK: the Freedom of Information Act 2000, and the Freedom of Information (Scotland) Act 2002. These Acts create a statutory right of *access* to information held by public bodies such as public authorities, publicly owned companies and other bodies performing public functions.

★★

gatekeeper *n. JOURNALISM & MEDIA STUDIES.* A person who controls the flow of information, not only but especially in the context of *news* editing. News editors and journalists occupy a classic gatekeeping role, though this is perhaps being progressively diminished by the rise of alternative sources of news on the *internet* as well as by the increasing adoption of user-generated content.

genderlects *n. pl. SOCIOLINGUISTICS.* A variety of language which is associated with a particular gender. Like other sociolects or social *dialects*, in which social class produces distinctive linguistic features, genderlects can be determined according to both passive acquisition of language use through immersion in a particular *community*, as well as active investment in particular spoken and written forms that signify identification with specific *groups*. => DIALECTS. *Further reading* Coates, J. and Pichler, P. (Eds.) (2011) *SJ*

genre *n. COMMUNICATION AND CULTURAL STUDIES, DISCOURSE STUDIES, FILM STUDIES, LITERARY LINGUISTICS, SOCIOLINGUISTICS.* A category of literature, music, film, *discourse* and visual art which shares conventions of form, *style* or subject matter. A work may be compatible with more than one genre. New genres may evolve, while old ones may fall out of favour. Mikhail Bakhtin's (1895–1975) concept of heteroglossia or 'speech genres' emphasises that genres, as modes of speaking or expression, are socially defined and recognised, in that formal and stylistic features respond to a particular communicative situation. Thus, a genre of discourse is a specific and recognisable configuration of discourse elements realising a particular communicative purpose or set of purposes and usually known amongst a language *community* by a widely shared label, such as 'advert', 'sermon', *gossip*, 'joke', or 'lecture'. Like structure, genre as a concept also faces two ways. "The constructional value of each and every element of a work can be understood only in relation to genre. . . . It is genre that gives shape and meaning to . . . a whole entity, and to all the elements of which that entity is comprised" (Medvedev, 1928, quoted in Titunik, 1973). One of the difficulties about the definition and application of the term genre is that genres are often unstable, in flux, with the boundaries dividing one genre from another tending to be indeterminate in practice. In *journalism*, for example, the notion of a 'news piece' is considered generically different from 'a feature'. The latter tends to be longer, less compressed, with less emphasis on current incident, more personal, with more focus on human interest and with greater allowance for the personal viewpoint of the journalist. 'News', on the other hand, is understood as generically opposed to 'feature', shorter, more impersonal and more focused on a particular event. Despite this there seems to be no contradiction involved in describing intermediate cases as a 'news feature'. So genre does not merely describe a patterned, recurrent configuration of elements or units but also encompasses shared understandings between producers and *audiences* about forms and the purposes they serve. In this sense, although genre is textually manifested in discourse, it may also be considered a process beyond the discourse itself involving a promise, by producers, and recognition, by audiences, of the type of discursive activity being performed. Genre is thus also a set of generative and interpretative procedures, a horizon of expectations against which any specific generic instance must be set. In this sense, genre is at once the sedimentation and routinisation of a set of practices and a backdrop against which innovation and change can take place. It should also be noted that well-defined discourse genres such as the lecture, the sermon, the debate, legal cross-examination or the medical consultation are often embedded in strongly institutionalised domains of social life such as medicine, education, law, politics and religion. They derive their purpose from their institutional position, at the same time as being the discursive embodiment of the institution. The productivity of genres, however, also allows for their migration across domains as models for newly discovered communicative purposes. Thus 'the lecture', 'the debate' and 'cross examination' have all had a life in *broadcasting* sometimes transformed into new genres such as the studio discussion or the political *interview*. => DIALECT, HYBRIDITY, REGISTER, STYLE. *Further reading* Biber, D. and Conrad S. (2009)

geodemographics *n.* GEOGRAPHY, SOCIOLOGY. As classifications which relate to the structure of populations, geodemography links the fields of demography, geography and sociology and seeks to study people based on where and how cities and neighbourhoods have formed. The foundations of geodemographic theory may be located in the work of Charles Booth (1840–1916) on impoverished neighbourhoods in London in the early 20th century, as well as of the Chicago School of Sociology, which respectively developed the ideas of 'classifying neighbourhoods' and 'natural areas' within cities. The idea that geographical sectors have particular socio-economic and cultural features has been also put to commercial use to tailor information and services towards *groups* based upon location and population characteristics. SJ

gesture *n*. INTERACTION. A form of non-verbal *communication* in which movements of the hands, face and other parts of the body communicate meanings that supplement, complement or work independently from spoken communication. => KINESICS, MULTIMODALITY.

ghost writer *np*. PUBLISHING. One who writes on behalf of another who is officially credited with authorship. The role is easier to acknowledge in certain *genres* of *writing* and tends to be associated with popular cultural forms, especially where individuals famous for exploits in ostensibly non-literary fields (e.g. sporting endeavours, screen-acting, entertainment, and so on) are commissioned to write an autobiography or *newspaper* column. The autobiographies of Ronald Reagan, Doris Day and Sophia Loren were penned by ghost writers. => AUTHOR, PARTICIPATION FRAMEWORK.

glasnost (*Rus*: 'openness') *n*. MEDIA. A policy adopted in the 1980s during the late period of the Soviet Union by its then president, Mikhail Gorbachev, where it was seen as a call for transparency in government as an antidote to corruption and the abuse of *power*. *Glasnost* went hand-in-hand with *perestroika* – the restructuring of Soviet society and economy. => CENSORSHIP, FREEDOM OF INFORMATION.

global media *np*. MEDIA & COMMUNICATION STUDIES. Large media conglomerates which have developed a global reach and range to their activities. In 2012 the five largest media conglomerates were The Walt Disney Company, News Corporation, Time Warner, Viacom and CBS Corporation. Of these, News Corporation, for example, owns *newspapers* such as the Wall Street Journal, television *networks* such as Star Asia, television *news* channels such as Fox News and entertainment media such as 20th Century Fox. Either its products are designed as much as possible for global *audiences*, with worldwide distribution rights (e.g. 20th Century Fox), or its ownership structures include local producers who create content adapted for local audiences (e.g. Star Asia). The largest media conglomerates, therefore, aim always to operate transnationally – as global media. => GLOBAL VILLAGE, GLOBALISATION. *Further reading* Miller, T and Kraidy (2016)

global village *np*. MEDIA & COMMUNICATION STUDIES. A metaphorical expression associated with the Canadian scholar and media theorist Marshall McLuhan (1911–1980). It was introduced in his books

The Gutenberg Galaxy (1962) and *Understanding Media* (1967) and encapsulates his view that the electronic media have changed the way we communicate with and relate to each other through their capacity for radically overcoming the pre-technological constraints of time and distance. The speed and reach of electronic media enable us to communicate in real time with others on the other side of the globe as if they were near at hand. They have also made possible many more interconnections between ourselves and others. In this sense they count, in another of McLuhan's phrases, as 'extensions of man' (the subtitle of *Understanding Media*): they not only simulate the speed of the central nervous system but re-configure the senses into new modalities of perception. The result is a global village in two ways. The world has become a village insofar as its inhabitants are (electronically) near at hand to each other for the purposes of *communication*. But we also exist in a world where we have a heightened sense of responsibility for those far away, as if they were our neighbour. The idea of the global village has been criticised for overlooking important issues of *access* to the electronic media – failing to recognise, for instance, differences between rural and urban populations with their different kinds of use of and access to the electronic media. Nonetheless, although McLuhan's coining of the phrase pre-dated the *internet* and the *World Wide Web* by at least a couple of decades, his visionary phrase in a very real sense anticipated the consequences of its widespread adoption. => GLOBALISATION, GLOBAL MEDIA, TIME-SPACE DISTANTIATION, WORLD WIDE WEB. *Further reading* Hafez, K. (2007); Miller, T. and Kraidy (2016)

globalisation *n.* MEDIA & COMMUNICATION STUDIES. Processes of *integration* on a global scale that include intensified economic, financial, political and cultural exchanges and which have led to increased interdependence between societies. => GLOBALISATION, GLOBAL MEDIA, TIME-SPACE DISTANTIATION, WORLD WIDE WEB. *Further reading* Hafez, K. (2007)

gossip *n.* COMMUNICATION AND MEDIA STUDIES, SOCIOLINGUISTICS. Communal speech event or *genre* that involves the sharing of information about an absent third party, one who may be described as the target or victim of gossip. Anthropological research suggests that single women, widows, daughters-in-law, teachers and doctors make ideal gossip victims. The subject or theme of gossip consists broadly of the faults, character flaws, behavioural inconsistencies, moral failings, bad manners or other shortcomings of the gossip victim. Gossiping makes an ideal accompaniment to repetitive tasks such as cleaning vegetables, sewing, or bread baking and is also associated with locations that members of a *community* routinely need to visit – such as the water cooler, the well, village shops, bars and barber shops. Indeed, it is prototypically associated with small-town or village life, but large organisations are not immune as long as there are places where members need to congregate or meet on a regular basis. While gossip may be seen primarily as a face-to-face activity, it also plays an important role in public *communication* to the degree that it becomes institutionalised in *newspaper* and *magazine* gossip columns where celebrities and politicians become prime targets. *Reality television* shows and *soap opera* may also be seen as forms of surrogate gossip material. => GENRE, SPEECH EVENT. *Further reading* Besnier, N. (2009); Thornborrow, J.T. and Morris (2004)

grammar *n.* LINGUISTICS, SEMIOTICS. A formal statement of the rules (or patterns or structural combinations) of a language that specifies in abstract terms all that a speaker needs to know to produce and recognise well-formed sentences. The overall statement of rules that make up a grammar is divided into subsets or components to deal with different aspects of language such as sound or meaning. Thus, grammars usually contain a component associated with the sounds of the language (phonology), the meanings of the language (*semantics*) and the constraints on the ordering of words (syntax or lexicogrammar). Formulating a grammar is the overall project of linguistics as a human science, though there are different schools of thought within linguistics about the precise nature of the project, especially at the level of syntax or lexicogrammar. Those working within a broadly Chomskyan paradigm tend to work deductively, thinking of this project in terms of the examination (by introspective assessment) of the native speakers' intuitions about what counts as a grammatical or well-formed sentence. Those associated with the neo-Firthian and structuralist paradigms tend to work inductively, building the grammar from observation of patterns of co-occurrence. The latter approach has been given fresh impetus by developments within *corpus linguistics* which use computational techniques to investigate linguistic patterns in large bodies of linguistic data. The aims of the two approaches are, however, quite different. Within the Chomskyan paradigm the ultimate aim is to define the properties or design features of a universal grammar that underlies the discrete grammars of individual languages and which therefore reflects fundamental characteristics of the human mind. The neo-Firthian approach tends to be more concerned with linguistic variation in context, and its modes of explanation are more sociological. In either case the focus, it should be noted, is resolutely descriptive rather than prescriptive, i.e. neither approach has any interest in imposing notions of correctness or in defining what language-users should do linguistically in order to be better communicators. The notion of a grammar, however, is sometimes used by extension to examine kinds of communicative activity other than the strictly linguistic. There have, for instance, been attempts to define the grammar of film or advertising as rule-governed systems of communicative behaviour, where the notion of an underlying grammar provides a useful way of pointing to the regularities, patterns and basic systematicities in their mode of composition. => CORPUS LINGUISTICS, FILM LANGUAGE, LEXICO-GRAMMAR, SEMANTICS. *Further reading* Yule, G. (2016)

groups *n.* SOCIOLOGY, SOCIAL PSYCHOLOGY. People or things that are classed together according to a common factor. For example, the classification of groups may be according to belief, occupation, age, gender, race or nationality. *SJ*

★★

habitus *n.* (*L.* 'habit, disposition') CULTURAL STUDIES, SOCIOLOGY. A way of describing the complex interrelationships between different kinds of *tastes* (or social preferences more generally) and social practices, especially as they centre on the body, when these form part of the social identity of a *group*. The term is particularly associated with the work of the French sociologist Pierre Bourdieu (1930–2002), for whom it provides an important mediating concept between structure on the one hand and agency on the other. For Bourdieu, a distinctive habitus may be seen as the outcome of choices in lifestyle (which may include, for instance, food preferences, pastimes and hobbies, leisure activities, ornamentation, furnishings and fashion choices, many of which are habitual and unconscious) even if to some degree for any individual the range of these choices is determined in advance by social position. In this way the choices that constitute habitus are generative, structuring but in the last analysis already structured in advance. => TASTE. *Further reading* Bourdieu (1977), (2010); Elias, N. (2000)

hard news *np.* JOURNALISM & MEDIA STUDIES. Hard news stories are distinguished from *soft news* stories by their seriousness and timeliness. Hard news is likely to be assigned a prominent position by *news* outlets either because of the scale of the event which it captures or because of its general significance in political, economic or social terms. Soft news, by contrast, lacks seriousness and timeliness, though it may be strong in human interest and thereby high in entertainment value. => INFOTAINMENT, NEWS VALUES, SOFT NEWS.

harijans *n. ANTHROPOLOGY, SOCIOLOGY.* A term meaning 'children of God' popularised by Mahatma Gandhi as a substitution for the pejorative 'untouchables' which refers to the *Dalits*, a caste traditionally discriminated against in India. => CASTE SYSTEM, DALITS. *SJ*

hegemony *n. CULTURAL STUDIES.* Term associated with the work of the Italian Marxist thinker Antonio Gramsci (1891–1937), who used it to explore how subordinate *groups* become reconciled to their position to the degree that they accept certain key ideas as commonplace and commonsense. For Gramsci, hegemony is a term that foregrounds the role of everyday *popular culture* in supporting relations of *power* and *domination*, though he also used it to emphasise the importance of cultural politics in resisting relations of power. => CONSENT, CONSENSUS, DOMINANT IDEOLOGY, IDEOLOGY, POPULAR CULTURE. *Further reading* Laclau, E. and Mouffe (2014)

hermeneutics *n. COMMUNICATION STUDIES, LITERARY STUDIES, MEDIA STUDIES.* The science or art of interpretation, its theory and its methodology. The term originated in the context of biblical criticism or the interpretation of esoteric and difficult *texts* – for example, philosophical texts – where the meaning was evidently important but not at all self-evident. The term played an important role in the work of the French philosopher Paul Ricouer (1913–2005), who explored in depth one kind of hermeneutic – the hermeneutics of suspicion. This, he suggested, (1974) characterised the work of – at least – three important thinkers: Nietzsche, Marx and Freud. None of these took reality or text for granted but drew out hermeneutically their hidden meanings. Freud, for instance, interpreted dreams as expressing the repressed contents of unconscious desires. Marx interpreted *ideology* as concealing the real relations of production in which working people were exploited. Scannell (1998), by contrast, following Ricouer, proposed an alternative hermeneutic – the hermeneutics of trust. He points out, drawing upon ethnomethodology and *conversation analysis*, that the natural attitude of members of society is to take meaning and reality for granted and that we need to be able to understand how ordinary interpretations are made before we can begin to critique the process. In this sense, in both media studies and communication studies, we need, suggests Scannell, a hermeneutics of trust before we can have a satisfactory hermeneutics of suspicion. => IDEOLOGY, INTERPRETIVE COMMUNITIES. *Further reading* Bell, A. (2011); Scannell, P. (1998)

high culture *np. CULTURAL STUDIES.* General term for those cultural artefacts (painting, music, sculpture, literature) judged to be of the highest value for a society. The term exists in contrast not so much to 'low' *culture* as to mass, *popular* or *folk culture*, though qualitative assumptions play an important part in the distinction. The value of high culture lies in its capacity to educate and refine the moral and aesthetic sensibility of those who can appreciate it, and the term carries (deliberate) connotations of exclusivity and elitism. For this reason, much cultural commentary in the latter half of the 20th century was devoted to finding different ways of organising the distinction between minority high culture and popular mass culture so as to rescue 'the popular' from the implied devaluation. => CULTURE, TASTE, CULTURAL CAPITAL, POPULAR CULTURE. *Further reading* Eagleton, T. (2000); Gans, H.J. (1999)

hot media *np.* MEDIA STUDIES. => COLD MEDIA.

hybridity *n.* ART, CULTURAL STUDIES, LITERATURE. In *culture*, a mixing of forms and *genres* often, but not invariably, associated with the avant garde. In literature, work that fuses elements of memoir, philosophical reflection and *narrative* (e.g. Maggie Nelson's *Argonauts*) may be said to display hybridity. Performance art, where the art-work is not fixed but displayed by the artist (or *group*) in the form of an activity, such as Spencer Tunick's nude gathering which featured thousands of participants painted blue in Gateshead, UK, is likewise a form of hybridity. However, hybridity flourishes in less obvious ways in many domains of *popular culture*, where it is a constant source of innovation and *creativity*. Computer gaming may be considered a hybrid form, as well as older forms such as docu-drama and *reality television*. => GENRE, POPULAR CULTURE, POSTMODERNISM. *Further reading* Kraidy, M. (2005)

★★

iconic *adj.* LITERARY LINGUISTICS, MEDIA STUDIES, SEMIOTICS. From icon, a type of sign studied in *semiotics* that gains meaning by virtue of a resemblance between what is signified by the sign and that which is used to signify it. Road signs are often iconic, and photography, film, cartoons and figurative painting all draw upon iconic signs. Often used more loosely to indicate an image, artefact or even performance considered to be representative of the times. => MULTI-MODALITY, SEMIOTICS. *Further reading* Fischer, O. and Nanny (Eds.) (2001)

identification process *n.* PSYCHOLOGY. A psychological process in which an individual's personality is constructed by becoming like or being like another. Identification occurs through a series of assimilations of aspects, attributes or properties of another's identity. => IDENTITY, INTERPELLATION, PERSONALITY. *SJ*

ideological state apparatus (ISA) => INTERPELLATION. *Further reading* Althusser, L. (1972)

ideology *n.* MEDIA & CULTURAL STUDIES. A set of interconnected concepts, beliefs, values and ideas about the world that serve to affirm or underpin the pre-eminence of a particular social *group*: in brief, 'meaning in the service of power'. The theory and analysis of ideology has been most developed within the Marxist tradition, building on or elaborating the basic premise that at any historical juncture the *dominant ideology* in a society will articulate the interests of the ruling class and be widely dispersed through the population. => DOMINANT IDEOLOGY, HEGEMONY, INTERPELLATION. *Further reading* Eagleton, T. (Ed.) (2013); Thompson, J.B. (1990)

imagined community *n.* MEDIA & CULTURAL STUDIES. A *group* whose ties of solidarity are based not upon routine contact and propinquity but primarily upon a shared and imagined sense of membership. Whereas the traditional definition of *community* applies most easily to spatially circumscribed and local entities, such as the village, neighborhood, parish or school, in which members recognise each other by name or appearance, an imagined community transcends these local particulars to form a fellowship in which members may never know or meet or even hear of their fellow-members but in which all may feel that they equally belong. The term was introduced by the Irish-Anglo-American political philosopher Benedict Anderson (1936–2015) to characterise the special mode of belonging that underpins the modern nation-state. Indeed, for him the nation is the quintessential case of an imagined community: "members of even the smallest nation will never know most of their fellow-members, meet them, or even hear of them, yet in the minds of each lives the image of their communion". So strong is this sense of identification that "regardless of the actual inequality and exploitation that may prevail in each, the nation is always conceived as a deep, horizontal comradeship. Ultimately it is this fraternity that makes possible, over the past two centuries for so many millions of people, not so much to kill, as willingly to die for such limited imaginings." While Anderson's work was principally concerned with historical conditions underlying the rise of the modern nation-state, the notion of the imagined community has enjoyed wide currency beyond his particular historical inquiry. => COMMUNITY, VIRTUAL COMMUNITY. *Further reading* Anderson, B. (2006)

immediacy *n.* BROADCASTING, MEDIA STUDIES. An effect of live television when the event is presented as if unfolding in the here and now without the intervention of a mediating agency. => LIVENESS, MEDIA

EVENT, REAL-TIME COMMUNICATION, TIME-SPACE DISTANTIATION. *Further reading* Scannell, P. (2014)

impartiality *n.* BROADCASTING, JOURNALISM STUDIES, MEDIA STUDIES. A journalistic convention that controversial topics, especially relating to matters of public policy, political debate or industrial relations, should be treated in an even-handed way. This requirement applies mostly to broadcast *journalism* (rather than the press) and may well be explicitly written into the *codes* of practice, especially of public service broadcasters. In the UK, the BBC, for instance, as a public service broadcaster, is regulated by charter and by an agreement with the Secretary of State for Digital, Culture, Media, and Sport of the UK government; and bearing in mind both the charter and the agreement, the BBC follows published editorial guidelines which require it to demonstrate 'due impartiality'. In practice, there can be uncertainties over the precise spheres or topics to which impartiality applies and how best to demonstrate it. During a general election campaign in the UK, a public service broadcaster will try and provide equivalent exposure to major political parties. In broadcast panel debates or current affairs discussions there will be attempts to balance the range of opinions. But, because impartiality in the final analysis is a matter of judgement, public service broadcasters routinely receive accusations of *bias* – often from opposite ends of the political spectrum or opposing sides of a controversy. In this sense, accusations of bias and the requirement to impartiality are two sides of the same coin. Interestingly, the notion of impartiality is not applied in the same way to *newspapers*, which are usually under commercial ownership, are often partisan, and widely assumed to be so. The nearest requirement to impartiality in press journalism, and one which is often written into general codes of journalistic practice, is a requirement to be objective. => BIAS, BROADCASTING, FAKE NEWS, OBJECTIVITY, PUBLIC SERVICE. *Further reading* Wahl-Jorgensen, Karin et al. (2017); www.bbc.co.uk/editorialguidelines/guidelines/impartiality

implicature *n.* LINGUISTIC PRAGMATICS. The kind of meaning conveyed implicitly rather than explicitly through an utterance. The term is important in *pragmatics* and derives from the work of the British philosopher H. P. Grice (1913–1988), who in a quite radical way contrasted the logic of philosophy with that of everyday *conversation*. In particular, he pointed out how utterances in everyday conversation often mean much more than they actually say. In order to explain how this can be, he proposed that conversation proceeds on the basis of a fundamental principle – the *principle*. This can be summed up using four basic maxims, or ground rules, which conversationalists tacitly follow:

- the *maxim of quality* states that speakers should be truthful and should not say things which they believe to be false or for which they lack sufficient evidence;
- the *maxim of quantity* requires that speakers should be as informative as is required for the purposes of the conversation and should say neither too little nor too much;
- the *maxim of relevance* states that what speakers say should fit in with and relate to the purposes of the conversation at that point;
- the *maxim of manner* requires that speakers should avoid obscurity, prolixity and ambiguity.

It is on the assumption that these maxims still hold in some way, even when they appear to have been 'flouted', that we make sense of conversation. What happens briefly is this: when a maxim has apparently been flouted by an utterance, we try to derive some meaning from it that will leave the maxim and the cooperative principle in place. This inferred, non-manifest meaning is the 'implicature'. Thus, B's reply in the following exchange does not seem literally to meet the terms of A's question:

A: Where's Bill?
B: There's a yellow VW outside Sue's house.

At first sight, it apparently flouts at least the maxims of quantity and relevance and thereby fails to conform to the cooperative principle. In practice, however, we assume B to be cooperative at some deeper level and look for a proposition that would link B's actual reply with some manifestly relevant and cooperative reply to the question. In this case B effectively conveys that 'if Bill has a yellow VW, then he may be in Sue's house'.

The notion of conversational implicature provides an important way of going beyond highly literal and strictly logical approaches to meaning: it is a way of emphasising how the meaning of an utterance lies not just in the words we use but in the deductions and inferences that may be made on the basis of them. But the idea is not without its difficulties. There is considerable debate about exactly how many maxims you need to define adequately the cooperative principle. Some commentators have proposed as many as eight or more. Others have suggested that they can all be reduced to the one maxim – 'be relevant'. Nor is it certain how strong the cooperative principle is in itself. Some *speech genres* — such as adversarial cross-examination in the courtroom, the combative political *interview* on television or the full-blown marital quarrel — would seem to exhibit serious, systematic and fundamental departures from such a principle. And yet, for the theory of implicature to work, it is not a principle that can be applied variably. => CONTEXT OF SITUATION, CONVERSATION, GENRE, MEANING, PRAGMATICS. *Further reading* Grice, H. P. (1975)

improvisation *n.* BROADCASTING. A performance given independently of a written *script* as if without prior planning. => PERFORMANCE

individualisation *n.* PSYCHOLOGY, SOCIOLOGY. The conferring of a singular, original or particular set of traits to a person or an entity. It can also refer to the discernment of an individual within a *group* or a species, as well as to sociological changes that result in individuals constructing their own lives. SJ

influence *n.* MEDIA & COMMUNICATION STUDIES. The mechanisms whereby social actors are led to conform to expectations of others, most commonly by the need to be liked or the need to be right. *Further reading* Katz, E. and Lazarsfeld, P. (1955)

informalisation *n.* CRITICAL DISCOURSE ANALYSIS, SOCIOLINGUISTICS. A growing tendency in public *discourse* to select more colloquial vocabulary and less formal grammatical structures than previously in settings where degrees of formality might have been expected. In such contexts, commentators (e.g. Baker and Ellece 2011) have noted, for instance, a shortening of terms of *address*, greater use of contractions and a preference for the active rather than the passive *voice* — features, incidentally, typically associated with *speech* rather than *writing*. There are two kinds of problem with the claims around informalisation. Firstly, it tends to see the changes as of fairly recent origin, stemming particularly from marketising and consumerist pressures under late capitalism. Sociolinguists, however, have charted shifts in formality from *power* to 'solidarity' — especially, for example, in terms of address — in 17th century England (Francis), 18th century France (Brown and Gilman 1972), 19th and early 20th century Russia (Friedrich 1972) and 20th century Iran (Ardehali, 1990) (all of them cases where there seems to be an incidental relationship with revolutionary social change). The unfolding of these changes, therefore, may have begun earlier and with a more extended period of development. Secondly, changes in the direction of informalisation and the democratisation of discourse may not only long pre-date marketising and consumerist pressures but also have a history which is uneven and discontinuous. Elias's (1996) encyclopaedic study of informalisation and civilisation in Germany draws attention to the ways in which extreme forms of both formality *and* informality can exist side by side within the same society (as was the case, he suggests, in 18th century Salzburg). => CONVERSATIONALISATION, MARKETISATION, PARA-SOCIAL INTERACTION, SPEECH. *Further reading* Fairclough, N. (1992), (2015) (3rd Ed.)

information and communications technology (ICT) *np.* INTERNET & *MEDIA STUDIES*. Knowledge, programmes and products that enable the storage, transmission, sharing and exchange of information using digital data. It includes telecommunications, computer *networks*, software, storage and audio-visual systems. => AFFORDANCE, DIGITALISATION, TECHNOLOGY. SJ

information commons *n.* COMMUNICATION STUDIES. Systems or spaces of shared information and knowledge, either physical, such as a library, or virtual, such as an online resource. The purpose of an information commons is to enable the producing, gathering, preservation and sharing of information and knowledge. => INFORMATION SOCIETY, KNOWLEDGE SOCIETY. SJ

information rich *n.* MEDIA. The capacity to have *access* to information through media such as the *internet*, television, radio, *newspapers* and other printed matter. Those who are information rich are able to act on the basis of what they know and what they can find out as opposed to those who are information poor who are restricted in informed action and vulnerable in changing circumstances. => INFORMATION SOCIETY, KNOWLEDGE SOCIETY. SJ

information society *n.* SOCIOLOGY. A society where the rapid accumulation, integration, manipulation and dissemination of information is a significant feature of economic, political and cultural life. => KNOWLEDGE SOCIETY, NETWORK SOCIETY. *Further reading* Webster, F. (2014)

information technology *n.* MEDIA. => INFORMATION AND COMMUNICATIONS TECHNOLOGY.

infotainment JOURNALISM & CULTURAL STUDIES. where *news* loses its capacity to inform about serious issues of the day and becomes instead a form of entertainment. The term is used mostly pejoratively to reflect a concern that a commitment to responsible journalism has been supplanted by a search for ratings and readership. => HARD NEWS, READERSHIP, SOFT NEWS, TABLOIDISATION.

inoculation effect *n.* SOCIAL PSYCHOLOGY. A theory proposed by the American social psychologist William J. McGuire (1925–2007) following the Korean War to explain how resistance to *persuasion* can be built up through a process of exposure to weak counterarguments.

Like a medical inoculation, which allows one to build up resistance to disease through exposure to small doses of a virus, attitudinal inoculation allows the individual to become actively defensive in strengthening beliefs, opinions and attitudes in anticipation of future attacks by *messages* or arguments. SJ

instant messaging *n. COMMUNICATION STUDIES, INTERNET STUDIES.* Uses the *internet* to communicate in real-time by typed *text* with another named party or parties. It enables *messages* to go back and forth between established contacts who are online at the same time. Instant messaging is different from email inasmuch as it requires both parties to be simultaneously online. It is also different from Internet Relay Chat where, although the exchange of messages takes place in real time, it does so pseudo-anonymously between relative strangers. => CYBERSPACE, MEDIATION, SYNCHRONOUS COMMUNICATION, TIME-SPACE DISTANTIATION.

integration *n. SOCIOLOGY.* The act or process of merging, homogenising or uniting people, *groups* or entities. In sociology, integration refers to the merging of ethnic, religious or economic minorities with the social mainstream. This process involves the acceptance by the minority of common values, laws and language, and it may allow the minority access to opportunities, services and rights. => INTERCULTURAL COMMUNICATION. SJ

intellectual property *np. PUBLISHING.* The creative products of mental activity considered as subject to laws of ownership. Under intellectual property law, producers are given ownership rights to a variety of creative assets such as discoveries and inventions, musical, literary and artistic works. Common types of intellectual property rights include patents, trademarks, copyright and industrial design rights. By virtue of intellectual property law, creators are given some guarantee of financial return on their creations. => CREATIVE AND CULTURAL INDUSTRIES, CULTURAL CAPITAL.

interaction *n. COMMUNICATION STUDIES.* Reciprocal or mutual action or *influence* between two or more entities or phenomena. Interaction refers to the ways in which entities or phenomena, such as objects, languages or social relations, affect each other through dynamic causal connections. => CONVERSATION, CONVERSATION ANALYSIS, DIALOGUE, INTERACTION, INTERACTIVE MEDIA, SOCIAL INTERACTION. SJ

interactive media *np. INTERNET AND MEDIA STUDIES.* Typically includes any digital medium which requires a high degree of input from the user for its main purpose to be realised. Examples include video games, *virtual reality platforms* and most *social media*. => INTERACTION, NEW MEDIA, SOCIAL MEDIA, SOCIAL NETWORK, WORLD WIDE WEB

intercultural communication *np.* COMMUNICATION & CULTURAL STUDIES. *Communication* between people of different *cultures*. Theories of intercultural communication recognise that within a common culture communication depends upon a shared language (or languages), shared norms of communication and behaviour, and a repository of shared knowledge, a great deal of which may remain implicit in any encounter. By contrast, intercultural communication, between members of different cultures, may need to proceed in the absence of shared norms and without background shared knowledge, even where there is a common language. Intercultural communication, therefore, is a special case of communication, one where particular skills of intercultural *competence* may be required. => COMMUNICATION, CULTURE, SUB-CULTURE. *Further reading* Piller, I (2017)

internet *n.* INTERNET & MEDIA STUDIES. A global *network* of computer networks linked by a broad array of wireless and optical networking technologies using software protocols that enable easy and almost instant transfer of information between all points or nodes of the network. Since the 1990s the internet has had a major impact on *culture* and commerce because of the way in which it enabled the rise of electronic mail, *instant messaging*, phone calls using voice-over-internet protocols (VoIP), two-way interactive video calls and most significantly the *World Wide Web*. => CYBERSPACE, DIGITALISATION, GLOBAL MEDIA, GLOBALISATION, SOCIAL NETWORK, WORLD WIDE WEB. *Further reading* Hine, C. (2015)

interpellation *n.* CULTURAL STUDIES, FILM THEORY, MEDIA STUDIES. Calling, hailing, addressing. As a technical term, interpellation, derived from the work of the French Marxist philosopher Louis Althusser (1918–1990), has proved important for conceptualising the unobtrusive, everyday workings of *ideology* and most significantly for suggesting how ideology as an imaginary relationship with the real conditions of existence is internalised by individuals. Ideology may offer frameworks of belief that seek to disguise or naturalise inequalities of *power*. But ideologies can only work if individuals and *groups* at specific historical junctures feel addressed (hailed) by them as somehow appropriate to their circumstances and social position. Ideologies in this sense, by apparently stating the obvious, constitute individual subjects as complicit in their occupation of a particular social position. Althusser was drawing on a more general sense of how the abstract subject becomes integrated into society by the acquisition of language. In the context of ideology, however, he was suggesting that *ideological state apparatuses* such as education, religion and the family (some would add the media) actively position individuals within the social order by a process of interpellation, calling them into place. There were two major advantages in developments of the Althusserian approach. First, it emphasised the pervasiveness of the workings of ideology and the ways in which it works actively and continuously to constitute us in our identities as women, men, black, white, Asian and so on. Secondly, ideology as understood within this framework became more than a set of propositions about the world (e.g. 'men are stronger than women') but the creation of forms of *subjectivity*, in which there is a double movement: ideologies interpellate us and define for us who we are; and because of who we are, we are interpellated by particular ideologies. The problem with the Althusserian approach is that ideology within this account becomes an all-embracing system and lacks any sense of where resistance to ideology can come from. If we are constituted as subjects within ideology, in what space can we take up a position to resist it? => DOMINANT IDEOLOGY, IDEOLOGY, IDENTITY, SUBJECT, SUBJECTIVITY. *Further reading* Althusser, L. (1972)

interpersonal communication *np.* COMMUNICATION STUDIES. One-on-one *interaction* between individuals within a society, including the processes by which people communicate thoughts, feelings and ideas to others, both verbally and non-verbally. Communicative acts may be direct or indirect, for example by face-to-face *conversation* or a computer-*mediated* exchange of *messages*. Successful interpersonal communication depends on the existence or creation of shared meanings and implications so that participants can effectively interpret elements including words, tones of *voice*, facial expressions, body language and clothing. => CONVERSATION, CONVERSATION ANALYSIS, DIALOGUE, INTERACTION, SOCIAL INTERACTION. *Further reading* Hartley, P. (1999) SJ

interpretive community *np.* LITERARY LINGUISTICS. A *group* constituted by shared ways of interpreting *texts*. The term has its origins in literary criticism, particularly in reader response theory. While it emphasises the importance of the reader in making sense of a text, it nonetheless avoids assuming that all reading is simply an arbitrary, individualistic and subjective process by situating the act of reading within a shared set of reading practices held in common by a specific *community*. The American literary critic and theorist Stanley Fish (b. 1938) is credited with first using the term, though rarely with any sociological or historically specific content. => ACTIVE READER, AUDIENCE, COMMUNITY, HERMENEUTICS. *Further reading* Fish, S. (1990)

intersubjectivity *n.* SOCIOLOGY AND COMMUNICATION STUDIES. A way of defining experience or knowledge in such a way that it transcends the polarities of *subjectivity* and *objectivity*. If the claim to *truth* can rest only upon objective knowledge, it denies the role of the knowing subject. If all knowledge is subjective, on the other hand, then there is no way of validating it. The notion of intersubjectivity underpins claims that some things can be known to be true because they are shared knowledge between knowing subjects. Intersubjectivity is a basic property of *dialogue*, which is only possible if participants share to some degree a fundamental reciprocity of perspectives. => DIALOGUE, INTERPERSONAL COMMUNICATION, OBJECTIVITY, SUBJECT, SUBJECTIVITY

intertextuality *n.* LITERARY LINGUISTICS, MEDIA AND CULTURAL STUDIES. The interrelationships between a *text* and other texts. Familiar examples of intertextuality would be *parody*, *irony*, allusion, reported *speech* and quotation, though these by no means exhaust the full scope of the term, which has its origins in the work of the Bulgarian-French semiotician and post-structuralist thinker Julia Kristeva (b. 1941). She uses it to emphasise the way in which no text is a bounded object, meaningful in and for itself, but exists in a creative interplay with a myriad of other texts from the *culture*. In her view, the meaning of a text lies not 'inside' it but in tension between, or in the space occupied between itself and other texts. The term has been widely applied in literary criticism, linguistics and media and cultural studies, though often simply to assert *influence* or connection between one text and another without clear principles of application. => COHESION, MULTI-ACCENTUALITY, PARODY, SATIRE, TEXT. *Further reading* Orr, M. (2003)

interview *n.* BROADCAST TALK, COMMUNICATION STUDIES. An institutionalised *speech genre* defined by the pre-allocation of the roles of questioner and answerer: the interviewer asks the questions and the interviewee answers them. The interview is widely used in a variety of institutional settings ranging from the forensic to the medical. In addition, it is commonly used when selecting candidates for a job and has become highly salient in both entertainment and current affairs television. => GENRE, TALK SHOW. *Further reading* Montgomery, M. (2008b)

intonation *n.* LINGUISTICS, SPEECH. Variation within the pitch, stress, pace and *voice* quality of an utterance that effects its meaning in systematic ways. Intonation has received most attention within linguistics, especially as a sub-branch of phonetics/phonology. =>

FACE-TO-FACE COMMUNICATION, GESTURE, KINESICS, PROXEMICS. *Further reading* Wichmann, A. (2000)

intrapersonal communication *np.* COMMUNICATION STUDIES. *Communication* that takes place within the self rather than between the self and another. Day-dreaming, interior monologue and talking to oneself are all examples of intrapersonal communication. => INTERACTION, INTERPERSONAL COMMUNICATION, INTERSUBJECTIVITY, PARTICIPATION FRAMEWORK.

irony *n.* PRAGMATICS, RHETORIC. Saying something in a context which calls the meaning of the utterance into question, often for humorous effect, sometimes in such a way that the intended (and inferred) meaning ends up as the opposite of what was said. Sarcasm is the most obvious kind of irony, but irony also includes dramatic irony and situational irony. In both everyday situations and in public *communication*, irony has the advantage of 'deniability'. As part of *satire* it can be used to ridicule while denying any intention to give offense. => PARODY, POSTMODERNISM, SATIRE. *Further reading* Hutcheon, L. (1994)

★★

Jakobson's model of communication *np.* COMMUNICATION STUDIES, LINGUISTICS. Recognised six key components of a *communication* situation: an addresser, an addressee, a *message*, a *code*, a channel and a context (or referent). From these components, the Russian-born linguist Roman Jakobson (1896–1982) derived six functions of communication – the emotive, the conative, the poetic, the metalingual, the phatic and the referential – each function related to a corresponding component. For instance, the phatic function is related to the channel component (or means of contact) of the communication situation: it is the function orientated to making contact or keeping open the channel of communication. Jakobson's account has been widely influential across the *communication sciences*, though it is interesting to note that his fullest statement of the model was designed to define and illustrate the poetic function – communication that calls attention to the form of the message for its own sake. => COMMUNICATIVE FUNCTIONS, DISCOURSE ACTS, PRAGMATICS. *Further reading* Jakobson, R. (1960)

jouissance *n.* (*Fr.* 'enjoyment', 'delight', 'bliss') LITERARY STUDIES. Used as a term by both the French psychoanalytic thinker Jacques Lacan (1901–1981) and the French semiotician Roland Gérard Barthes (1915–1980), in both of whose work it stands in contradistinction to 'plaisir' (pleasure). For Barthes, the activity of literary reading is broadly of two kinds depending on a distinction between two types of *text*, the readerly and the writerly. A readerly text is one whose meaning is relatively accessible to the reader and which thereby makes less demand of him or her, the reward for which is plaisir. A 'writerly' text, on the other hand, is one whose meaning is more uncertain and which thereby requires greater involvement and effort from the reader, the reward for which is jouissance. => AESTHETICS, CLOSED TEXT, OPEN TEXT. *Further reading* Barthes, R. (1990)

journalese JOURNALISM STUDIES *n*. Clichéd *style* of *writing* associated with *journalism*. The term is pejorative and refers particularly to the use of standardised phrases (e.g. 'war-torn', 'military strongman', 'not available for comment', 'it remains to be seen', 'on the brink') rarely found outside journalism itself. *Further reading* Cotter, C. (2010); Smith, A. & Higgins, M. (2013)

journalism *n*. JOURNALISM STUDIES. The recording or reporting of current events deemed to be of interest to a wide public. The term may be used to designate the professional institution of those who report events (similar to the notion of 'the press') or as a collective name for the reports themselves. => DOCUMENTARY, NEWS. *Further reading* Allan, S. (Ed.) (2011)

★★

kernel (of narrative) => NARRATIVE KERNEL.

knowledge society *n*. MEDIA. A society in which innovation in and the circulation of knowledge is the predominant source of economic growth. => INFORMATION SOCIETY, NETWORK SOCIETY. *Further reading* Stehr, N. and Meja, V. (2017)

★★

labeling process *np*. CULTURAL STUDIES, SOCIOLOGY. A sociological theory that explains how the behaviour and *self-identity* of individuals or minorities may be informed and defined according to the terms used to describe and categorise them. Theories of the labeling process maintain that deviant behaviour is not inherent in an act or individual but can be explained as the propensity of the majority to negatively label minorities or those perceived as not conforming to socially and culturally normative behaviour. The origins of labeling theory are attributed to Émile Durkheim (1858–1917), who analysed crime as an act that affronts society, rather than as a violation of a penal *code*, and therefore argued that deviant labeling fulfills society's need to control behaviour. The work of sociologists such as Howard Saul Becker (b. 1928) in the 1960s was highly influential in developing theories of the labeling process. => FOLK DEVILS, MORAL PANICS. *Further reading* Bettie, J. (2014)

language pollution *n*. SOCIOLINGUISTICS. Folk belief that a language is deteriorating because users are importing foreign material from another language (or languages) or failing properly to follow the rules of their own. In either case the pollution is often associated with the spread or *influence* of material from less favoured, more informal, colloquial linguistic varieties in a way that is seen as undermining the purity of the *standard language*. => ANTI-LANGUAGE, DIALECT. *Further reading* Cameron, D. (1995)

langue *n.* (*Fr.*) LINGUISTICS & SEMIOTICS. In Saussurian linguistics, the abstract system of signs and conventions underlying individual acts of speaking. The role of langue, therefore, may be seen as analogous to that of the musical score that underlies individual performances of a symphony or the rules of chess that make possible an unlimited variety of actual games. The symphony, for instance, exists independently of its individual performances – in which false notes may occur, distinctive choices of tempo may be adopted and so on. Likewise, chess may be played with many different sequences of moves, on many sizes of board, with different kinds of pieces, and yet remain chess as long as the basic rules of the game are observed. In the same way, for English or Swahili or Gujarati, there is a common storehouse of basic, necessary conventions or rules which speakers of that language follow when framing their utterances. It is these conventions that constitute the langue for that language, and it is by following such shared conventions that intelligibility is guaranteed between speakers of that language. In this sense, langue is very much a social product shared between members of a social body as a whole and out of the *control* of any one individual. As with so many important terms in modern linguistics, the notion of langue was developed initially in the work of the Swiss linguist Ferdinand de Saussure (1857–1913). For him, contrasting langue with *parole* was an important methodological step in isolating the object of linguistic enquiry by focusing on the *institution* (langue) rather than the event (parole). The distinction is similarly formulated in much modern linguistics, whether as *competence* versus performance in the work of the American linguist Naom Chomsky or as potential linguistic behaviour versus actual linguistic behaviour in the work of the British linguist Michael Halliday (1925–2018). In *structuralism* and in semiotics the notion of langue was extended to embrace other kinds of the sign than the purely linguistic one. Thus, patterns of kinship and the social organisation of furniture, food and fashion have all been considered as examples of underlying systems. => CODE, COMPETENCE, PAROLE. *Further reading* Culler (1976); Harris, R (2003); Hawkes, T. (2003); Saussure (1974)

leak *n. JOURNALISM, PUBLISHING.* The unauthorised release and publication of embargoed or confidential information.

legitimation *n. POLITICS & COMMUNICATION, SOCIOLOGY.* The process of making an action, a structure, a set of beliefs or a particular social arrangement normatively acceptable to society as a whole. The term has achieved particular currency and importance based on the work of the German political philosopher and social theorist Jürgen Habermas, who has argued that structures of governance in late modernity are undergoing a legitimation crisis because they are no longer held to serve the ends for which they were designed, and their legitimacy, therefore, becomes a source of dispute. => DOMINANT IDEOLOGY, HEGEMONY, IDEOLOGY, INTERPELLATION. *Further reading* Habermas, J. (1988)

libel *n. JOURNALISM & COMMUNICATION STUDIES.* Written *communication* that makes purportedly factual claims about a person or collectivity which are derogatory, or otherwise suggest a negative image, and which are untrue. => DEFAMATION.

linguistic determinism *np. ANTHROPOLOGICAL LINGUISTICS, CRITICAL DISCOURSE ANALYSIS.* The view that our language determines our thought. => LINGUISTIC RELATIVITY, POSTSTRUCTURALISM. *Further reading* Lucy, J. (1992)

linguistic relativity *np. ANTHROPOLOGICAL LINGUISTICS, CRITICAL DISCOURSE ANALYSIS.* A hypothesis that different languages give rise to different views of the world. According to this hypothesis we do not experience the world in a direct and straightforward fashion. On the contrary, the language that we use shapes and even creates the conditions for our experience. Thus, there is no absolutely neutral and disinterested way of apprehending and representing the world, because the particular language that we habitually use points us towards certain types of observation and predisposes certain choices of interpretation. This may be partly a question of vocabulary. Thus, different languages carve up areas of experience in different ways. Russian, for example, divides up the colour spectrum with 12 basic colour terms, whereas English segments the same domain with 11 basic terms, using only one basic colour term for 'blue' in place of the two available in Russian. In an Australian aborigine language called Pintupi there are 10 discrete expressions for types of hole, many of which can be translated into English only by elaborate paraphrase: for example, *katarta* means roughly 'the hole left by a goanna when it has broken the surface after hibernation'. Languages, however, differ in more than the organisation of their respective vocabularies. They also differ in their characteristic ways of forming sentences – in their *grammar*. The system of tense in one language may be very different from that of another: English grammar, for instance, provides at least two tenses, present and past, but Hopi – a North American language – seems to operate without tenses at all. Instead, its verb forms distinguish between what is subjective and what is objective. It seems likely, therefore, that the different grammars of these two languages make available for their speakers quite different senses of time. On the basis of such evidence, the American linguist B. L. Whorf (1897–1941) concluded that "all observers are not led to the same picture of the universe . . . Users of markedly different grammars are pointed by their grammars toward different types of observations and different evaluations of externally similar acts of observation, and hence are not equivalent as observers" (Whorf 1956, p. 214). Whorf's original formulation of the hypothesis (it is sometimes referred to as the Sapir-Whorf hypothesis in deference to himself and a distinguished anthropological linguist – Edward Sapir (1884–1939) – who was his intellectual mentor) was published roughly 80 years ago (see Whorf, 1940). But controversy has remained strong ever since over its central claims. It is not easy, for example, to provide clear empirical support for linguistic relativity. Critics point to the fact of translation between languages, which should not be possible if one's native language totally constrained one's thought-world. However, the burgeoning of interest in language, and in linguistic models, as evidenced in movements such as *structuralism* and *post-structuralism*, has given new impetus to forms of the linguistic relativity hypothesis. When a poststructuralist literary critic argues that a novel is a discursive (linguistic) artefact that constructs a reality as much as it *mediates* it, she is espousing a form of linguistic relativity. => LINGUISTIC DETERMINISM. *Further reading* Lucy, J. (1992)

literary agent *n.* PUBLISHING. A person who, acting in a professional capacity, represents the interests of individual authors in securing publication and remuneration for their work. Authors, as clients, pay a levy or fee to *agents* for their services.

live/liveness *n.* MEDIA & COMMUNICATION STUDIES. The quality attributed to a public performance or act of *communication* that takes place simultaneously with its reception by an *audience*. The term is particularly important in the study of *broadcasting*, where it stands in contradistinction to 'recorded' – a default condition for much broadcast output. Nonetheless, liveness is a particular quality of the shared experience that broadcasting was able to deliver of bringing an unfolding, usually significant, event to an audience as it occurs in real-time even though the audience is physically far removed and separated in spatial terms from each other and from the event itself. In broadcast *news*, in particular, switching from studio presentation and pre-recorded reports to an unfolding live event helps to guarantee the *immediacy* and veracity of the news. Furthermore, in an age of *mediated communication*, the quality of a live performance precisely as 'non-mediated' can take on special value – witness the large crowds which can be drawn to public events such as concerts, festivals and campaign rallies. => BROADCASTING, MEDIA EVENTS, MEDIATION, SYNCHRONOUS COMMUNICATION, REAL TIME, TIME-SPACE DISTANTIATION. *Further reading* Marriott, S. (2007); Scannell, P. (2014)

localisation *n.* CULTURAL STUDIES. The *adaptation* of cultural products to specific locales and regions in order to take account of local languages and *cultures*. => GLOBALISATION.

★★

magazine *n.* JOURNALISM, PUBLISHING. Printed publication that contains articles and features, often illustrated, on a range of topics usually focused around a theme or interest. This may be very broad, as in 'women's magazines', or more specialised, as in photography or yachting. Magazines are financed through a combination of advertising, subscription or a cover price at the point of sale. Occasionally, as in the case of in-flight magazines, they are distributed for free in restricted locations. The magazine market tends to be dominated by large publishing conglomerates, each of whom may own and publish several hundred titles, and who may have other media interests such as newspapers and broadcasting.

mainstream media *np.* MEDIA & COMMUNICATION STUDIES. Refers to cultural output or forms that command widespread recognition and/or acceptance within a *culture*. When used of the media it carries the implication of orthodoxy, *consensus* and conformism in the service of either commercial imperatives or popular appeal. In this sense it is used variously of cinema, the press and popular music. However, it may also be used to describe the representation of movements in politics, science, religion, education and the arts, indicating those areas of belief or practice that have become conventional or orthodox.

manufacture of consent *np. JOURNALISM STUDIES, POLITICAL COMMUNICATION, SOCIOLOGY.* Phrase used in the book *Public Opinion* (1922/2004) by the American writer and public intellectual Walter Lippman (1889–1974) to refer to the necessary and important processes of informing the public in a modern democracy. The phrase was subsequently adapted by the American scholars Noam Chomsky (b. 1928) and Edward S Herman (b. 1925) for the title of their book *Manufacturing Consent*, (1988), in which they posit a *propaganda* model to explain the output of the North American *news* media as serving mainly corporate interests and as therefore systematically biased. => BIAS, CONSENSUS, DOMINANT IDEOLOGY, HEGEMONY. *Further reading* Herman, E. & Chomsky, N. (1988)

marketing *n. BUSINESS AND CULTURAL STUDIES.* The processes involved in communicating and spreading the value of a service or product to customers and target markets. Successful marketing involves understanding consumer buying behaviour, creating connections with customers, the development of strong brand identities and sustaining long-term growth for a product or service. *SJ*

marketisation of discourse *np. CRITICAL DISCOURSE ANALYSIS.* Transformations of public *discourse* that reflect increasing pressure on public institutions (such as health, education, *broadcasting* and local government) to adopt market models of delivery in which competition and customer service have become increasingly salient. In communicating with the public, therefore, such institutions adopt discursive practices increasingly similar to advertising and other *genres* of promotional discourse such as the use of personal and familiar *modes of address*. The term was adopted and popularised by the British critical discourse analyst, Norman Fairclough (b. 1941). => CONVERSATIONALISATION, INFORMALISATION, MARKETING, MARKETISATION. *Further reading* Fairclough, N. (1992)

market research *np. BUSINESS STUDIES.* Research on customers and markets used to gain advantage over competitors. It involves systematically gathering information about factors such as competition, market size and market need and using analytical and statistical methodologies to interpret this information. *SJ*

mass audience *np. MEDIA STUDIES.* A large audience to which a work of *mediated communication* is addressed. The concept of a mass audience has been somewhat undermined by the development of *new media* which encourage a much more differentiated sense of audiences and publics. => ACTIVE AUDIENCE, AUDIENCE, BROADCASTING, MASS

COMMUNICATION, NARROWCASTING, NEW MEDIA, PERSONAL MEDIA, SOCIAL MEDIA.

mass communication *np.* MEDIA STUDIES. The study of how information is conveyed through the *mass media* to large *audiences*, sometimes *live*, but usually with a only a short time lapse between sending and receiving. As a field of study it is generally considered to include *newspaper, magazine* and book publishing as well as radio, television and film, especially insofar as these are media for disseminating *news, editorial* and advertising. In the U.S. academy there has long been a concern with how the content of mass communication affects the behaviour or attitudes of its audiences. This concern with effects has been accentuated - not only in the U.S. but elsewhere - with the rise of *social media*, even though the latter do not fit easily within older models of mass communication. => BROADCASTING, MASS AUDIENCE, MASS MEDIA.

mass media *np.* MEDIA STUDIES. Ways of communicating publicly with indefinitely large *audiences*, often over a short period of time. Traditional mass media, such as print, film and *broadcasting*, are based upon capital-intensive technologies and institutionalised techniques for distributing a standardised product, at relative speed, over wide distances. The term itself comes to refer not only to the technologies (e.g. print, radio, television) but also to the institutions that use the technologies and the forms carried by them. Increasingly, the mass media have come to be distinguished from the newer digital and *social media*, which are seen as more expressive, interactive and *community*-based than traditional mass media. => BROADCASTING, MASS AUDIENCE, MASS MEDIA, NARROWCASTING, PRESS, SOCIAL MEDIA.

mass production *np.* SOCIOLOGY. Technique for making multiple copies of a standardised product, usually by using an assembly line in which the product passes from worker to worker who each contribute partially and sequentially to its completion.

McLuhanism *n.* MEDIA STUDIES. Phrase, concept or saying derived from the work of the Canadian media theorist Marshall McLuhan (1911–1980). As one of the most important 20th century philosophers of the media, McLuhan set out to chart their respective influences. These he described in technologically deterministic terms. Some of his insights he summed up in pithy sayings such as "news, far more than art, is artifact"; "all advertising advertises advertising"; and, most famously, "the medium is the message". => TECHNOLOGICAL DETERMINISM. *Further reading* McLuhan, M. (2001)

meaning *n.* HERMENEUTICS, LINGUISTICS, PHILOSOPHY. The sense or import of an expression. Meaning in human interaction is rarely a fixed entity but is best understood as the product of a process of 'making sense' from the perspective of both the sense-maker and the sense-receiver; and in this way it is both the outcome of an interpretation on the one hand, and of the intention to communicate something on the other. Inevitably, there can occur gaps between what was intended and what was interpreted, so there are often struggles over meaning, reflecting the social positions and the respective perspectives of participants. *Pragmatics* and *semantics* aim to offer ways of understanding and analysing meaning by distinguishing between different types of meaning and by describing the parameters through which meanings are made and interpreted in human communication. => DECODING, DISCURSIVE GAP, ENCODING, HERMENEUTICS, INTERPRETIVE COMMUNITY, PRAGMATICS, SEMANTICS.

meaning potential *np. DISCOURSE STUDIES, LINGUISTICS.* The range of meanings associated with the language habitually used in the performance of a particular activity type or *context of situation*. In Hallidayan linguistics the overall context of *culture* is considered to be composed of typical contexts of situation for each of which certain kinds of language use (or *registers*) are found to be appropriate and recurrent. These linguistic choices will draw upon and enact a range of meanings typically associated with that context. For any typical context of situation, Halliday modelled the range of meanings likely to occur in terms of sets of choices or options comprised of semantic networks which, taken together, defined the potential meanings 'at risk' in the situation. These semantic networks could be stated for different levels or components of the overall semantic system – for instance, in terms of likely *discourse acts*, or in terms of choices within the system of appraisal. => GENRE, REGISTER. *Further reading* Halliday, M.A.K (1973), (1978)

media events *np. pl. BROADCASTING, MASS COMMUNICATION, MEDIA STUDIES, TELEVISION STUDIES.* Events that attract a distinctive kind of media coverage because of their sheer scale and public interest and in which the media (especially broadcast media) play a special role in bringing them to the attention of a *mass audience*. The term was developed particularly in the work of the American and Israeli media studies scholar Elihu Katz (b. 1926) and may be exemplified by events such as the moon landing, the coronation of Elizabeth II, Princess Diana's funeral or the Beijing or London Olympics. To qualify as a media event for Katz they should be planned in advance and scheduled for mass viewing: in other words, they do not happen out of the blue (as, for instance, in the case of the destruction of the twin towers of the World Trade Center on 9/11). They should be broadcast *live* for a mass audience, and viewing should be considered for some reason mandatory. As an event they need to be bounded in time and space with the capacity to be focused for *broadcasting*. They need to embody a degree of ritual or dramatic significance, and they need to feature a public, highly visible *personality* or *group*. => BROADCASTING, MEDIATION, MEDIATISATION. *Further reading* Katz, E. (1980); Dayan, D. and Katz, E. (1994)

media of communication *np. pl.* MASS COMMUNICATION, MEDIA STUDIES. The plural noun of 'medium' (drawing on the word's Latin origins), it is used in three main ways. (1) To refer to the technical means of transferring *messages* from a sender to a receiver across a spatial and temporal gap. In this sense smoke signals, the telegraph, VHF radio, the *internet* and semaphore are all examples of media of communication. (2) The historically specific kinds of social organisation devoted to supporting the technical means for transferring messages across time and space. In this sense print, *broadcasting* and electronic media are all media of communication, and the evolution from media of *mass communication* (e.g. broadcasting) to new electronic media (e.g. *social media* such as Twitter or Facebook) amounts to more than a change in the technical means of *communication* but to large-scale transformations of the social organisation that underpins and is implicated in communication. (3) The media as a term is also used in informal ways – equivalent to 'organs of public opinion' – to refer to the professionalised *groups* and bodies who assume responsibility for *framing* and articulating public *discourse* in late modern societies. Used in this way, it embraces a diverse array of groups such as journalists, advertisers, *public relations* experts, and bloggers (but not, for instance, politicians, teachers, doctors, clergy or union officials). It implicitly distinguishes between those who habitually use institutionalised media of communication for professional purposes as opposed to other influential groups in society, such as 'politicians', whose professional focus lies elsewhere (in education, workers' rights or government). => MASS COMMUNICATION, MAINSTREAM MEDIA, MEDIASPHERE. *Further reading* McLuhan, M. (2001); Scannell, P. (2007)

mediasphere *n.* MEDIA AND INTERNET STUDIES. The totality of *mediated communication* especially as it has developed in the age of the *internet*. The term has gained currency by extending the notion of the *public sphere*, which applied most obviously either to public gatherings or to print communication, to the age of digital communication. => CYBERSPACE, PUBLIC SPHERE.

mediate/mediated *v.* To act as an intermediary, to come between separate parties or entities in order to reconcile or otherwise bring

them together, to intercede – perhaps by conveying a gift. These senses, stemming from the 16th and 17th centuries, still distantly echo in more modern senses of *mediation* and *mediated communication.*
=> MEDIATION, MEDIATISATION, MEDIATED COMMUNICATION.

mediated communication *n.* COMMUNICATION STUDIES, MEDIA STUDIES. The transfer of a *message* between participants by technical means, such as *writing*, telephony or the *internet.* => FACE-TO-FACE COMMUNICATION, MEDIATION, MEDIATISATION, TIME-SPACE DISTANTIATION

mediation *n.* COMMUNICATION STUDIES, CULTURAL STUDIES, MEDIA STUDIES, SOCIOLOGY. *Communication* by means of any medium that allows meanings to be exchanged across time and space between people who are not physically co-present to each other. The material basis of mediation includes mechanical, electronic and digital modes of transfer or exchange and would accordingly include such diverse means as telephone, telegraph, semaphore, print, radio, TV and the *internet.* All of these media enable mediation to take place. In this way mediation is not restricted to the simple transfer of *messages* by technical means but includes the work that goes into the process of meaning-making by shaping and interpreting the material that is *mediated.* As Silverstone (1999) comments: "Readers, viewers and audiences are part of this process of mediation, because they continue the work of the media in the ways they respond to, extend and further communicate what they see and hear on the world's multitude of screens and speakers." If the making and exchanging of meanings amounts to a fundamental human capacity, then mediation may be understood as an extension of what it is to be human. This developed sense of the term may even be seen to overlap with an alternative, older, but still common use of the word to mean 'reconciliation' or 'the adoption as an intermediary of a middle position between contending or opposed parties'. It can also be contrasted with a recent coinage, *mediatisation.* => MEDIA EVENT, MEDIATED COMMUNICATION, MEDIATISATION. *Further reading* Couldry, N. (2008b); Silverstone, R. (1999); Williams, R. (1983, pp. 204–207)

mediatisation *n.* COMMUNICATION STUDIES, CULTURAL STUDIES, MEDIA STUDIES, SOCIOLOGY. The impact on society of the widespread *mediation* of social processes. Politics, in particular, has received much attention for the way in which mediation and media institutions have affected the ways in which political processes of various kinds are conducted. Political events – campaign rallies, debates, the workings of the legislature – are increasingly subject to media coverage to the degree that they become staged in such a way as to extract from *audiences* and political subjects the maximum political capital for political actors. Indeed, the *personalisation* of politics – the emphasis on personalities rather than policies – has been traced to the growing role of the media in articulating and representing the political process. The impact of mediatisation, however, far transcends the political process itself and enters many arenas of social life, including, for example, economic and financial processes. Trading in securities has been mediatised to such an extent that some steep and unexpected downward movements in stock market value are now described as a 'flash crash' – a by-product of semi-automatic, digital trading. More fundamentally the concept is used to highlight the transformative effects of mediation on social processes more generally to the extent that they come to exist primarily – almost exclusively – in their *mediated* form. => MEDIA EVENT, MEDIATED COMMUNICATION, MEDIATION. *Further reading* Couldry, N. (2008b); Schulz (2004); Silverstone, R. (1999); Williams, R. (1983)

melodrama *n.* FILM, MEDIA AND LITERARY STUDIES. Language, events, behaviour or a dramatic *genre* that relies upon exaggerated character types or plots in order to arouse and appeal to the emotions. The term originates from the French word '*mélodrame*', which derives from the Greek '*melos*', music, and the French '*drama*', from the Greek '*drān*', to perform. In the 18th and 19th centuries, music or song accompanied spoken recitation, such as in Jean-Jacques Rousseau's *Pygmalion*, first staged in 1770. Hollywood melodrama is a sub-genre of film-making which often features a central female protagonist struggling against the effects of alcoholism and domestic violence. => COMEDY, GENRE, SOAP OPERA. *Further reading* Mercer, J. & Shingler, M. (2004)

membership categorisation device *np.* CONVERSATION ANALYSIS, ETHNOMETHODOLOGY, SOCIOLOGY. The knowledge drawn upon by members of a society in labelling and typifying others according to categories (e.g. mothers, parking wardens, swimmers, doctors, students) in ways designed to allocate persons to membership of a *group* but simultaneously project the kind of activities that would be appropriate to the label. Accordingly, the normal application of a membership categorisation device usually draws upon a set of (stereotypical) assumptions about appropriate behaviours performed by members of a category. Thus 'mothers' as a membership category are assumed (among other things) to nurture children, 'doctors' (among other things) to care for patients, and so on. Activities or actions conventionally linked with the selected membership are regarded as 'category-bound activities' for that membership. Headlines often highlight activities which seem discrepant with the membership category: e.g. 'Jailed mother admits murdering baby son'; 'Junior doctors plan week of all-out strikes'. => STEREOTYPE. *Further reading* Fitzgerald, R. & Housley, W. (Eds.) (2015)

message *n.* COMMUNICATION STUDIES. Information coded for *communication* by transference between a sender and a receiver.

meta-communication *n.* COMMUNICATION STUDIES. The provision of information about the scope, nature or application of *communication* itself: literally, 'behind, or about, communication'. It is usually seen as a secondary or ancillary kind of communication that offers additional information on how the primary communication itself should be understood. As a term it has been usefully applied to the study of non-verbal, paralinguistic communication where this supplies an additional set of signals confirming, modifying or contradicting the meaning of verbal communication itself. => GESTURE, KINESICS, METADISCOURSE.

metadiscourse *n.* DISCOURSE STUDIES. A kind of *discourse* that refers not so much to things outside the discourse but to the discourse itself. Metadiscourse often fulfills an organising role in relation to discourse providing information about its status and direction. => GESTURE, KINESICS, METACOMMUNICATION.

modernism *n.* LITERARY & CULTURAL STUDIES. Literary and artistic movement broadly of the first half of the 20th century, committed to experiment and innovation in form and *style* and finding expression in theatre, film, literature and painting. It tended to reject realism, naturalism and conventional *narrative* in favour of abstract forms and aligned itself with the avant-garde not only in form but also in politics. => POSTMODERNISM. *Further reading* Butler, C. (2010)

modes of address *np.* CULTURAL & DISCOURSE STUDIES, MEDIA STUDIES. The ways in which *texts* establish their relationship to their *audience*. Texts generally imply a position from which they are most intelligible, and this is constructed and made manifest through the text's habitual modes of address, which may be direct or indirect, visual or verbal. The most obvious form of visual address involves the speaker looking directly towards his or her audience or interlocutor. Television *news* presenters, for instance, in looking through or beyond the *autocue* to the camera lens, use direct visual address as if they were talking directly to the audience. Direct verbal address, on the other hand, as a discursive practice will use verbal means to the same effect: this may involve selection of an interlocutor or audience member by name, pronoun or other descriptor (e.g. 'the gentleman with his hand raised in the back row . . . yes, you sir'); or *discourse acts* such as greetings, questions and commands, all of which strongly select not only intended recipient but also next action. It is possible to accentuate directness in one modality (see multi-modality) by corresponding directness in the other. Thus, direct visual address coupled with direct verbal address carries maximum effect. However, direct visual and verbal address need not coincide. In the case of bulletin television news, for the most part we have direct visual address accompanied by indirect (or implied) verbal address, except possibly at openings, closings or transition points in the programme where greetings or valedictions may take place ('Good evening, this is the ten o'clock news . . .') so that only at these points do visual and verbal direct address coincide. Promotional and advertising discourse tends to be strong in direct address. The famous World War I recruitment poster featuring General Haig gazing out from the poster at the reader/viewer over the caption "Your Country Needs You!" is a clear example of direct verbal and visual address. Any text, however, may feature complex variations in its mode of address, including modes of indirect address to an implied audience which in itself is not explicitly addressed, either verbally or visually. Poetry, popular song, drama and fictional *narrative* will often rest upon direct address within the world of the song, poem, drama or narrative (from one character to another, for instance) but on indirect address to an implied reader or audience who are thereby positioned as onlooker, voyeur or overhearer. => INTERPELLATION, PARA-SOCIAL INTERACTION,

montage *(Fr) n.* FILM STUDIES. Way of editing film so that the succession of images encourages the viewer to infer more of the action than he or she actually sees. The concept and its associated practice was developed by the Russian film-maker and theoretician Sergei Eisenstein (1898–1948) and is well illustrated by a famous scene called the Odessa Steps sequence from his film *Potemkin*, where the Tsarist troops advance down the steps firing at and scattering civilians before them. In one close-up shot we see a woman wearing a pince-nez looking upwards in horror. In the immediately following shot we see the same face of the same woman in close-up but now with one lens of her pince-nez shattered. As Eisenstein commented: we have the "impression of a shot hitting the eye", even though this particular action – of the shot hitting the eye – is not revealed to us in an image. This element of the action is implicit rather than explicit, unlike in contemporary cinema, such as *Saving Private Ryan* or *Dunkirk*, which will often draw on special effects to show the impact of a bullet on a body. The significance of montage, however, goes well beyond the *affordances* of film as a medium. Indeed, Eisenstein suggested that notions of montage underlay the way in which Japanese and Chinese ideographic *writing* worked, where many written characters are based on ideas or images (rather than sounds). To interpret a pictographic or ideographic script depends upon *decoding* each character in its relation to other characters in the same *message* so that the reader finds meaning as much in the space between the characters as in each character taken in isolation. In this way, he argued, "the principle of montage is the basic element of Japanese ... (and Chinese) ... representational culture". Montage may also be seen as a cultural resource in the process of *bricolage*. => BRICOLAGE, CONTINUITY EDITING, FILM LANGUAGE, MODERNISM. *Further reading* Monaco, J. (2009)

moral panic *n.* JOURNALISM & CULTURAL STUDIES, MEDIA, SOCIOLOGY. The identification by the media of an issue – usually, but not always, bound up with the actions of a specific *group* – that is described with disproportionate concern as posing a fundamental threat to the moral order of society. The term derives from work in the sociology of deviancy by the South African sociologist and criminologist Stanley Cohen, in particular a classic study – *Folk Devils and Moral Panics* (1972/2002) – of street violence on public holidays in seaside towns on England's south coast. In this study Cohen describes how two groups of primarily working-class male youths – 'mods' and 'rockers' – become the focus of *newspaper* concerns about social disorder. The theory has been variously applied since this original study to groups such as weekend 'binge drinkers' in British cities, working-class single mothers, 'benefit cheats', and most recently 'asylum seekers'. Debates in Britain about remaining or leaving the European Union were coloured by concerns over levels of immigration, and slippage between terms such as 'immigrant', 'economic migrant', 'refugee' and '(failed) asylum seeker' heightened opposition to the EU's commitment to free movement of workers and helped to underpin the vote to leave. In this context, the leave campaign's poster of thousands of refugees queuing to cross the border into Slovenia – overlaid with captions such as "Breaking Point"; "The EU has failed us all"; "We must break free of the EU and take control of our borders" – condensed several themes into a *message* that helped confirm a moral panic about immigration. => DEVIANCE, FOLK DEVILS, NEWS VALUES, TABLOIDISATION. *Further reading* Critcher, C. (2003), Critcher, C. et. al. (2013)

multi-accentuality *n.* LINGUISTICS, PRAGMATICS, SEMIOTICS. The potential for the meaning of a word, or more generally a sign, to vary according to social context, especially as a result of contending social forces or interests. A property of signs, consisting in the capacity every sign has to signify more than one meaning depending on the circumstances of its use. The term was coined by the Soviet Russian linguist V.N. Voloshinov (1895-1936) as part of an argument which sought to show how the meaning of signs is fixed not by the abstract system of language (*langue*), but by the dialogic *interaction* of social relations within which the potential for meaning is fixed. Indeed, particular signs at particular historical junctures can become the site of a struggle over their meaning. After the UK European Union referendum in 2016, in which there was a narrow vote to leave, the new British Prime Minister declared, apparently unequivocally, that "Brexit means Brexit". This tautological claim did not, however, successfully close down, or restrict, the meaning of the word. Indeed, the meaning of Brexit remained in flux during the next two years, with different *groups* interpreting the word in soft terms, clean terms and hard terms. In principle, multi-accentuality is a property of all signs, but in practice most signs are not constantly the object of active struggle. However, the concept remains useful in accounting for such phenomena as *anti-languages* or languages of resistance such as those of slaves in the Caribbean or southern states in the 18th and 19th centuries, which are characterised by complete inversions of existing signs and their values (thus 'black' is inverted to become the sign for 'good', 'powerful', 'sacred' and so on). *Feminism* too has demonstrated that apparently neutral signs ('he', 'man', 'mankind') are ideologically loaded and can reflect social *power* relations. => LANGUAGE, MEANING, PRAGMATICS, SIGN. *Further reading* Voloshinov, V. (1973)

multi-modality *n.* CRITICAL DISCOURSE ANALYSIS, DISCOURSE STUDIES. Recognition by discourse analysts that the textual realisation of meaning can incorporate many elements that go beyond the simply verbal but can include various 'modes' such as the visual (illustrations, pictures, diagrams, gestures, photos, etc.) and the aural (music, sound effects, variations in pitch and tempo, etc.). Multi-modal analyses attempt to integrate the many ways in which texts make meaning into a unified approach, one which has been given added impetus by the digitalisation of communication. Social media platforms and internet web-sites provide prime examples of multi-modal texts. => INTONATION, KINESICS, MEANING, MULTI-ACCENTUALITY, SOCIAL MEDIA. *Further reading* Jewitt, C. (2014)

myth *n.* ANTHROPOLOGY AND CULTURAL STUDIES, SEMIOTICS. In anthropology, a traditional story designed to explain the origins of things, usually featuring supernatural or fantastical characters and sacred elements. Myths may play a role in ritual, carry important *truths* and ideals from one generation to another and are usually endorsed by leading figures of a society. The term is used in a more technical sense by leading structuralists such as the French anthropologist Claude Lévi-Strauss (1908–2009) and the French semiotician Roland Barthes (1915–1980). For Lévi-Strauss, myths express fundamental laws of human thought and are constructed around underlying oppositions, alongside other elements that reconcile them. In this way they resolve important paradoxes of the human condition. The basic mechanisms of myth are universal so that, underlying their apparent diversity, a few highly abstract structures may be discerned. Lévi-Strauss's examples came from *oral cultures*. Roland Barthes applied his basic insights to elements of *popular culture* such as the output of the film, entertainment and fashion industries. Indeed, the *narratives* of popular culture are seen by some scholars as a continuation of myth. => IDEOLOGY, NARRATIVE, STRUCTURALISM. *Further reading* Barthes, R. (2012)

★★

narration *n.* DISCOURSE STUDIES, FILM & LITERARY STUDIES, MEDIA & CULTURAL STUDIES. Techniques for telling a story that may involve variously the use of temporal dislocation, such as presenting events out of their chronological sequence through *flashbacks* or flashforwards, variations in *point of view* and the use of different kinds of narrator, such as reliable versus unreliable, omniscient versus restricted, and telling rather than showing. => FOCALISATION, NARRATIVE, POINT OF VIEW. *Further reading* Toolan, M. (2001)

narrative *n.* CULTURAL, FILM, DISCOURSE, MEDIA AND LITERARY STUDIES. A sequence of at least two events, involving human or anthropomorphic actors, told as a story. The simplest narratives express some kind of consequential or logically connected relationship, such as 'complication-resolution' or 'puzzle-solution', between its core events. Core events are termed *narrative kernels* and are crucial to the advancement of the story, providing nodes or hinge points in its development. Narratives may also contain minor or subsidiary events, termed *narrative satellites*, that fill out the spaces between kernels, containing information about scene or character without playing a crucial role in advancing the story. Without kernels there would be no story. Most scholars also make a fundamental distinction in some way within narrative between the story itself and the manner of its telling, between the tale and its teller and between story and *narration*. => FILM LANGUAGE, NARRATION. *Further reading* Toolan, M. (2001), Chatman, S. (1980)

narrative codes *n. DISCOURSE STUDIES, FILM & LITERARY STUDIES, MEDIA & CULTURAL STUDIES.* Associated particularly with the work of the French semiotician and literary theorist Roland Barthes (1950–1980) and his detailed analysis of a short story by Honore de Balzac. Barthes identified five *codes* for the purpose of his analysis: the hermeneutic code, the proairetic code, the cultural (or referential) code, the semic code and the symbolic code. The hermeneutic code is the code of puzzles or enigmas (particularly important in detective stories); the proairetic code is the code of actions in which any *narrative kernel* action sets up expectations of a further narrative action; the cultural code makes reference to and draws upon established frameworks of knowledge and science; the semic code organises the connotations used to give emotional colour and value to characters and scenes; the symbolic code organises the elements in a *narrative* that generate meaning through symbols, metaphors and oppositions. These codes operate like threads that, woven together, constitute the totality of the narrative *text*. => FILM LANGUAGE, FOCALISATION, MYTH, NARRATION, NARRATIVE, POINT OF VIEW, STRUCTURALISM. *Further reading* Barthes, R. (1990)

narrative kernel *np. DISCOURSE STUDIES, FILM & LITERARY STUDIES, MEDIA & CULTURAL STUDIES.* => NARRATIVE.

narrative satellite *np. DISCOURSE STUDIES, FILM & LITERARY STUDIES, MEDIA & CULTURAL STUDIES.* => NARRATIVE.

negotiated reading *np. CULTURAL AND MEDIA STUDIES.* => DECODING.

netizen (digital native) *n. INTERNET STUDIES.* A portmanteau term combining 'citizen' and 'net' to refer to those who take an active interest in developing the *internet*. It is now used most frequently by mainland China–based English language media to mean simply 'internet users' as the widely accepted translation of two separate terms *wǎngmín* (网民, literally 'net-people') and *wǎngyǒu* (网友, literally 'net-friend'). => DIGITAL MEDIA, SOCIAL MEDIA, VIRTUAL COMMUNITY.

network[1] *n. BROADCASTING AND MEDIA STUDIES.* A way of distributing or sharing programme content across several separate television stations, especially in relation to *news*.

network[2] *n.* => NETWORK SOCIETY, SOCIAL NETWORK.

network society *np.* => *INTERNET STUDIES.* Forms of social organisation that have been made possible by the *internet* and the digitally coded exchange of information. Prime examples of the network society in action may be seen in *social media* such as Facebook and Twitter but also in the use of personal blogs, *instant messaging* and email. Together these allow for the creation of online communities that metaphorically congregate around particular issues and interests on an occasional and informal basis. Characteristics of the network society include interactivity, informal non-hierarchical modes of organisation and the use of microelectronic telecommunications for its basic infrastructure. => INSTANT MESSAGING, NEW MEDIA, SOCIAL MEDIA. *Further reading* Castells, M. (2009);Van Dijk, Jan A.G.M. (2012) (3rd Ed.)

neutralism *n.* CONVERSATION ANALYSIS, JOURNALISM SOCIOLOGY OF NEWS. The adoption by broadcast journalists of an apparently neutral position when reporting events or when interacting with public figures about them. The term was developed by Clayman and Heritage (2002) in their analysis of *news interviews* to highlight those verbal practices developed by interviewers to avoid openly taking sides or expressing personal points of view. The term applies particularly to broadcast *journalism* rather than print or online journalism, where more allowance is given for the expression of partisan opinion; but the limits of neutralism have been tested by recent developments in political *discourse* where public figures have routinely advanced claims in denial of expert opinion. The complementary rise of 'fact-checking' by media organisations can be seen as a formally neutral response to lying in public life. => BIAS, IMPARTIALITY, OBJECTIVITY, TRUTH. *Further reading* Clayman, S. and Heritage (2002)

new media *np.* INTERNET AND COMMUNICATION STUDIES. One of a set of overlapping terms, which include *personal media* and *social media*, used to describe the characteristic types of media in the digital age. The transition from analogue to *digital* means for the reproduction and dissemination of *messages*, coinciding with the widespread adoption of the *internet* and *World Wide Web*, seemed to inaugurate a new age of networked *communication* – highly mobile, interactive, compressing time and space – marking a break with the dominant modes of *mass communication* previously dependent on print and *broadcasting*. => CYBERSPACE, NETWORK SOCIETY, PERSONAL MEDIA, SOCIAL MEDIA, VIRTUAL COMMUNITY. *Further reading* Flew, T. (2014) (4th Ed.); Lister, M. et. al. (2008)

news *n.* JOURNALISM. Information and commentary on contemporary events as subjects of ongoing public interest. Most media channels – whether print or *digital* – contain a high proportion of this kind of output, which has a long history of being institutionalised and controlled for commercial gain, for reasons of state or supposedly in the public interest. => DOCUMENTARY, NEWS VALUES, OBJECTIVITY. *Further reading* Allan, S. (Ed.) (2011)

news anchor *np.* BROADCAST JOURNALISM, SOCIOLOGY OF NEWS. One who presents a broadcast *news* programme (usually television, but also radio) and who may read the lead items of news at intervals during the news programme but whose prime responsibility is to provide news updates as well as *continuity* during the programme by interviewing experts, witnesses, affiliated journalists and other social actors who can make a contribution to contextualising the news. The news anchor manages the transition from one such news participant to another but effectively becomes the public *face* of the news provider for the duration of the programme. As such, his or her *personality* becomes the guarantee of the *truth* and the relevance of the news as broadcast and the programme itself may be named after its news anchor, a practice more common in the US than elsewhere. => AUTOCUE, MODES OF ADDRESS, NEWS READER, PARA-SOCIAL INTERACTION, PERSONALISATION.

newscaster/newsreader *n.* BROADCAST JOURNALISM, SOCIOLOGY OF NEWS. Someone – usually familiar to the *audience* – who reads the main items of broadcast *news* in an institutional *voice* with little personal inflection. Occasionally this person also doubles as the *news anchor*, adopting the lead position and providing *continuity* throughout the news programme, but quite often these roles are kept separate. => AUTOCUE, MODES OF ADDRESS, NEWS READER, PARA-SOCIAL INTERACTION, PERSONALISATION. *Further reading* Montgomery, M. (2007), Montgomery, M. and Shen Jin (2017)

newspaper *n.* JOURNALISM. A printed publication issued at regular intervals (such as daily or weekly) that provides wide coverage of a range of topics of immediate public interest. The emergence of the modern newspaper is closely linked to the introduction of the printing press, though many newspapers are now transferring their publishing activity online while striving to maintain their traditional print identity. => NEWS, NEWS VALUES, PRESS. *Further reading* Conboy, M. (2004); Schudson, M. (1981); Williams, K. (2010)

news presentation *np.* BROADCAST JOURNALISM, SOCIOLOGY OF NEWS. Standard way of delivering the lead information for the main items of *news* on radio and television, using one or more *newsreaders* or *newscasters* to read the items, usually scripted in advance, assisted by a teleprompter or *autocue* if reading to a camera in order to heighten the sense of direct visual *address* to the *audience*. The look-to-camera on television news is regarded by some as the characteristic look of television, rarely found, for instance, in fictional film. => MODES OF ADDRESS, NEWS ANCHOR, NEWS READER, PARA-SOCIAL INTERACTION. *Further reading* Montgomery, M. (2007), Montgomery, M. and Shen Jin (2017)

news values *np.* JOURNALISM, DISCOURSE STUDIES, SOCIOLOGY. A way of describing 'newsworthiness' in terms of the qualities or factors that inform the selection of items for the *news*. Events become news to the extent that they satisfy the following criteria.

Recency/Timeliness. News, as the name implies, deals by definition with 'the new' ("new information of recent events", as the Shorter Oxford English Dictionary puts it). Accordingly, news items have a limited life-cycle, with their news value dwindling rapidly over time. *Intensity/Discontinuity.* The sharper and more temporally bounded the event, the easier it is to integrate it into the temporal rhythms of news. *Scale/Scope.* Events need to be of a scale large enough to warrant attention. "The stronger the signal, the greater the amplitude, the more probable that it will be recorded as worth listening to" (Galtung and Ruge 1965: 64). *Conflict.* Conflict between opposing parties is newsworthy. Strong oppositions serve not only to dramatise individual events but also provide overarching *frames* for organising diverse material. *Personalisation.* The news is more interested in 'persons' than 'processes'. People provide points of identification, and they help to dramatise conflict. "News has a tendency to present events as sentences where there is a subject, a named person or collectivity consisting of a few persons, and the event is then seen as a consequence of the actions of this person or these persons" (Galtung and Ruge 1965: 66). *Power.* The *salience* of news material is enhanced if it involves people with power – however this may be defined. The actions of presidents, princesses, prime ministers and popes generally attract more notice than those of plumbers, porters, park-keepers and pensioners. *Negativity.* Bad news makes good news. War reporting is one of the earliest historical examples of news; but crime, fatal accident, famine, earthquake, execution, epidemic and disaster are staple elements of the news. *Unexpectedness.* Routine events are difficult to assimilate to the news, which favours the novel, the atypical and the unusual. As the old joke has it: 'Man bites dog' is a more likely news item than 'Dog bites man'. *Proximity/Cultural relevance.* The further removed an event from the news centre the less relevance it has for the news outlet. This is partly a question of literal, geographical distance. Distance may also be understood metaphorically, in cultural terms, as well as literally. Societies and figures that are remote in cultural terms from the norms of broadcasters feature less prominently than those which have a great deal in common with the news centre. *Meaningfulness/Unambiguity.* News prefers material whose meaning can be presented as if clear-cut and unambiguous rather than cloudy and complex. "An event with a clear interpretation, free from ambiguities in its meaning, is preferred to the highly ambiguous event from which many and inconsistent implications can and will be made" (Galtung and Ruge, 1965: 64). *Composition/Fit*. In any bulletin particular slots carry particular values. It is common, for instance, for some broadcasters to finish their bulletin with a relatively quirky, 'upbeat', human-interest story. In the final slot such material is likely to take precedence over an accident or injury story. There may also be considerations of balance within a bulletin as a whole between, for example, domestic news and international news, political news and sporting news. News values may also be encoded differentially into different news media. Television has an obvious predilection for *actuality* footage. A news story with strong pictures is likely to take precedence over one without footage, all else being equal. => NEWS, PERSONALISATION. *Further reading* Bednarek, M. and Caple, H. (2012), Bednarek, M. and Caple, H. (2017)

★★

op-ed *adj.* JOURNALISM, PRESS. A *genre* of *writing* found in *newspapers* where a named author offers an opinion on a topic of current interest in their own name rather than in the name of the publication itself. In this way, an op-ed piece is distinct from an *editorial* piece in a newspaper which is not authored by a named individual but is attributed to an editorial board writing on behalf of the publication. The name op-ed may derive from the habitual position of such pieces on the page opposite the editorial. => EDITORIAL.

open text *np.* LITERARY LINGUISTICS. Any *text* that seems designed to sustain a variety of interpretations, the availability of which may be said to enrich (rather than diminish) the reading experience. Umberto Eco, the Italian semiotician (1932–2016), thought of the work of art as an 'open work', which he described as a dynamic 'work in movement', effectively open to an unlimited range of interpretations and possible readings. See also Barthes's study *S/Z* and his concept of the writerly text. => CLOSED TEXT, HERMENEUTICS, JOUISSANCE. *Further reading* Eco, U. (1981)

objectivity *n.* JOURNALISM & COMMUNICATION STUDIES. Criterion used for judging the truthfulness of various kinds of *text* but most particularly those of *journalism*. Statements that are objective are faithful to the object or phenomena that they describe which they capture without personal prejudice and uninfluenced by emotion. Objectivity is often explicitly incorporated into the *codes* of professional journalism as a guarantee of *truth* but also to foreground the merits of journalistic independence. => BIAS, IMPARTIALITY,

NEUTRALISM, SUBJECTIVITY. *Further reading* Tuchman, G. (1980); Schudson, M. (2011)

opinion poll *np*. POLITICAL COMMUNICATION. A survey of opinion of a given population. Polls may be carried out verbally, through ballots or through telecommunications. => PUBLIC OPINION. SJ

oppositional reading *np*. CULTURAL STUDIES. => ENCODING/DECODING, HERMENEUTICS, INTERPRETIVE COMMUNITY, OPEN TEXT.

oral culture *np*. ANTHROPOLOGY, CULTURAL STUDIES. A *culture* that depends primarily on word of mouth for the transmission of knowledge, values and beliefs. Oral cultures are typically described by contrast to literate cultures in which knowledge and beliefs are codified and transmitted by means of writing and written *text*. Putative differences between oral and literate cultures have been of keen interest to anthropologists, sociologists and literary-cultural theorists since at least the mid-20th century. Oral cultures are thought to be more empathetic and participatory, to depend more on associative and analogical lines of reasoning than the more linear and syllogistic modes encouraged by literacy and to favour implied rather than explicit meanings. In practice, many cultures seem to exist on a continuum between the two types. Indeed, one of the most influential accounts of *orality* and literacy, by the American Jesuit literary and cultural historian Walter J. Ong (1912–2003), suggests that the *influence* of digital *communication* on contemporary literate cultures may be re-emphasising the oral in a phase that Ong calls *secondary orality*. => DIGITALISATION, ORALITY, SPEECH, WRITING. *Further reading* Ong, W.J. (2012) (2nd Ed.)

orality *n*. ANTHROPOLOGY, CULTURAL STUDIES. A quality of those *cultures* or *groups* that have been largely untouched by the knowledge and use of *writing* and print. Under conditions of orality, knowledge and traditions are passed on by word of mouth rather than codified in written *text*. => FACE-TO-FACE COMMUNICATION, ORAL CULTURE, SPEECH, WRITING. *Further reading* Ong, W.J. (2012) (2nd Ed.)

other *n*. COMMUNICATION, CULTURAL AND LITERARY STUDIES. Perhaps the most important but problematic term in the contemporary social and human sciences, 'the other' has been a significant focus of discussion in sociology, anthropology, philosophy, psychoanalysis and literary studies. In sociology, for instance, the American sociologist George Herbert Mead (1863–1931) proposed that for the socially constituted 'self' to emerge within *socialisation* some notion of a 'generalised other' is required: in other words, for the child to act as a social agent or being it has to come to an appreciation of the nature of the other roles that make up any social activity in which it is engaged. In this sociological tradition, therefore, 'the other' exists as a necessary and complementary counterpart to 'the self'. In a radically different idiom the French psychoanalyst Jacques Lacan (1901–1981) proposed that the subject only comes to full self-consciousness and discovers a sense of its own identity when it recognises the fundamental difference from the self of 'the Other'. In Lacan, therefore, as for Mead, recognition of 'the other' is a necessary and inevitable part of the individual's development. In anthropology and literary studies, however, 'the other' emerges as an epiphenomenon of the contact between *groups* and peoples. Anthropology's emphasis on the customs and mentalities of pre-historical societies led to an assumption of difference in which the object of study was constructed as distant, strange and exotic. This process itself, however, becomes the focus of attention in literary (especially post-colonial) studies where a prevailing tendency to construct 'the other' as inferior is subjected to extensive critique. Subordinate groups (whether they be identified in terms of race, sex, class, religious *affiliation* or some other attribute) have tended to be represented as 'other' – often drawing upon a range of overlapping terms (e.g. irrational, lazy, sensual, impulsive, exotic, violent, submissive, enigmatic) – from the perspective of a dominant group (members of which are assumed to share positive qualities such as rationality, industriousness, self-control, normality and so on). Whether the dominant group is the coloniser, the ruling class, male, heterosexual or white, the processes seem to be similar, so that a general term 'othering', has been coined. In short, powerful groups come to a positive definition of themselves by projecting negative qualities onto others. => SELF-CONCEPT, SELF-PRESENTATION. *Further reading* Fabian, J. (2014); Levinas, E. (1987)

★★

para-social interaction *np.* MEDIA & COMMUNICATION STUDIES, PSYCHIATRY, SOCIAL PSYCHOLOGY. A way of describing the *interaction* between the broadcast media and their *audiences*. The notion is particularly apposite in the case of television where the television *personality* or performer may seem to be directly addressing the audience and where the television image makes available to the audience details of expression and *gesture* that typically function as important cues in real-time, face-to-face social interaction. Indeed, both radio and television have fostered a way of talking, apparently personal and private even though to large anonymous audiences, as part of an illusion of 'intimacy at a distance'. The notion of para-social interaction was developed in an article by Horton and Wohl (1956), where they suggested that television's attention to the expressive surfaces of the face – especially when the speaker is looking to camera – reproduced the kind of attention we give to an interlocutor in day-to-day interaction, and thereby concluded that "this simulacrum of conversational give and take may be called *para-social interaction*." It is this, some commentators believe (e.g. Frosh, 2009), which lies at the root of the *sociability* of television (and *broadcasting* more generally) and its characteristic *communicative ethos*. => FACE-TO-FACE COMMUNICATION, INTERACTION, MODE OF ADDRESS. *Further reading* Horton, D. and R. Wohl (1956), Frosh, P. (2009)

parody *n*. FILM & TELEVISION STUDIES, MEDIA & COMMUNICATION STUDIES. A *text* in which the *style* of a particular writer, period, *genre* or *register* is reproduced in an exaggerated fashion for comic effect, especially when the parody is applied to ludicrously inappropriate subject matter. Parody often features in the armory of *satire*, especially as a weapon for ridicule, and may be put to effective use in film, television and radio as well as in the more traditional literary genres of poetry, drama and the novel. Although it receives little critical attention, there is a substantial body of work from Hollywood that offers parodies of mainstream films, for instance, *Fifty Shades of Black* (2016) as a parody of *Fifty Shades of Grey* (2015). The satirical *magazines The Onion* in the US and *Private Eye* in the UK both deploy parodies of various styles – especially *news* styles – sometimes to satirise public figures, and sometimes the news media themselves. In the UK, *Brass Eye* (Channel 4, 1997–2001), and its predecessor *The Day Today* (BBC2, 1994), mocked current affairs television and *celebrity culture* but operated precariously on the boundaries of 'good taste'. As a form of satire, parody relies upon informed *audiences* with a high degree of media literacy capable of recognising existing styles and genres and appreciating their re-inflection into different situations, contexts and subject matters. => INTERTEXTUALITY, IRONY, *PASTICHE*, SATIRE. *Further reading* Gray, Jonathan (2006)

parole *n*. (*Fr*.) COMMUNICATION STUDIES, LINGUISTICS, SEMIOTICS. In Saussurian linguistics, the activity of speaking. The term was used by the Swiss linguist, Ferdinand de Saussure (1857- 1913), to separate those variable and accidental aspects of *speech* that were to be excluded from the focus of linguistic enquiry. As such, parole needs to be understood in relation to its contrasting term, *langue*. Parole amounts to individual instances of speaking; langue to the abstract system that underlies it. Although what people actually do when speaking may be of interest to the physiologist or the behavioural psychologist, it cannot form the basis of linguistic study, because – for Saussure – it is subject to too much random fluctuation. Instead, linguistics should focus on the underlying sets of rules and conventions that make parole possible and guarantee its intelligibility. There is none the less a close and complementary relationship between langue and parole. Parole may be seen as a continual implementation of the underlying system constituted in the langue; but conversely the continual practice of speaking affirms and adjusts the langue, moulding it gradually into a different form. No one individual can control or shape the langue, but generations of speakers can and do alter it from one historically specific state to another. Like many of the terms originally developed in Saussure's lectures between 1906 and 1911, langue and parole achieved new currency during the 1960s and 1970s with the emergence of semiology as the study of sign systems. In this study, a particular film or fashion garment could be seen as an individual instance of parole against the backdrop of the underlying system of *film language* or fashion *codes*. One difficulty with this application of the term is that it was much more difficult to think of ways in which film as a system of *signification* was available for study except through its parole, whereas language was more generally available through introspection because of its mental basis. => CODE, COMPETENCE, LANGUE, PERFORMANCE. *Further reading* Harris, R. (2003); Hawkes, T. (2003); Saussure (1974); Culler (1976)

participation framework *np.* COMMUNICATION STUDIES, DISCOURSE STUDIES, SOCIOLOGY. The possible configuration of parties or roles in *communication*. The term derives from the work of American sociologist Erving Goffman (1922–1982), who used it to distinguish different kinds of *footing* which can be adopted in the production or reception of an utterance. Hearers, for instance, may include over-hearers as well as ratified participants. And the act of speaking itself may refer to not merely the one who utters the words (for Goffman, the *animator*) but also the one who composes them (the 'author') and the one who bears responsibility for them (the 'principal'). => FOOTING. *Further reading* Dynel, M. and Chovanec, J. (2015); Goffman, E. (1981)

pastiche *n.* CULTURAL STUDIES, FILM & LITERARY STUDIES. A literary or artistic composition that imitates the *style* and form of a pre-existing work in a knowing and deliberate fashion, often in homage to the original. Sometimes it will incorporate different styles or *registers* from a variety of sources to humorous effect. Indeed, for pastiche to be successful the *audience* needs to be able to appreciate the relationship between the original source and the derived work. This re-working or simple reiteration of previous styles and forms has been associated with *postmodernism*, which is content to recycle previous work (as in *bricolage*) without striving – like *modernism* – for originality. Unlike *parody*, pastiche is not satirical in its intent but is respectful to its sources. => ETHICS, INTERTEXTUALITY, IRONY, MODERNISM, PARODY, SATIRE. *Further reading* Dyer, R. (2006)

persistence of vision *np.* MEDIA STUDIES, TECHNOLOGY. An early theory of how the *projection* of successive images (e.g. frames of a film or cartoon) could create the sense of continuous motion. It maintained that the retina of the eye retained each projected image for a fraction of a second before the next image followed in quick succession. Although the theory has survived in some accounts of film, psychologists have long explained the sense of continuous motion in terms of the brain making sense of perceptual data rather than the retina retaining an after-image. => MONTAGE, ZOETROPE.

persona *n.* COMMUNICATION, CULTURAL AND DISCOURSE STUDIES. Usually a fictional identity assumed for the sake of *mediated* public performance. The use of a recurrent persona is a common feature of British television and radio comedy, especially when it involves camp or drag comic routines. Examples would be Mrs Merton, Lily Savage, Dame Edna and Ali G. More fundamentally, in dramaturgical theories of social interaction all behaviour in public requires the assumption of a persona fashioned for the occasion but distinct from the 'real' or inner self. => IDENTITY, PERFORMANCE, SELF-CONCEPT. *Further reading* Tolson, A. (2001b)

personal influence *n.* MEDIA STUDIES. Recognises that *messages* from the media do not simply have effects directly on individuals, either as isolated recipients or as an aggregated mass, but are further *mediated* by informal 'opinion leaders' who filter, interpret and disseminate what they see and hear to their personal networks. The idea was most fully articulated in a book of the same name by the American sociologists Elihu Katz (b. 1926) and Paul Lazarsfeld (1901–1976) published in 1955. => INFLUENCE. *Further reading* Katz, E. and Lazarsfeld, P. (1955)

personalisation *n.* DISCOURSE STUDIES, JOURNALISM. The tendency to design public *discourse*, especially *news* discourse, so that it seems to be directly addressed to individual persons rather than abstract *audiences*. A range of discourse practices are associated with this tendency, such as the use of familiar forms of *address*, questions, commands and informal colloquial usage. The term can also be used to apply not only to *styles* of address but also to ways of *framing* topics so that they are articulated in personal terms. Policy issues, for instance, are likely to be reported using indicative case studies, *vox pops*, and a focus on the effects of change on individuals. => MODES OF ADDRESS, NEWS

VALUES, PARA-SOCIAL INTERACTION, SYNTHETIC PERSONALISATION. *Further reading* Landert, D. (2014)

personality *n.* COMMUNICATION AND CULTURAL STUDIES. A person well known by virtue of their frequent appearances on television or more generally in the media. Television personalities may exhibit particular kinds of excellence in a field such as cookery, sport or music, but they typically project a certain kind of approachable, warm and friendly ordinariness. They may be extremely talented in a field, but they also excel at 'being themselves' on television. => CELEBRITY, PERSONA, SYNTHETIC PERSONALITY. *Further reading* Tolson, A. (1991)

personal media *np.* MEDIA & INTERNET STUDIES. Any form of media designed for use on a person-to-person basis allowing for the reciprocal exchange of *messages* between individuals or small *groups*. Typical forms of personal media include *instant messaging*, email, and blogs. => DIGITALISATION, MEDIATION, NEW MEDIA, SOCIAL MEDIA, TECHNOLOGY. *Further reading* Rasmussen, T. (2014)

personal space *n.* PROXEMICS. The space surrounding a person which they normally regard as their own. Entering someone's personal space may send signals of closeness, even intimacy, and, if unwarranted, may cause irritation or anxiety. => PROXEMICS.

persuasion *n.* RHETORIC. A mode of *communication* purposefully designed to change the attitudes, actions or beliefs of an *audience*. Closely allied to *propaganda* and *public relations*. => INFLUENCE, PERSONAL INFLUENCE, RHETORIC.

platform => DIGITAL PLATFORM.

point of view *np.* FILM AND CULTURAL STUDIES, LITERARY. The role played by a particular angle of vision in the depiction of an object or an event. The term has a wide currency in the visual arts where it is used to emphasise ways in which any representation must adopt a particular perspective on its subject matter and in doing so constructs a position from which the spectator will view it. By extension the term is used in *film theory* and criticism for the kind of camera work that provides a shot of a scene as if from the position of a character within it, the so-called 'point of view' shot. More generally, the term plays a key role in studies of prose fiction in describing the role of different kinds of narrator in telling a story. None of these uses is far from a metaphorical application meaning broadly 'framework of belief'. => FOCALISATION, NARRATION. *Further reading* Scholes, R. (2009)

popular culture *np.* CULTURAL STUDIES. The common arts, artefacts, forms of entertainment, folklore, frameworks of belief, games, music, *myths,* expressive *styles,* sports and values of ordinary people. The field of popular culture gains definition by contrast with minority or *high culture* whose objects and values tend to attract official endorsement and in the appreciation of which accrues *cultural capital.* Popular culture, instead, has often been dismissed as a *culture* of commercially debased products and simplified, stock responses. => COUNTER CULTURE, CULTURE, HIGH CULTURE, ORAL CULTURE, SUB CULTURE. *Further reading* Storey, J. (2015)

postmodernism *n.* CRITICAL THEORY, CULTURAL CRITICISM, CULTURAL STUDIES. Philosophical and cultural response to social changes which accelerated during the latter half of the 20th century. The increasingly *mediated* nature of much of social and public life suggests that a great deal of personal experience takes place no longer in an immediate and first hand fashion. As a result, the *genres* and forms through which it is communicated become the focus of self-conscious understanding and reflection, leading to the avoidance of straightforward commitment to the content of *communication* and the adoption instead of forms of playfulness and detachment – especially *irony, pastiche* and *bricolage.* Postmodernism, indeed, should not be seen as a coherent, internally consistent philosophy but rather as a loose label for tendencies in cultural form and production which can be understood in part as a reaction to previous cultural tendencies and movements such as *modernism* and the Enlightenment more generally. Thus, postmodernism distrusts the kind of grand *narratives* that see history moving inevitably towards the amelioration of the human condition. It distrusts the application of reason as the best, most reliable answer to human problems. It celebrates the surfaces of *culture* and makes no claim for a core of inner significance where the purpose of the 'outside' is to express the real meaning of the 'inside'. In this way, shifting notions of postmodernism have come to inform commentary on a variety of cultural forms including art, architecture, film, music, literature, politics and the blogosphere. As an idea and as a movement it is not without its critics. For the Marxist literary critic Frederic Jameson, it is 'the cultural logic of late capitalism', and its freewheeling, 'liquid' approach to questions of *truth,* value and human relationships raise serious issues for those more wedded to objectivism rather than relativism in knowledge and ethics. => ETHICS, MODERNISM, PASTICHE, POST-STRUCTURALISM, PARODY, SATIRE. *Further reading* Baumann, Z. (2000); Harvey, D. (1990); Jameson, F. (1991); Lyotard, J.-F. (1984)

post-structuralism *n.* CRITICAL THEORY, CULTURAL CRITICISM, CULTURAL STUDIES. Intellectual movement emerging in France in the

1960s and 1970s, typically associated with the work of Michel Foucault (1926-1984) and Jacques Derrida (1930-2004), that defined itself negatively against the tenets of *structuralism*. Derrida in particular took issue with the structuralist tendency to see cultural activity in terms of sets of binary oppositions (such as *speech* versus *writing*, system versus event, signifier versus signified, synchronic versus *diachronic*, masculine versus feminine, reason versus emotion). For one thing, there was often an implicit, covert hierarchy at work in the way the oppositions were formulated, in which one side was valued over the other. For another thing, the nature of the oppositions tended to conceal or suppress what might be of interest in the space between the opposing terms (e.g. do the terms masculine and feminine exhaust all forms of gender identity?) Foucault's difficulties with structuralism might be best traced to issues of history and change. For Foucault, the past genealogy of forms and practices is crucial to understanding the present, whereas structuralism in its purest forms tended not to be interested in change but in cultural systems as they operate as if at a single point in time. => DECONSTRUCTION, POSTMODERNISM, STRUCTURALISM. *Further reading* Belsey, C. (2002)

power *n.* CRITICAL DISCOURSE ANALYSIS, MEDIA & CULTURAL STUDIES. The capacity or the potential for action by a social actor by virtue of their agency within social structure. Some theories of language, of the media and of society conceptualise power primarily in terms of *control*, emphasising the capacity of actors or institutions to influence and constrain the behaviour, attitudes and options of others even in spite of their resistance. In other ways, however, the power of actors or institutions may be considered productive and enabling. => CONTROL. *Further reading* Thornborrow, J. (2002); Van Dijk, T. (2008)

pragmatics *n.* LINGUISTICS. The systematic study of the interpretation of utterances and more specifically how the *context of situation* influences their meaning. Traditionally the study of meaning in linguistics has focused upon the meaning of words or sentences as if meaning inhered within the linguistic expression itself and was ultimately determined by the linguistic system. Pragmatics, however, emphasises the role of context in determining meaning. It had long been recognised that linguistic items such as deictics and other indexical expressions depend for their meaning on the context of situation. In particular, deictics such as the personal pronouns 'I' and 'you' and indexical expressions such as 'tomorrow' all depend for their meaning on the circumstances in which they are uttered. Thus, the precise meaning of 'I'll visit you tomorrow' will vary depending upon who actually is speaking to whom and on when the utterance takes place. Even apart from *deixis*, however, many words have multiple senses. Even a simple item such as 'coach' has several senses, including 'a mode of transport' and 'someone who trains people in a particular sport'. Its use, therefore, in an utterance such as 'Look out for the coach' is potentially ambiguous, and we rely upon context to select the relevant sense. Pragmatic issues, however, go far beyond issues of word meaning to include consideration of complicated kinds of contextual effect where the meaning of an utterance is much more than what is literally said. If in a review of an opera we read that 'Mr Jones sang a series of notes which corresponded to those of an aria from Rigoletto', we infer that he sang badly, even though the utterance does not actually say so. Similarly, if while driving in a strange town we ask someone, 'Is there anywhere we can get petrol round here?' and they reply 'There's a garage just round the corner', we assume that it is the type of garage that sells petrol (not that it is one for parking your car) and that it is open. These kinds of inferences that go beyond the literal meaning of what is said are known as *implicatures*. A further kind of contextual effect relates to the notion of *speech act*. Directives, for instance, are a commonly occurring type of speech act designed to get someone to do something. An utterance such as 'Play the piano, Elton' is likely to be a directive whatever the circumstances of its occurrence. But utterances such as 'Would you mind playing the piano, Elton?', 'Can you play the piano, Elton?', 'The piano, Elton', etc., may or may not prove to be directives depending on the context of situation. If a teacher in a music lesson says to a pupil, 'Can you play the piano, Elton?', with the piano waiting for someone to play it, then it is most likely to be heard as a directive. If, on the other hand, a group of acquaintances are discussing what instruments they can play and one asks of another 'Can you play the piano, Elton?' then s/he would most likely be heard as requesting information rather than making a directive. In this way, what an utterance is heard as doing (in other words, what speech act it is performing) can vary according to its context of situation. The aim of pragmatics is in the first place to describe these various kinds of contextual effect; but more significantly it aims to explain how language users actually make sense of each other's utterances in the face of the various kinds of indeterminacy and ambiguity outlined above. The contribution of pragmatics to *communication* studies more generally is potentially considerable, although not always realised, since it goes to the heart of some of the most troubling issues surrounding *text* and interpretation (e.g. 'Where is meaning – in the text; or in the context?'). At the same time, however, pragmatics has become closely associated more recently with the interests of cognitive science and the study of artificial intelligence. Such links tend to produce a strong emphasis on the supposed rationality of communicators, and on the *universality* (or not) of the interpretative procedures that they adopt, so that much work remains to be done on the socially structured distribution and organisation of pragmatic knowledge and procedures. => CONTEXT OF SITUATION, CONVERSATION ANALYSIS, DECODING, DISCOURSE ACT, HERMENEUTICS, IMPLICATURE, MEANING, MULTI ACCENTUALITY, NEGOTIATED READING, OPEN TEXT, SEMANTICS, SPEECH ACT. *Further reading*: Leech (1983); Levinson (1983)

preferred reading *np.* MEDIA & CULTURAL STUDIES. When members of an *audience* interpret a media *text* in the way that its producers intended => DECODING. *Further reading* Hall, S. (2007); Morley, D. (2004)

press officer *np.* POLITICAL COMMUNICATION. Person charged with the official role of liaising with *news* media on behalf of a large organisation such as a corporation, government department or royal household. => PUBLIC RELATIONS (PR).

primary orality *np.* => ORALITY.

projection *n.* FILM AND MEDIA STUDIES. In cinema the process of displaying film for public viewing by projecting light on to a screen through a continuously moving film strip at a constant rate usually of 24 frames a second. *Further reading* Monaco, J. (2009)

propaganda *n.* POLITICAL COMMUNICATION. Public *communication* designed to influence the views or actions of an *audience* principally for ideological or political purposes by the use of systematically biased *messages*. => BIAS, MANUFACTURE OF CONSENT. *Further reading* Herman, E. S., & Chomsky, N. (1988)

protocols of use *np.* MEDIA & COMMUNICATION STUDIES, TECHNOLOGY. Communicative technologies require certain kinds of taken-for-granted habitual and conventional understandings about their use. These can be simultaneously restricting and/or enabling, explicit or implicit. *Writing* systems and scripts, for instance, can be laid out and read in a variety of ways according to different protocols of use. The Latin alphabetic script (adopted here) is read from left to right, working in horizontal linear fashion from the top of the page to the bottom. Other major scripts, such as Hebrew or Arabic, on the other hand, are read from right to left. Chinese characters are usually read from left to right, but they can alternatively be set out in columns and read vertically from the top of the page to the bottom. Egyptian hieroglyphs could be read vertically, horizontally, from left to right or from right to left, depending on which direction the signs themselves (often including animal or human figures) were facing: if the signs faced right, they should be read from left to right. Chinese *newspapers* sometimes combine all three directions on the same page. These scripts, therefore, do not just vary from alphabetic to pictographic or ideographic: they also vary in their taken-for-granted protocols of use. Protocols, however, may be more explicit and clearly articulated in the use of the chosen medium and its associated *technology*. *Communication* between air-traffic control and aircraft is subject to carefully designed verbal protocols of use. For instance, the following radio voice *message* from an aircraft to a flight centre follows various established protocols for use: "MIAMI CENTER BARON FIVE SIX THREE HOTEL, REQUEST VFR TRAFFIC ADVISORIES, OVER." According to protocol, the name of the centre being called comes first: "Miami Center". This is followed by the individual call sign of the calling aircraft: "Baron five six three hotel" (equivalent to 'B563H', using the agreed phonetic alphabet of words for initial letters). This in turn is followed by the core content of the communication: "Request VFR traffic advisories" (equivalent to 'I request visual flight rules traffic advisories'). The end of the message is marked by the standard pro-term for use in two-way radio communication, "Over". Protocols of use – such as Twitter's initial restriction to 140 characters – may be relatively simple, or highly complex – such as rules of *impartiality* for public service *news* broadcasters. Every major technology of communication, however, is only able to achieve its communicative potential by developing and adhering to such protocols => AFFORDANCES, SPEECH, TECHNOLOGY, WRITING.

proxemics *n.* COMMUNICATION. The study of the roles played by space and physical distance in social *interaction*. The negotiation of mutual distance between parties provides important cues about social distance. => FACE-TO-FACE COMMUNICATION, INTERPERSONAL COMMUNICATION, REAL-TIME COMMUNICATION.

public opinion *np.* POLITICAL COMMUNICATION. The assumed view of most people about some issue of *community*-wide relevance. The reality is that there are many publics and manifold opinions. There are few issues that command a general *consensus* in a really sizeable majority of a nation-wide community, except perhaps in the unifying case of war or disaster. So what counts as public opinion is usually the outcome of a relatively limited exercise assessing the opinions of perhaps some thousands of respondents, often by automated technologies. The most frequently encountered method of assessing public opinion is an *opinion poll*, usually administered by agencies recruited to survey matters such as political voting intentions, purchasing patterns, preferred television programmes, and the like. Where a high degree of consensus is found and publicised, this itself can become a biasing factor in constructing public opinion. To maintain democratic independence, some countries forbid the publication of opinion poll findings about voting intentions in the immediate run-up to a political election. The largest scale test of public opinion is a governmental election or a national referendum on matters such as the *powers* or structural make-up of a state. => HEGEMONY, MANUFACTURE OF CONSENT, OPINION POLL, PUBLIC SPHERE. *Further reading* Glynn, C.J. et. al. (3rd Ed.) (2016)

public relations (PR) *np.* POLITICAL COMMUNICATION. Often referred to simply as 'PR', public relations are conducted by professional communicators (usually called consultants, often former journalists) on behalf of large organisations such as governments and multi-national corporations who seek to manage the media so as to maintain good relations between themselves and the public at large. => PROPAGANDA, SPIN DOCTORS.

public service broadcasting *np.* MEDIA, CULTURAL & COMMUNICATION STUDIES. The provision of television and radio services funded by public subscription or levy through a licence fee which is then in turn used to fund an approved broadcaster. In the UK this arrangement is managed within the terms of a charter between the government and a broadcaster, in this case most typically the BBC. Public service broadcasting, within this model, is treated as a public good that needs to be provided, maintained and distributed relatively free of direct government *control* and commercial imperatives. Thus, the model is designed to allow broadcasting a degree of relative autonomy in which it, on the one hand, escapes state ownership and control and pressures to provide *propaganda* and, on the other hand, remains independent of the exigencies of the media market place and a consequent drive to maximise ratings. The model has been widely adopted, and versions of it may be found in Scandanavia, for instance, or the Netherlands, the US, Hong Kong and Macau, usually playing a greater or lesser role in a mixed media economy. The *digitalisation* of the media poses some challenge to the concept of public service broadcasting. The BBC, for instance, has responded to digitalisation by successfully moving its services online, adding to and enriching many of them. This, however, has inevitably raised issues about the practicalities of the licence fee as a form of funding when the broadcaster's output, programming and content more generally may be received on smartphones, tablets and laptops rather than – as formerly – on a radio or television. In addition, *terrestrial broadcasting* had a limited but well-defined geographical reach, while the reach of online services is potentially unlimited: how, therefore, does one ensure that those using the service are paying for it? And, finally, commercial broadcasters argue that, in this changing environment, the competition from public service providers with – for the time being at least – a stable source of funding is unfair. => BROADCASTING, CENSORSHIP, DIGITALISATION, PROPANGANDA, PUBLIC SPHERE. *Further reading* Scannell, P. and Cardiff, D. (1991)

public sphere *np. MEDIA & COMMUNICATION STUDIES.* A social discursive space in which members of civil society can engage in identifying and discussing common areas of concern that form *public opinion* and that can relate to political action. The collective body of the 'public' is constituted by the processes of articulation and negotiation that take place within this sphere. In theories of democratic governance, the public sphere connects the state with the interests of society by spanning both the private sphere of social labour and commodity exchange as well as the sphere of public authority vested in the state. Most theories of the public sphere are influenced by the German sociologist and critical theorist Jürgen Habermas's *The Structural Transformation of the Public Sphere: An Inquiry into a Category of Bourgeois Society* (1989), which analyses the evolution of a new civic society in Europe in the 18th century due to the growth of commercial needs, literacy rates and the development of a critical social *discourse* of the people. New resources that arose in the 18th century such as print *journalism* and the press were instrumental in the establishment of the bourgeois public sphere. Subsequently, according to Habermas, the dominance of consumer desire over political action in a burgeoning capitalist economy led to the downturn in the *power* of a rational and inclusive public sphere. As such, the media became increasingly fashioned as a tool of advertising and political forces rather than a medium through which the public could access information on political concerns. Growing media power in the public sphere signified a new *influence* and *control* over *communication* flows. => INFOTAINMENT, VALIDITY CLAIMS. *Further reading* Calhoun, C. (Ed.) (1992); Habermas, J. (1989) *SJ*

publishing industry *n. PUBLISHING.* Those companies devoted to the large-scale reproduction and dissemination of information, ideas, literature, music and other forms of *intellectual property*. Typical products of the publishing industry have traditionally included books, *magazines*, directories, journals and *newspapers*. However, the emergence of multimedia formats and digital online publishing as an alternative to print is changing the nature of the industry to include services as well as products. *Further reading* Benjamin, W. (2008)

**

questionnaire *n.* A research tool or mechanism that consists of a set of printed or written questions, designed in order to gather information from respondents and often devised for the purposes of statistical study. A questionnaire may offer a choice of standardised answers to facilitate the collection and organisation of data. SJ

**

rapport-talk => REPORT-TALK.
readership *n.* COMMUNICATION & CULTURAL STUDIES. The collectivity of readers of a published resource such as *newspaper, magazine* or book. It can also refer to the state or quality of being a reader. => CULTURAL CAPITAL, INTERPRETIVE COMMUNITY, READING PUBLIC. *Further reading* Radway, J. (1992) SJ
reading public *n.* LITERARY & CULTURAL STUDIES. Those who are equipped by education and social background to form an *audience* for certain kinds of literary production. The rise of the novel, for instance, has been identified with the growth of a bourgeois middle class with the requisite resources of time and money to read, often in private, extended prose *narratives.* => CULTURAL CAPITAL, INTERPRETIVE COMMUNITY, READERSHIP. *Further reading* Radway, J. (1992); Watt, I. (2015)
real-time communication *n.* CONVERSATION ANALYSIS, SOCIAL INTERACTION, VERBAL INTERACTION. The exchange of meanings between interlocutors that unfolds at the pace of ordinary *interaction* without rapid acceleration or long delays. *Conversation,* or *talk-in-interaction,* takes place in real-time where participants must compose and interpret simultaneously with the flow of *speech.* The pressures of doing so in real-time lead to both *redundancy* and occasional dysfluency in production as well as ad hoc and unreliable inferencing in interpretation. Real-time communication can be contrasted with the kind of *asynchronous communication* that takes place in digital exchanges like text-messaging, micro-blogging and email, where delays may interrupt, sometimes indefinitely, the flow of *communication* and where inputting *text* is slower than the instantaneous quality of speech. => ASYNCHRONOUS AND SYNCHRONOUS COMMUNICATION, COMMUNICATION, CO-PRESENCE, FACE-TO-FACE COMMUNICATION, TIME-SPACE COMPRESSION AND DISTANTIATION.
reality television *n.* MEDIA AND CULTURAL STUDIES. A hybrid, generically diverse form that purports to present a slice of life in an

unstructured, unscripted, almost naturalistic fashion. While it has roots in *documentary* and other forms of realism such as *actuality* cinema, reportage and even the realist novel, it has become a widespread form of entertainment on broadcast television, as exemplified by programmes such as *The Apprentice, Airport, Saving Lives at Sea, Big Brother, Simple Lives, Love Island, Survivor, The X Factor, Hell's Kitchen, Supernanny, The Hotel* and *Wife Swap*. Various sub-*genres* have been defined, such as the 'Game-doc', in which contestants are eliminated until a winner is declared (*The Apprentice, Big Brother*, or *Survivor*); dating programmes (*Love Island*); occupational docu-soaps (*The Hotel, Paddington Station 24/7*); and the makeover programme (*Hell's Kitchen*). The focus is usually on so-called 'ordinary people' (though sometimes celebrities can be persuaded to take part, as in *Simple Lives* or *Celebrity Big Brother*) finding their way in challenging or difficult circumstances. Despite the invocation of 'reality' in the general title of these shows, they have attracted criticism, or at least debate, for reducing reality to its surfaces and offering distortions or manipulations of it. Certainly, footage is often patently edited, usually with some kind of *narrative* trajectory in mind, and *continuity* between sections of a programme and clarity of exposition may need to be supplied by *voice-over narration*. More problematic is reality TV's sense of 'behind the scenes'. In an episode of *Paddington 24/7* ("inside one of Britain's busiest railway stations") staff are shown struggling with the effects of signalling failures near Heathrow, for instance, which have a knock-on effect throughout the rail network, stopping all rail movement in and out of Paddington station on successive days for four of five hours at a time during commuting periods. The immediate cause of the crisis is ultimately traced (off camera) to electronic components in the signalling system. But there is no exploration of the industrial, economic or organisational realities that lie behind this failure. Causation is perfunctorily treated, and the focus instead remains resolutely on the effects on people (commuters, passengers) and the crisis management efforts of individuals in dealing with them. The realities of reality TV are carefully circumscribed. Despite their prevalence in the schedules and the *hybridity* evident amongst examples of the type, they stand in marked contrast to fictional programming with its dependence on *scripts*, plotting, ostensible acting by recognised actors and so on. While it might be regarded as a form of voyeurism, it also carries a strong sense of depicting ordinary people even if in unusual circumstances. In Britain, a strong tradition of gritty social realism in television drama has almost been supplanted by reality TV. => ACTUALITY, AMBIENT SOUND, DIEGETIC SOUND,

DOCUMENTARY, NARRATIVE. *Further reading* Biressi, A. and Nunn, H. (2005); Lorenzo-Dus, N. & Blitvich, P. (2013) (Eds.)

reciprocity of perspectives *np.* SOCIOLOGY a fundamental premise of social interaction. The concept is derived from the work of the Austrian phenomenological sociologist, Alfred Schutz (1899-1959), who maintained that social interaction was only possible if grounded in the assumption of the interchangeability of standpoints – effectively 'if you were where I am, you would see what I see, and vice versa'. In addition, parties to an interaction should share the same or a similar system of relevances for the purposes at hand. These fundamental premises of interaction need to be assumed for all practical purposes, despite the fact that we have individual biographies with the many differences of perception and understanding that may flow from this and so the actual perspectives of interactants may not precisely match. => DISCURSIVE GAP, INTERPERSONAL COMMUNICATION, INTERSUBJECTIVITY, SUBJECTIVITY.

redundancy *n.* COMMUNICATION STUDIES. Elements of a *message* whose information value is relatively low and, therefore, on the face of it, not strictly necessary for *communication*. The concept derives ultimately from the mathematical theory of communication and implies that not every element is high in information, while, conversely, some elements are fairly predictable and hence redundant. In written English *text*, for instance, roughly half the letters could be deleted and its meaning would still be recoverable. Unscripted spoken English often uses a high degree of verbal repetition. Additionally, redundancy can be built into the language system itself, allowing – for example – the question function to be signalled both by *grammar* and *intonation*. This does not imply that informationally redundant elements are unnecessary for communication. Duplication, double coding and so on are necessary for various reasons – notably to overcome what has been referred to as 'noise' in the system or – more generally – impediments to communication. => SHANNON AND WEAVER. *Further reading* Cherry, C. (1978)

reflexivity *n.* COMMUNICATION STUDIES. Circuits of cause and effect wherein both cause and effect shape one another. As a methodological issue in the social sciences, reflexivity implies self-consciousness and self-reference where investigation or action refers back to the presence of the investigator, thereby complicating explanation, prediction and *control* as objective outcomes of study. => SELF-IMAGE, SELF-CONCEPT. SJ

register *n.* LINGUISTICS, SOCIOLINGUISTICS. Stylistic variation in language according to its *context of situation*. The selection of words and structures by the language user is influenced strongly by features of the situation. Indeed, utterances typically carry the imprint of their context so markedly, and we are so attuned to contextual variation, that we can often infer features of the original context of situation from quite fragmentary, isolated linguistic examples. For instance, most readers will feel confident that they can reconstruct crucial features of the original context of situation for the following examples:

(1) I'm going to give you a prescription for the pain.
(2) New Tubifast. The tubular dressing retention bandage. No sticking. No tying. No pinning.

The first is from a doctor-patient *interview*, and the second is taken from a *magazine* advertisement. What is more difficult to explain is how we intuitively recognise aspects of the original context in each case. Why, for example, is (1) unlikely to be from an advertisement, and why is (2) not from a discussion between two nurses in casualty? Part of the explanation lies in the use of deictics ('I' and 'you') in the first example, and their absence in the second example, in which moodless clauses on the other hand highlight a three-part parallelism.

The fine-tuning that goes on between language and its context of situation operates along three independent parameters. First, the activity or topic on which the *talk* is based influences the kind of language used, particularly in the selection of vocabulary. Second, the nature of the social relationship will affect the language: talk between friends, for instance, is likely to avoid formal expressions, unless for ironic effect. Finally, the medium of *communication* adopted – whether face-to-face *speech*, written *text*, telephone, dictaphone, etc. – will affect the way all utterances are formed. These three parameters are known as *field*, *tenor* and *mode*, respectively. Collectively they shape the register of a particular text. => CONTEXT OF SITUATION, GENRE. Further reading Eggins, S. and Martin, J.R. (1997)

reinforcement *n.* PSYCHOLOGY. The process of encouraging, establishing or strengthening a belief, behavioural pattern or memory, particularly through the use of positive stimuli such as a reward or encouragement. Conversely, negative reinforcement depends upon painful or otherwise distressing stimuli. *SJ*

report-talk *n.* SOCIOLINGUISTICS. Used alongside the companion term *rapport-talk*, a way of characterising the contrasting *conversational styles* of men and women. According to the American linguist Deborah Tannen (b. 1945), men use *conversation* more typically to exchange information impersonally (report-talk), whereas women more typically use conversation to focus on personal feelings and to build relationships (rapport-talk). Her claims, though interesting, are still regarded as unproven by some linguists and sociolinguists. => RAPPORT-TALK. *Further reading* Tannen, D. (1992)

representation *n.* DISCOURSE STUDIES, LINGUISTICS, SEMIOTICS. The use of signs to stand in for and take the place of something else; a sign, image, symbol, statement or *text* that stands in place of some other absent aspect of reality so as to make it present. => LANGUE, STRUCTURALISM.

resemiotisation *n.* DISCOURSE STUDIES, LINGUISTICS, SEMIOTICS. The transfer of meaning from one communicative event or *message* into another, often involving a shift of medium or mode, in ways which may also include a change from one sign system or *code* to another. Linguistic translation provides a fairly obvious case of resemiotisation, one in which standard protocols emphasise the importance of trying to preserve the meaning of the source *text* in translating it for the target language. Other examples are provided by the translation of a drama *script* into a staged performance, or alternatively the reworking of a novel into a script, story board and ultimately a filmic text. Resemiotisation may involve the attempt to preserve meaning throughout the process from one stage to another. Equally, however, the process may engender marked differences in the passage from one stage of resemiotisation to the next. As Iedema, an early proponent of the term, comments: "A semiotic mode is ... hard pressed to provide an unproblematic, transparent, and accurate translation for the meanings from another mode. Transposition between different semiotics inevitably introduces discrepancy, and resemiotisation is necessarily a process which produces not exact likenesses, but which represents 'a multi-channel set of directions'" (Iedema, 2003). In this way, the concept encourages attention, not only to the particulars of texts in transition from one mode (or code) to another, as well as to the *affordances* of the different modes, but also to elements of the context in which these changes occur. => INTERTEXTUALITY, MODE, SOUND-BITE. *Further reading* Iedema, R. (2001), (2003)

residual culture *np.* CULTURAL STUDIES. Frameworks of belief, values, meaning and social practice which remain active within the cultural field even in the face of the emergence of newer cultural forms. => DOMINANT CULTURE, DOMINANT IDEOLOGY, EMERGENT CULTURE. *Further reading* Williams, R. (2003)

resistive reading *np.* MEDIA & CULTURAL STUDIES. => DECODING, ENCODING, HERMENEUTICS.

response token *np.* => BACK CHANNEL BEHAVIOUR.
rhetoric *n.* COMMUNICATION STUDIES. The practice of using *communication* for the purpose of *persuasion*.
royalties *n.* PUBLISHING. Payments at a fixed rate (usually a percentage of the sale price) for the right to profit from the use or distribution of assets usually in the form of *intellectual property*. Thus publishers of books commonly pay royalties to their authors, although royalties may also be paid for music, for patent rights and even for the exploitation rights of natural resources such as oil. => AUTHOR.
rumour *n.* ETHNOGRAPHY, INTERNET STUDIES, SOCIOLINGUISTICS. An uncorroborated, usually anonymous, claim which circulates freely between people about a person, event or state of affairs. The most potent rumours relate to issues of public concern and add a satisfying twist to an existing *narrative*. While *gossip* traditionally has provided an apt relay or *diffusion* mechanism for the circulation of rumour, the *internet* has vastly increased the potential of rumour for strategic effect, particularly in the area of political *communication*. => DIFFUSION, GOSSIP. *Further reading* Bergmann J. (1993)

★★

salience *n.* Information or the state of being important, prominent and conspicuous. It is a concept used in the fields of semiotics, linguistics, *communication*, psychology and sociology, among others. SJ
salutation display *np.* SOCIAL INTERACTION. A standard formula of words used, for example, as a greeting or courtesy title in electronic communications. => CONVERSATION ANALYSIS. SJ
satellite (of narrative) => NARRATIVE SATELLITE.
satire *n.* CULTURAL AND LITERARY STUDIES, MEDIA. A *genre* devoted to ridiculing the follies, foibles, vices and abuses of humanity often by caricature, exaggeration, *parody*, *irony* and sarcasm. The genre has long-established literary antecedents going back to classical times (for example, the Roman writers Horace and Juvenal), and more recent examples within the novel would include George Orwell's *Animal Farm*, Joseph Heller's *Catch 22* or Malcolm Bradbury's *Eating People is Wrong* (itself an allusion to Jonathan Swift's (1729) satire, *A Modest Proposal for preventing the Children of Poor People From being a Burthen to Their Parents or Country, and For making them Beneficial to the Publick*). More generally, satire finds expression in various forms and media including painting, illustration, cartoon, *magazine*, film and drama, including television drama. Hogarth's depiction of the dreadful consequences of dependency on gin (*Gin Lane*, 1751) along with

SELF-CONCEPT

other work such as *The Four Stages of Cruelty* (1751) are sometimes described as the beginnings of political satire, finding contemporary parallels in the cartoons of U.K. *newspaper* cartoonists Martin Rowson, Steve Bell and Gerald Scarfe. And the election of President Trump in 2016 in the US seems to have energised late night TV comedy shows with satirical riffs on the week's political *news* provided by high-profile presenters such as *The Last Week Tonight with John Oliver*, *The Late Show with Stephen Colbert* and *Late Night with Seth Myers*. These offer a highly politicised take on recent political events, consistently from a partisan (usually leftist) perspective. There may well be a division in media output between satirical material that is highly politicised and embedded in the moment, on the one hand, and more generalised satire of human nature. Thus, while Monty Python's particular brand of satire occasionally included quite specific political references (see, for instance, 'Mr Hilter and the Minehead by-election'), the satirical target seemed to be more generally the absurdities of human nature. This would be true also of a comedy series such as *The Office* (UK BBC2, 2001) (US NBC, 2005–2013), which used the setting of a stationery office to focus on traits of human behaviour such as self-importance and conceit. => GENRE, PARODY, PASTICHE. *Further reading* Simpson, P. (2003); Gray, J. et. al. (Eds.) (2009)

scopophilia *n.* FILM THEORY. The pleasure derived from watching, or looking at, another person. The concept plays a pivotal role in the work of the British feminist film theorist Laura Mulvey, who argued that mainstream Hollywood narrative cinema is structured around the male gaze and thereby routinely depicts women voyeuristically as objects of (male) desire. => CONTINUITY EDITING, FILM LANGUAGE, INTERPELLATION. *Further reading* Mulvey, L. (1990)

script *n.* FILM AND MEDIA STUDIES. The written version, prepared in advance, of an announcement, *dialogue*, *speech*, programme or other form of language-based, public performance. Usually specifies the words that will be delivered but may also encompass a range of non-verbal and visual information including pace, rhythm, graphics and scenery. In film and media production a shooting script will also include information about lighting, camera angle, shot sequence, etc. While much *mass communication* is scripted in advance, a great deal of effort is made to avoid the presence of a script being too obvious, for example, by use of autocue or 'sincerity machine'. => AUTHENTICITY, PERFORMANCE, REAL-TIME COMMUNICATION, SINCERITY.

secondary orality => ORALITY.

self-concept *n.* COMMUNICATION STUDIES, PSYCHOLOGY, PHILOSOPHY. The idea of the self's unique identity based upon the beliefs one holds about oneself and the responses of others, combining both self-perceptions as well as social identity. Self-concept can be informed of past or future selves, for example, what one hopes to become or what one fears becoming. Self-assessment of one's skills, physical features and personality, among other factors, shapes self-concept. *syn. self-image.* => SELF-DISCLOSURE, SELF-PRESENTATION, SELF-MONITORING. SJ

self-disclosure *n.* MEDIA. The revealing or communication of information about oneself to others, including one's thoughts, emotions, preferences, fears, failures, dreams and goals. It is both a conscious and subconscious act that occurs upon initial encounter and during the development of a relationship with another. => SELF-CONCEPT, SELF-MONITORING, SELF-PRESENTATION. SJ

self-identity *n.* MEDIA => SELF-CONCEPT.

selfie *n.* INTERNET AND MEDIA STUDIES. Selected by Oxford Dictionaries as 'word of the year' in 2013 and defined by them as "a photograph that one has taken of oneself, typically one taken with a smartphone or webcam and shared via social media", selfies have become a routine component of *communication* on social networking sites. They tend to depict the subject in a characteristic posture looking towards the camera lens held at arm's length from the face, or alternatively as posed in a mirror with the smartphone held in hand. The rapid rise of the selfie and its prevalence in *social media* have raised concerns about narcissism and *self-image*, especially among young people – women in particular. However, the performative aspect of the selfie needs to be considered as well as its manifest content. Selfies are used in a variety of ways that transcend any simple communicative act such as 'look at me'. For one thing, many selfies obscure features of the image-taker and perform a variety of other communicative acts such as 'see where I am', or 'see who I am with' or 'see what I am doing'. As such they can be highly economical, shorthand, documentary ways of performing a diary, or journal entry or travelogue for friends and family. Considered performatively, they are not just a form of self-regarding but also a form of self-sharing or self-disclosure. => NEW MEDIA, PERSONAL MEDIA, SOCIAL MEDIA, SOCIAL NETWORKING. *Further reading* Storr, Will (2017)

self-image => SELF-CONCEPT.

self-monitoring *n.* PSYCHOLOGY. A personality characteristic that explains an individual's tendency to engage in expressive *self-presentation* controls. High self-monitors engage in careful expressive control by closely monitoring themselves in relation to context; they are receptive to situational and social cues and adapt themselves in order to project positive public self-images. The expressive controls of low self-monitors are linked to their internal states, for example, their beliefs and attitudes; as such these individuals are less concerned with social norms and with adapting to notions of public propriety than with consistency to their worldview. => SELF-CONCEPT, SELF-DISCLOSURE, SELF-PRESENTATION. *SJ*

self-presentation *n.* SOCIAL INTERACTION A conscious or unconscious process by which individuals influence and control perceptions of themselves, closely related to impression management, which refers to the set of communications and *public relations* practices that corporate bodies such as companies and organisations use to manage their public image. Self-presentation strategies are aimed at establishing and maintaining impressions that are consistent with the perceptions one wishes to give the public. They can be broadly categorised as defensive (e.g. avoidance, self-handicapping) or assertive (e.g. self-idealisation, use of status symbols). Erving Goffman's (1922–1982) *The Presentation of Self* (1959), which emphasises performativity as a strategy of social identity and *interaction*, has been influential in the conceptualisation of this sociological and social psychological theory. => SELF-DISCLOSURE, SELF-PRESENTATION, SELF-CONCEPT. *SJ*

semantic prosody *np.* CORPUS LINGUISTICS, LINGUISTICS. Associations that may accrue to a word of which language users may not be consciously aware and which transcend the received, normal dictionary definition of the word, but which specialist tools from *corpus linguistics* can display. Corpus linguistics is able to bring hitherto unnoticed aspects of the meaning of a word into view because it allows many examples of the occurrence of a word in actual contexts to be assembled, drawing upon large bodies of data (normally consisting of millions of words of running *text*). When these occurrences are inspected side by side, regular features of the context may show that specific words may be used regularly with a positive meaning, for instance, or with a negative one. For example, the verb 'cause' when used in context is often used negatively in phrases such as 'cause a rift', 'cause damage', 'cause misery' and 'cause outrage'. Since 'cause', when examined in this way, habitually occurs in the environment of negative expressions, these negative meanings are shown to be part of the meaning of the word and are said to contribute to its negative semantic prosody. The notion of semantic prosody is important for showing how meanings can accrue to a word (or expression) through the relations it establishes with other words in context. Meaning belongs not so much to isolated words but spreads, prosodically, from one word or expression to another. =>

MEANING, MULTI-ACCENTUALITY, SEMANTICS. Hunston, S. (2007); Sinclair, J. (2004)

semantics *n. LINGUISTICS.* The study of meaning from a linguistic perspective. Semantics aims to analyse and explain how meanings are expressed in language. Research is focussed around three important distinctions.

(a) *Sense versus reference.* The meaning of a linguistic expression – a word, for instance – can be treated in terms of its correspondence with extra-linguistic reality. Thus, the meaning of the word 'chair' lies in its capacity to refer outwards form the language to objects such as the one on which you may be sitting as you read this entry. From a different perspective, however, the meaning of a word can be considered in terms of its relationship to other words in the language. Thus, the meaning of the word 'chair' lies in its relationship with other words such as 'furniture', 'table', 'seat', 'bench', etc. The distinction between sense and reference may be further illustrated by the way in which, objectively, the same planet – Venus – can be referred to equally appropriately as 'the morning star' and 'the evening star', since it has the capacity to shine brightly both in the morning sky and in the evening sky, and it is designated equally well by both expressions. Thus, the two expressions – 'the morning star' and 'the evening star' – have an identical referent, although the sense of each expression is of course quite different. Greater attention in semantics has been given to the area of sense relations than to that of reference, in line with Wittgenstein's dictum: 'the meaning of a word is its use in the language'.

But ignoring either side of the contrast between sense and reference tends to lead to unbalanced theories of meaning, and this can have consequences that go beyond the domains of linguistic theory. It is worth noting, for instance, that rival aesthetic theories can be divided into two camps depending upon whether they tend to favour one or the other side of the distinction between reference and sense: realist theories favour art that appears to mirror or reflect reality in as direct a way as possible; other more Formalist theories, however, stress the conventionality of artistic *representation* and see art, and more particularly literature, as a continual experiment with meaning (or 'sense'). Contemporary critical theory tends to be very strong on the conventional bases of meaning, so much so that at times it seems to deny the possibility of any reality at all outside language. At the very least, it insists that reality is not *mediated* to us directly, but is constructed through acts of meaning, so that we have no direct access to it outside of language. One pitfall of this position is that it can lead to a species of idealism in which reality is spoken into existence through language, and arguments about interpretation become avowedly subjective, to the exclusion of *culture* and history as material process.

In modern semantics sense relations have been treated in terms of the following major relationships that words can have with each other.

- *Synonomy*: expressions which can be used in identical ways are considered synonymous, by which criterion an expression such as 'to ponder' is held to be synonymous with 'to meditate', or 'loutish' is held to be synonymous with 'uncouth'.
- *Antonymy*: expressions which reverse the meaning of each other in some way are considered to be antonymous. Thus, the pairs 'woman/man', 'fast/slow', 'up/down' and 'good/bad' all express relations of antonymy.
- *Hyponomy*: expressions may also operate in hierarchical relations of meaning where the meaning of the expression includes that of another. Thus, the expression 'dog' is a hyponym of the expression 'animal', the latter being a superordinate term for a range of hyponyms with 'dog', such as 'cat', 'monkey', 'giraffe', 'rabbit'. 'Dog' itself, of course, is a superordinate term for another range of hyponyms such as 'terrier', 'hound', 'retriever', etc.

Synonymy, *antonymy* and *hyponomy* consist, therefore, of differing kinds of sense relations possible within the vocabulary of a language. They provide a way of conceptualising the construction of meaning as it goes on within the linguistic system. In this respect it is worth emphasising that they display linguistic and not 'real-world' classification. There is no reason in the real world why terms for animals should be organised in the particular types of sense relation adopted in English, as becomes immediately apparent when comparisons in particular areas of meaning are made between languages. According to Whorf (1956), the Hopi tribe of North America used one word, '*masaytaka*', to designate all flying objects except birds. Thus, they actually designated an insect, an aeroplane and an aviator by the same word, whereas English provides quite separate lexical items.

(b) *Word meaning versus sentence meaning.* Other approaches to the meaning of words involve notions such as semantic features and *collocation*. Whatever approach is adopted, however, it does not seem possible to account for the meaning of a sentence merely by building upwards from the individual words that make it up, irrespective of the order in which they occur. Otherwise 'Man bites dog' would mean the same thing as 'Dog bites man'. Nonetheless, it seems possible that there may be parallels between the kind of sense relation we have described between words and those that exist between sentences. A sense relation such as synonymy, for instance, may be considered to hold not only between individual words but also between whole sentences. Thus 'Sidney sold the book to Sheila' may be considered to be synonymous with 'Sheila bought the book from Sidney', and the same kind of relation can be claimed between 'The police arrested the miners' and 'The miners were arrested by the police'. As sentences, therefore, they are synonymous. Other kinds of relationship that can hold between sentences are those of *entailment* and *presupposition*. *Entailment* is a relation whereby, given two sentences A and B, A semantically entails B if under all conditions in which A is true, B is also true. Thus, a sentence such as (A) 'Achilles killed Hector' entails (B) 'Hector is dead'. In such cases B follows from A as a logical consequence. If it is true that Achilles killed Hector, then Hector must as a logical consequence be dead. *Presuppositional* relations are somewhat different. Basically, whereas negation will alter a sentence's entailment, it will leave presuppositions in place. Consider the sentence: (i) 'Sidney managed to stop in time'. From this we may infer both that (ii) 'Sidney stopped in time' and that (iii) 'Sidney tried to stop in time'. These inferred sentences, however, do not behave in quite the same way. Sentence (ii), 'Sidney stopped in time', follows logically from sentence (i): it is an entailment from sentence (i). As such, (ii) does not hold if (i) is negated. Sentence (iii), however, is not so much an entailment from (i) as a presupposition. As such it is possible to negate (i) and for (iii) to still remain true. In other words, the original entailment of (ii) from (i) may no longer hold; but the presupposition that (iii) 'Sidney tried to stop in time' will still survive intact.

These kinds of distinctions are important for the analysis of meaning in all kinds of *discourse*. Ideological claims, for instance, are often promoted implicitly rather than explicitly, covertly rather than overtly; and they often need to be recovered from the presuppositions or entailments of a discourse rather than from its surface assertions. Thus, when a Ministry of Defence pamphlet urged that "Britain must do everything in its power ... to deter Russia from further acts of aggression", various unargued propositions were merely presupposed; notably, for example: (i) 'Britain has power' and (ii) 'Russia is committing acts of aggression'.

(c) *Text versus context.* The third major area of inquiry and debate is concerned with issues such as how much of meaning is created and carried by the linguistic system and how much and in what way it is determined by crucial characteristics of the context in which any utterance is grounded. Indeed, some aspects of meaning previously considered to be semantic – i.e. part of the linguistic system itself – are now being treated as part of *pragmatics*.

The history of linguistics during the last 60 years can be read in terms of a continual deferral of the study of meaning. Indeed, the progression during this time has been very much from the smaller units of linguistic organisation, such as the phoneme, to the larger, such as the *sentence* or text; it has also been a progression from substance (phonology) to significance (semantics). Meaning, however, has at last come centre stage, and the last 10 years has seen an immense burgeoning of work in both semantics and pragmatics. Meaning, of course, cannot be other than the ultimate goal of linguistic inquiry, and findings in this area undoubtedly have important consequences for associated areas of scholarship such as media studies, literary criticism, interpretive sociology or cognitive science, in all of which issues of meaning are often at the centre of debate. => DISCOURSE ACT, MEANING, MEANING POTENTIAL, MULTI ACCENTUALITY, PRAGMATICS, SEMANTIC PROSODY, SEMIOSIS. *Further reading* Lyons (1981); Saeed, J.I. (2016)

semiosis *n.* COMMUNICATION STUDIES, LINGUISTICS. The production of meaning within the constraints and possibilities of a sign system. The term derives from the work of the American philosopher, logician and scientist Charles Sanders Pierce (1839–1914), amongst whose writings can be found perhaps the first systematic attempt to develop a theory of semiotics or sign systems. His approach in the event proved complementary to that of the Swiss linguist Ferdinand de Saussure's (1857–1913) account of semiology proposed in his Course in General Linguistics given at the University of Geneva between 1906 and 1911. In addition to outlining the basis of linguistics as a systematic approach to language as an object of study, Saussure also made the case for semiology as 'a science that studies the life of signs within society'. Together, Pierce and Saussure can be considered the founders of semiotics/semiology. Semiosis refers to the capacity of sign systems to produce and convey meaning. => ICON, LANGUE, MEANING. *Further reading* Cobley, P. (ed.) (2010)

sexism *n.* Discrimination against a person or persons on the grounds of their sexual identity; traditionally applies to discrimination against women but can in principle be applied to other forms of sexual identity.

Shannon and Weaver's model of communication *np.* COMMUNICATION STUDIES. Uses a mathematical formula to measure the flow of information in a *message* or *signal* between a source and a receiver. The model acknowledges the possibility of interference (or 'noise') in the channel of *communication* and measures the value of bits of information in terms of their relative predictability and unpredictability. Predictable bits of information may be redundant but necessary because of accompanying noise in the channel. => INFORMATION, MESSAGE, REDUNDANCY, SIGNAL. *Further reading* Cherry, C. (1978)

signification *n.* COMMUNICATION STUDIES. The act or process of signifying by means of signs or other symbol systems. => ICON, LANGUE, MEANING, SEMANTICS, SEMIOSIS. *Further reading* Cobley, P. (ed.) (2010)

signifying practice *np.* COMMUNICATION STUDIES, SEMIOTICS. A way of using a sign system, such as language, in order to make and convey meanings. The signs of a system carry meaning in part by their place within the system but also by virtue of their characteristic patterns of usage, including their habitual modes of interpretation. => HERMENEUTICS, ICON, INTERPRETIVE COMMUNITY, LANGUE, MEANING, SEMIOSIS. *Further reading* Cobley, P. (ed.) (2010)

silence *n.* SOCIAL INTERACTION, TALK-IN-INTERACTION. => STRATEGIC SILENCE.

sincerity *n.* COMMUNICATION, CULTURAL & MEDIA STUDIES. The quality of straightforwardness in relationships; the absence of dissimulation, deception or false feelings. As a term it has gained some importance in the discussion of *mediated communication*, especially in cases where this exhibits characteristics of *para-social interaction*. In this context, sincerity is the capacity to faithfully express on the surface an interior, subjective emotional state. Television and radio as communicative media both seem to foreground the importance of sincerity in those who gain pre-eminence in either medium, in part at least, through their emphasis on the spoken *voice* and (in the case of television) the expressive modalities of the face. Thereby, sincerity, normally a quality of private relationships, becomes projected as an important quality that needs to be exhibited by performers in the public domain. Indeed, the German sociologist and critical theorist, Jurgen Habermas, drawing on *speech act* theory, has suggested that sincerity is one of three major claims to *validity* that utterances can make: in addition to their *truth* value and their appropriateness they will be judged as valid or otherwise in terms of their perceived sincerity. In the *mediated public sphere*, of course, this entails a performative paradox in which the requirement to be sincere runs the risk of appearing to be its opposite. Sincerity might be seen as a salient and important quality of the *communicative ethos* of broadcasting. In the digital spaces of *social media* it has been complemented by *authenticity*. => AUTHENTICITY, COMMUNICATIVE ETHOS, PARA-SOCIAL INTERACTION, PARTICIPATION FRAMEWORK, PERSONALISATION, SYNTHETIC PERSONALISATION, VALIDITY CLAIMS. *Further reading* Habermas, J. (1979); Montgomery, M. (1999); Trilling, L. (1973)

slander *n.* COMMUNICATION AND JOURNALISM STUDIES. => DEFAMATION.

soap opera *np.* MEDIA & CULTURAL STUDIES. Episodic work of dramatic fiction serialised on radio or television. The term derives from their emergence on radio programmes in the US that were sponsored by soap manufacturers. Plots are open-ended, with each episode ending on a note of suspense. Typically soap operas are broadcast several times a week, with some of the most famous continuing for several years or even decades. => GENRE, MELODRAMA. *Further reading* Allen, R. (ed.) (1994)

sociability *n.* BROADCASTING, COMMUNICATION & MEDIA STUDIES. A quality of relationship displayed by some media. Whereas, traditionally, print as a medium has been associated with individualism, both in terms of its modes of authorship and *readership*, Scannell (1996) has argued that the characteristic *communicative ethos* of *broadcasting* – especially radio – is sociability. This is partly evident in the way that some broadcast events have a quasi-ritual, communal aspect in which large *audiences* switch on for a *live* transmission knowing that friends, relatives and maybe a whole nation are doing likewise. The classic examples of this kind of broadcast event are state funerals (e.g. the funeral of Princess Diana) or major sporting events (such as the Beijing or London Olympics), but also programmes with very wide social appeal such as *Strictly Come Dancing* or *The Great British Bake Off*. However, the sociable character of broadcasting can also be evident in the intrinsic character of significant sections of output where the emphasis falls on lively exchanges between people doing 'ordinary' sociability, such as story-telling, sharing personal experiences, friendly banter and so on. Thus, in *talk shows* and *reality television* both radio and television foreground sociability in the form of broadcast *talk* as an important quality of the medium. Sociability, of course, goes beyond broadcasting and can be associated with the emergence of older media such as the telephone but also newer media such as the personal and *social media* of Twitter, Sina Weibo, Facebook, WeChat and Instagram. As with broadcasting, however, it should be noted that modes of sociable inclusion have as their counterpoint modes of exclusion, and the other side of sociability can well take the form of social antagonism, as evidenced in *trolling*, *fisking* and *flaming*. => COMMUNICATIVE ETHOS, FISKING, FLAMING, MEDIA EVENTS, PERSONAL MEDIA BROADCASTING, SOCIAL MEDIA BROADCASTING, TROLLING. *Further reading* Higgins, M. and Angela Smith (2017); Moores, S. (2007); Morley, D. (2004); Scannell, P. (1996)

social media *np. COMMUNICATION, CULTURAL AND MEDIA STUDIES*. Collective name for a set of *digital platforms* or websites such as Facebook, Instagram, Twitter, WeChat, WhatsApp and Sina Weibo which feature an overlapping set of *affordances* that allow or encourage *interaction* between people online using short message systems (sms), microblogging and the re-circulation of digital material from one person or *group* to another, as well as the posting and sharing of images. Previously known as *new media*, or *personal media*, they have increasingly foregrounded the possibilities of interpersonal connection not only between people such as family or friends who are already affiliated in established relationships of everyday life but also between relative strangers who can 'follow' each other online and become 'friends' by means of the use of deliberate marking and overt signs of connectivity offered by the platform. In this way social media offer a special form of online presence geared particularly to an ethos of *sociability*, sometimes focused and direct, as between family and friends where there is already direct connection and interaction between members of a defined and bounded network, and sometimes much more loosely, as in a form of *ambient affiliation* where users of a particular platform follow the actions of other members of the platform without necessarily contributing directly to the ongoing social *conversation*. It is difficult to understate the rapid rise, reach and effect of social media. Facebook, for instance, provides apparently a well-designed way for people to get in touch and stay in touch on the *internet*. In practice it is big business: valued at US$180 billion when it was brought to market in 2013, Facebook was considered to be worth US$300 billion only three years later. It is reputed to have two billion registered users and handles about a third of the mobile advertising revenue. It is used as a tool in advertising, *marketing* and in political campaigning. It has been credited with results such as the election of Donald Trump in the US and the rise of Jeremy Corbyn in the UK. More generally, social media and microblogging seem to have led to new forms of activism to the extent that the influential media theorist, Elihu Katz, can comment: "If *broadcasting* took politics into the home, social media have taken politics into the street". Also, social media have been associated with the rise of identity politics on the one hand, and with and sub-national or small-nation politics on the other. Some commentators credit social media with a fragmentation of the polity. If the nation as an *imagined community* was a product of the *newspaper* and the novel, social media seem to have reinvigorated a politics of identity. => COMMUNITY, NEW MEDIA, ONLINE COMMUNITY, PERSONAL MEDIA, VIRTUAL COMMUNITY. *Further reading* Fuchs, C. (2017)

social network *n.* MEDIA & INTERNET STUDIES. The overlapping dyadic interrelationships between a determinate set of social actors within a defined social space such as a city, kinship system, friendship *group* or *virtual community* online. Social network analysis attempts to model the ties between members of the network along parameters such as strength, durability and frequency. => COMMUNITY, NETWORK SOCIETY, ONLINE COMMUNITY, VIRTUAL COMMUNTIY. *Further reading* Castells, M. (2009), Van Dijk, Jan A G M (2012)(3rd Ed.)

socialisation *n.* COMMUNICATION AND CULTURAL STUDIES, SOCIOLOGY. The ongoing process that an individual participates in throughout his or her life of inheriting, learning and promulgating norms, values, behaviours, customs and ideologies. Socialisation can be described as a process of reciprocal social learning that occurs in order that an individual may effectively participate and assimilate with his or her *culture* and society. SJ

soft news *np.* JOURNALISM STUDIES. => HARD NEWS.

sound bite *np.* JOURNALISM STUDIES, POLITICAL COMMUNICATION. Usually a phrase or sentence excerpted from a longer *speech* or *interview* that somehow fixes verbally the content or tone of the speaker's utterance and is used as a form of highly condensed quotation of prominent political figures in order to capture the essence of their position, most usually for subsequent new reports. Examples include "axis of evil" (George W. Bush); "the economy, stupid" (Bill Clinton); "ich bin ein Berliner" (J.F. Kennedy); "the pound in your pocket" has not been devalued (Harold Wilson); "this lady's not for turning" (Margaret Thatcher); "Brexit means Brexit" (Theresa May); and "an act of pure evil" (Donald Trump). The press, and *news* media in general, treat any major statement by a political figure as an occasion for quotation, which preferably needs to be pithy, colourful or otherwise memorable. Political figures and their speech-writers in turn hope to provide headline-writers, leader-writers, bloggers and columnists with a shorthand phrase that sums up their *message*. An effective sound bite will have a long afterlife and may well circulate and re-circulate well beyond their original context. As the name implies, the term originated in the context of *broadcasting*, where it often took the form of an audio or video clip used subsequently in a news report. In the age of *digital media* – with the enhanced potential for tweeting and re-tweeting fragments, phrases and sayings – the term has a slightly anachronistic ring to it, even though the similar communicative economies and pressures may underlie the relay and re-circulation of wordings. => INTERTEXTUALITY.

source *n.* JOURNALISM STUDIES. In *journalism*, a person, publication, document or other record that provides newsworthy information. Especially on controversial matters, journalists are expected to use multiple sources and to distinguish between information that is offered on the record (where the source can expect to be named and cited) as opposed to off the record. => ACCESSED VOICES, GATEKEEPER.

speech *n.* BROADCAST TALK, LINGUISTICS, SOCIOLINGUISTICS. The spoken medium of *communication*. Long recognised as the primary means of human communication, it is considered to be a feature of all, or nearly all, human societies. In species terms, the human vocal tract, and the wide range of the sounds that it is capable of producing, are unique to humans. While it is not the only medium of human communication – there are several alternatives such as sign-language or *writing* – the alternatives are underpinned by the use of a shared system of *encoding* meanings by way of sentence structure, or syntax, into material form such as *gesture* (in sign language), durable marks (in writing) or articulated sounds (as in speech). Thus, the use of these varying possibilities for communication is underpinned by a general language system or language faculty which they hold in common and without which none of them would be effective. All the same, it has long been recognised that choosing between alternative means or *media of communication* will draw on the common language system in different ways. Thus, the choice of writing instead of speech as a medium of communication may entail particular grammatical, syntactic or lexical preferences over others. Indeed, some work suggests that certain kinds of linguistic patterning may be distinctive to particular media (e.g. Biber 1988). From this perspective, speech, or the spoken medium, is associated with lexical repetition, low lexical density, vague or indefinite expressions ('sort of', 'whatsit'), a higher incidence of coordinated clauses linked by common conjunctions ('and', 'but') and selection of the active rather than the passive *voice*. The nature of these differences has led the British linguist Michael Halliday (1925-2018) to characterise speech as a process (as opposed to writing as a product) (Halliday, 2014). The predilection for certain kinds of linguistic patterning in spoken *discourse* stems in part from the fact that speech typically takes place between interlocutors who are in some way co-present to each other, and this enables them to adjust their utterance in the light of the apparent reactions of the other. Furthermore, the process of composing and planning speech goes hand in hand with the act of speaking, and speaking, in turn, goes hand in hand with the process of interpretation that must keep pace with it. There is no time lag between production and reception. Instead, speech is temporally bound, transient and dynamic, rooted in an unfolding context, with paralinguistic behaviour providing an important supplementary layer to communication. By comparison, writing as a semi-permanent product opens up radically different *affordances*: for instance, it enables a gap across time and space to open up between participants. Writing, consequently, is forced to be less reliant on its immediate context for its meaning. => REAL-TIME COMMUNICATION, SYNCHRONOUS COMMUNICATION, WRITING. *Further reading* Cornbleet, S & Carter, R. (2001)

speech act *np.* CONVERSATIONAL ANALYSIS, DISCOURSE ANALYSIS, LINGUISTICS, PRAGMATICS, PHILOSOPHY. The action performed by an utterance as part of an *interaction*. The concept developed out of the work of the British philosopher J.L. Austin (1911–1960), who demonstrated that many utterances are significant not so much in terms of what they say but rather in terms of what they do. Indeed, in the case of many utterances it makes more sense to ask, 'What is this utterance trying to do?' than to ask, 'Is what it says true or false?' – as may be seen if we consider the following examples of everyday utterances:

> 'I bet he won't turn up.'
> 'Hello.'
> 'Please keep your seat belts fastened.'
> 'Okay.'

These utterances exemplify a whole range of speech acts, including those of *betting, greeting, requesting an action, acknowledging*. None of them is limited to asserting some kind of propositional *truth*. This kind of observation led Austin to the conclusion that stating or asserting (in ways that can be judged true or false) is only one of many kinds of action (or speech act) that language makes possible – actions as diverse as warning, promising, naming, exemplifying, commenting and challenging. Significantly, for many of these actions it is difficult to envisage how else they might be performed except in words. Since Austin's pioneering work, most attention has been devoted to trying to identify a determinate range of speech acts, as well as trying to specify precisely the recognition criteria for the most common speech acts, such as questions or commands.

The concept is an important one for *communication* and cultural studies, partly as a way of countering simplistic linear flow models of communication that see it simply in terms of 'information transfer' or 'exchanging ideas'. It has also been influential in studies of social interaction by providing an analytic tool for a variety of research traditions ranging from *discourse* and *conversation analysis* to the *ethnography* of communication. => CONVERSATION ANALYSIS, DISCOURSE ACT, ETHNOGRAPHY OF COMMUNICATION. *Further reading* Morris, M. (2007)

speech balloon *np.* COMMUNICATION & CULTURAL STUDIES. A graphic device used mostly in comics and cartoons, in which a figure's *speech* is enclosed in a diagrammatic balloon, often complete with signs of emphasis (bold and/or large type), or indications of swearing (a random sequence of non-alphabetic punctuation signs, usually enlarged, with at least one exclamation point). The fact that a particular individual is speaking is shown by a tail to the balloon, linked to or near to the mouth of the speaker. A similar convention graphically suggests a depicted person's thinking process in a *thought balloon*. The mechanism is the same as for a speech balloon, except that the tail of the balloon is usually a trail of ever-smaller separate balloons back to the thinker. *Further reading* Cohn, N. (2013)

speech (/language) community *np.* LINGUISTICS, SOCIOLINGUISTICS. A *group* of people who share a common language or linguistic variety. A speech community in the strongest sense will also display common ways of using the shared language and common attitudes towards it within a given society. The term is important for highlighting the way in which language exists not just as an abstract system, codified in *grammar* books and dictionaries; it is integral to everyday social life and belongs ultimately to its *community* of users. It is they who make and remake it in their everyday encounters.

At the same time, it is a term beset with difficulties. First, the reference to 'speech' recalls earlier societies based on face-to-face contact, and this seems inappropriate for societies in which print and electronic means of *communication* have opened up a whole range of *mediated* transactions that do not rely on speech. Some linguists now use the term 'language community' instead.

Second, the reference to 'community' seems something of a misnomer under late capitalism. This is not just a question of the division of labour. In the case of UK society, for example, it is now clearer than ever that gross inequalities of material advantage continue to accumulate around the divisions of ethnicity, gender, class and region. And if the society displays not only diversity but also fundamental division, then verbal practices themselves will not just be held in common but will come to operate actively in contradistinction to each other. => COMMUNITY, LANGUE, ONLINE COMMUNITY, SPEECH, VIRTUAL COMMUNITY. *Further reading* Morgan, M. (2014)

sphere of consensus *np.* COMMUNICATION STUDIES, JOURNALISM STUDIES. Conceptual space in which ideas are uncontroversial. The term was developed by the American communication studies scholar Daniel C. Hallin alongside two other terms, the sphere legitimate controversy and the sphere of *deviance*. These spheres are organised as concentric circles moving from the sphere of consensus outwards through the sphere of legitimate controversy to the sphere of deviance. Fundamentally, these spheres of consensus, controversy and deviance are necessary for understanding aspects of the relationship of *journalism* to *public opinion*. While there is a general requirement on quality journalism to treat ideas in the public realm neutrally, impartially and objectively, it is impossible to treat all ideas in practice with the same weight. And how *objectivity* or *impartiality* is applied in any single case is affected by an estimate of the place of a proposition within Hallin's spheres. Indeed, ideas may move as a result of shifts over time in public opinion, as well as the journalistic presentation of debate, from one sphere to another. By way of illustration, take the U.K. example of Brexit (according to which Britain is leaving the European Union): the proposition that the likely result of Brexit is damaging for the U.K. economy belongs currently (in 2017) to the sphere of legitimate controversy, so it tends to be reported as if there are arguments to be made on both sides of the proposition. However, if evidence of damaging consequences continues to accumulate, the claim may shift to the sphere of consensus, at which point it may become reported as fact. In the year following the

U.K. referendum the proposition that Brexit could be reversed was considered impossible and was only reported as deviant. But if the damage to the U.K. economy of Brexit becomes part of the sphere of consensus, then ideas concerning the reversibility of Brexit may move from the sphere of deviance to the sphere of legitimate controversy. => IMPARTIALITY, NEUTRALISM, OBJECTIVITY, PUBLIC OPINION, PUBLIC SPHERE. *Further reading* Hallin, Daniel (1986), pp. 116–118

spin *n. POLITICAL COMMUNICATION.* A form of *public relations* that attempts to influence how the *news* media represent events, actions or persons by using specialists (such as government *press officers*) to manage the flow of information and more particularly to interpret policy or behaviour in the best possible light through official or unofficial briefings. The term is nearly always used pejoratively, with the implication that exponents of spin transform public relations into a form of *propaganda*. => PROPAGANDA, PUBLIC RELATIONS, SPIN DOCTOR.

spin-doctor *n. POLITICAL COMMUNICATION.* Someone that utilises techniques and tactics of creative *representation* of facts, disingenuousness, misinformation or deception in order to interpret *news* or events in such a way as to move *public opinion* in favour of or against public figures or organisations, such as politicians or governments. => SPIN.

standard language *np. LINGUISTICS, SOCIOLINGUISTICS.* A *dialect* that has assumed ascendancy within a language or *speech community* to such an extent that its internal rules become the standard of correctness for the whole *community*. A standard language tends to have arrogated more prestige and authority to itself than the varieties with which it competes, principally because it usually emerges from the dialect of the dominant *group*. The emergence of a standard language is often related to the process of nation-building; and just as nations are imaginary communities within the social sphere, so standard languages are imaginary systems within the linguistic sphere – not many of us actually speak the standard language, although most of us either think that we do or believe that we should. Their imaginary nature is suppressed by elaborate processes of codification in prescriptive *grammar* books, guides to usage and dictionaries. => ACCENT, DIALECT GENRE, REGISTER. *Further reading* Milroy, J. and Milroy, L. (2012)

strategic silence *np. SOCIAL INTERACTION.* Calculated and tactical uncommunicativeness. Silence can be used to place emphasis on what has already been stated or to increase the strength of a position in an argument. Silence may also be used to open up reflective space for the reception of ideas and arguments. *SJ*

striptitle *n. FILM AND TELEVISION STUDIES.* An alternative, explanatory or subordinate title in a book or film, also referred to as subtitles.

Striptitles may be used to provide a sense of the theme of a work or to denote instalments in a series of works. Striptitles also refer to the captions displayed on a film or television screen that translate or transcribe *dialogue*. => SUBTITLE. SJ

structuralism *n.* CULTURAL & LITERARY STUDIES, LINGUISTICS. Linguistic, literary and cultural theory that emerged in France in the 1950s and 1960s based on Ferdinand de Saussure's linguistics. Saussure (1857–1913), in his *Course in General Linguistics*, first published posthumously by two of his students in 1916, established the scientific study of language on a set of new principles based on sets of interlocking dichotomies. One of these was a distinction between the abstract underlying system of language (*langue*) and any individual act of speaking (*parole*). Individual acts only become possible and meaningful on the basis of the underlying system. The system belongs not to any one individual but to the collectivity of users of the language and in this way to society as a whole. While Saussure's main aim was to establish a framework for the scientific study of language, he simultaneously recognised that there were other aspects of society that could be understood in similar ways because they were structured like a language. He proposed that there should also be a general science of the life of signs in society, semiology; and this began to consolidate in France about a half-century later in structuralism and semiotics as his approach to linguistics began to be applied to literature, to film, to anthropology, to *myth* and to *popular culture*. In literature, media or film, for instance, cultural *texts* were held to be possible and meaningful by a pre-existing system consisting of conventional techniques and devices such as the conventions of *genre* and the general symbolic *codes* of a *culture*. => BRICOLAGE, GENRE, POST-STRUCTURALISM, SEMIOTICS. *Further reading* Harris, R (2003); Hawkes, T. (2003)

structures of feeling *np.* CULTURAL & LITERARY STUDIES, SOCIOLOGY. Salient ways of organising experience (expectations, fears, desires, preferences, as well as feelings and values more generally) at a particular historical moment or period. Structures of feeling current at any historical moment offer solutions to lived contradictions in experience and typically find expression in particular cultural forms. As structures they represent common, shared patterns across and within a *culture* at the same time as they reach into and pervade the interior *subjectivity* of individuals. Although a structure of feeling may animate and inform our subjectivity, they extend far beyond us as discrete individuals. In addition, as structures, they organise a particular cluster of feelings into a complex array. => CULTURE,

COMMUNICATIVE ETHOS, SUBJECTIVITY. *Further reading* Williams, R. (2003) pp. 128–136

style *n.* CULTURAL & MEDIA STUDIES, LINGUISTICS, SOCIOLINGUISTICS, STYLISTICS. A particular and recurrent set of selections from the total repertoire of meaningful communicative behaviour which becomes associated with an individual or *group*. The term is used informally to refer to a specialised way of doing things or a particular kind of 'look' or appearance. More technical usages draw on this sense but attempt to apply it systematically to discrete areas of communicative behaviour. Thus, in linguistics and sociolinguistics it is used to refer to the way in patterns of linguistic choice become clustered in the *speech* or *writing* of individuals or groups to the extent that they convey or project identifiable social meanings or values. The most common kind of social meaning conveyed by stylistic choice from a sociolinguistic perspective is 'formal' versus 'informal', in which two utterances can be alike in their referential meaning but convey a quite different effect, as for instance in (i) 'Give the windows a wipe, will you?' versus (ii) 'Would you mind very much cleaning the windows?'. In this respect different ways of saying 'the same thing' may carry quite different stylistic meanings and effects. Style is also studied at the intersection of linguistics and literature by focusing on patterns of linguistic choice peculiar to a writer (for example, William Shakespeare or Emily Dickinson), a group of writers (e.g. the Beat poets) or a period of writing (e.g. Renaissance Drama). By extension the notion of style has applications in media and cultural studies. Nichols (2010), for instance, identifies six main styles or modes of *documentary* film: poetic, observational, expository, reflexive, participatory and performative. However, style can also be a form of distinctive expression and appearance for whole groups who mark their distinctive sub-cultural identity by their choice of clothing, music, ornament and speech => ANTI-LANGUAGE, BRICOLAGE, HABITUS, SUB CULTURE. *Further reading* Gelder, K. (ed.) (2005) (2nd Ed.); Hall, S. & Jefferson, T. (eds.) (1993); Mortensen, J. & Coupland, N. (eds.) (2017)

sub-culture *n.* MEDIA. An oppositional or marginal social *group* defined by distinctive frameworks of belief, musical preferences, expressive *styles*, leisure pursuits and values that set them apart from mainstream society. => STYLE. *Further reading* Gelder, K. (ed.) (2005) (2nd Ed.); Hebdige, D. (1979)

subjectivity *n.* CRITICAL THEORY, PHILOSOPHY, PSYCHOANALYSIS, STRUCTURALISM. The self-conscious awareness of an individual.

subliminal *adj.* COMMUNICATION STUDIES, PSYCHOLOGY. Stimuli and *messages* that are subconscious, unconscious or hidden. While they may not be strong enough to produce conscious response, subliminal stimuli can influence mental processes and behaviour. *SJ*

suture *v.* MEDIA. The process whereby the cinema *audience* is 'stitched into' the experience of watching and making sense of a film by techniques of *continuity* editing. => CONTINUITY EDITING, FILM LANGUAGE, SCOPOPHILIA. *Further reading* Monaco, J. (2009)

synchronous communication *np.* SOCIAL INTERACTION. Direct *communication* where the communicators are time-synchronised so that all parties involved in the communication are co-present at the same time. This includes, but is not limited to, a telephone *conversation* (but not texting), a company board meeting, video conferencing, a *chat room* event and *instant messaging. Asynchronous communication*, by contrast, does not require that all parties involved in the communication be co-present at the same time. Some examples are e-mail *messages*, discussion boards, blogging and *text* messaging over cell phones. => ASYNCHRONOUS COMMUNICATION, REAL-TIME COMMUNICATION, TIME-SPACE DISTANTIATION.

synthetic personalisation *np.* CRITICAL DISCOURSE ANALYSIS. The simulation of private face-to-face *discourse* in public mass-*audience* discourse. Despite the apparent anonymity of *mass communication*, there is a noticeable tendency for some kinds of *communication* in the *public sphere* to incorporate features of local, small-scale *interaction* as if there was a personal rather than an anonymous relationship in play. The term was first used by the critical discourse analyst Norman Fairclough, who described it as "a compensatory tendency to give the impression of treating each of the people 'handled' *en masse* as an individual." => CONVERSATIONALISMATION, INFORMATIONALISMATION, PARA-SOCIAL INTERACTION, PERSONALISATION,. *Further reading* Fairclough (2015)

★★

tabloid *n.* JOURNALISM STUDIES, NEWSPAPERS, PRESS. A kind of *newspaper* printed in a format normally measuring 430 x 280 mm (16.9"x 11.0"), about half the size adopted for *broadsheet* newspapers. Compared with broadsheets, tabloid newspapers have tended to reach larger *readerships* and have drawn on a different mix of *news values*, emphasising particularly show-business, sport, *popular culture*, crime, *personalisation* and human interest stories. => BROADSHEET, NEWS VALUES, PERSONALISATION, TABLOIDISATION. *Further reading* Conboy, M. (2005)

tabloidisation *n.* JOURNALISM STUDIES, NEWSPAPERS, PRESS A process whereby the *style* and content of *tabloid journalism*, including *news* *values* such as *personalisation*, sensationalism and prurient populism are considered to be affecting *news* output more generally. In the UK concerns about tabloidisation reached a peak around the turn of the century, though little concrete evidence has been accumulated to prove the point. => BROADSHEET, NEWS VALUES, PERSONALISATION. *Further reading* Zelizer, B. (ed) (2009)

talk *n.* COMMUNICATION STUDIES CONVERSATION ANALYSIS. Apparently unscripted exchange of utterances between conversationalists, broadly synonymous with 'chat': a serious object of study since most of social life depends upon it. Ubiquitous in *broadcasting* across a range of formal and informal *genres*, including *talk shows, chat shows* and 'talk radio'. => CHAT SHOW, CONVERSATION, CONVERSATION ANALYSIS, TALK-IN-INTERACTION, TALK SHOW. *Further reading* Hutchby, I. (2006); Scannell, P. (ed.) (1991); Tolson, A. (2005)

talk-in-interaction *n.* CONVERSATION ANALYSIS. Includes *conversation* but also embraces various kinds of institutional *talk*, such as doctor-patient consultations, classroom *interaction*, media *interviews*, service transactions and so on, where talk – whatever business is getting done – serves as the primary medium of interaction and is subject to variation in the primary rules of conversation. => CONVERSATION, CONVERSATION ANALYSIS, TALK, TALK SHOW. *Further reading* Drew, P. et al. (2006)

talk show *n.* CONVERSATION ANALYSIS, LINGUISTICS, MEDIA AND CULTURAL STUDIES. *Genre* or format, associated mostly with television, in which the performance of *talk* is the focus of the show. Talk show formats are highly variable. In the main, however, the talk takes place between selected participants, including those in the role of guest(s) and a host (whose name often provides the eponymous title of the show, e.g. Oprah, Parkinson, Andrew Marr, Jerry Springer), who orchestrates the talk. The talk may take place before a studio *audience*, especially when its key or tone is one of lively humorous banter, and entertainment, in which case appreciation of the talk will be shown by audience laughter and applause. The key, tone and topical range of talk shows may vary as much as their format. While some are devised to be light and entertaining, others are devoted to issues of human interest, current affairs or lifestyle issues, in which case some degree of expert opinion may well be inserted by way of commentary. But whatever the degree of variation between examples of the talk show, talk – relatively unscripted and momentarily unpredictable – remains their defining characteristic. => TALK, TALK-IN-INTERACTION. *Further reading* Hutchby, I. (2006); Scannell, P. (ed.) (1991); Tolson, A. (ed.) (2001a); Tolson, A. (2005)

taste *n. AESTHETICS, CULTURAL STUDIES, SOCIOLOGY.* A structured preference for certain kinds of aesthetic objects or experiences over others. The term plays an important role on the work of the French anthropologist and sociologist Pierre Bourdieu (1930–2002), especially in his work *Distinction: A Social Critique of the Judgment of Taste* (1984). In this work he proposed that "taste classifies and classifies the classifier": in other words, judgments of taste reflect the social position of those who make them as much as distinctions in the objects or experiences that are the target of them. Indeed, in a class society the exercise of taste is also the exercise of different degrees of *cultural capital* that separate and maintain the hierarchical distinctions between *groups*. => CULTURAL CAPITAL, HABITUS, HIGH CULTURE, POPULAR CULTURE, STRUCTURE OF FEELING. *Further reading* Bourdieu, P. (1984)

technological determinism *np. ECONOMICS, HISTORY, MEDIA STUDIES, SOCIOLOGY.* A view that social change and the evolution of society is driven by technological innovation. Karl Marx may be considered an early proponent of technological determinism in his belief that changes in modes of production affect developments in the rest of society. In the field of media studies, perhaps the best known proponent of technological determinism is Canadian media theorist Marshall McLuhan (1911-1980) as expressed in his dictum that "the medium is the message" (McLuhan, 1964): it is not so much the content of any medium that is important but rather the kind of participation and sensory focus that each medium demands of its users. In his view, different media, insofar as they are "extensions of man", emphasise different perceptual and cognitive capacities, with far reaching social and cultural effects, so that he could claim, for example, that "[t]he technique of the suspended judgment is the discovery of the twentieth century", brought on by the bard abilities of radio, movies and television. Many critical responses to the rise of *digital media* presuppose a kind of technological determinism in which, for instance, the *internet* and *social media* are blamed for shortening our attention span and for changing reading habits. In this vein, the American social psychologist Sherry Turkle's work warns that the constant connectivity of the tablet and the smartphone may be endangering our capacity for friendship, empathy and intimacy (Turkle 2011, 2015). => COLD MEDIA, GLOBAL MEDIA, HOT MEDIA, TECHNOLOGY.

technology *n. MEDIA AND CULTURAL STUDIES, SOCIOLOGY.* Derived from the Greek words '*techne*' – art, skill, craft (from which technique and technical are also derived) – and '*logia*' – the systematic treatment or study of something. Everyday definitions of technology tend to stress its role in those engineered devices – prototypically tools, engines or machinery – that replace or extend human muscle-power, usually by the application of scientific knowledge. This kind of definition of technology as amplifying control of the natural world seems less than fully apt for those technologies that relate more particularly to *communication*. These are, of course, diverse, ranging from the stylus and pen through the printing press to radio and television, and from personal computer to smartphone. In all of these, what is at stake is not so much using a device to manipulate the natural world, but the development of ways of enhancing, accelerating or extending the reach of *text* (i.e. different kinds of signifying material) through time and space. With its roots in the notion of a tool, the term 'technology' tends commonly to be understood in terms of hardware or concrete objects. In the digital age, however, technology increasingly incorporates intelligent systems pre-programmed to extend the capacities of the physical apparatus, with the boundary between hardware and software increasingly blurred. McLuhan (2001) wrote of different media (visual, oral, aural, oral-aural), especially electronic media, as "extensions of man", or "extensions of our central nervous system"; and this is all the more true of communicative technology in the digital age. Indeed, while a smartphone may be considered primarily as a configuration of screen, processor, battery, camera, microphone and speaker, its potential depends crucially on applications pre-loaded or added to it. => AFFORDANCE, DIGITALISATION, INFORMATION TECHNOLOGY, MEDIATION, TECHNOLOGICAL DETERMINISM, WRITING. *Further reading* Lin, C. and Atkin, D. (eds.) (2009)

telex *n.* TECHNOLOGY. A *network* of teleprinters that is capable of sending *text*-based *messages*. Beginning in Germany in 1926, telex preceded the telephone network as the first medium for international *communications* through its use of standard signalling techniques and operating criteria. Although still in operation in certain industries, such as maritime and aviation, the use of telex has been largely superseded by fax and email systems. *SJ*

text *n.* LITERARY AND CULTURAL STUDIES, MEDIA STUDIES. Traditionally refers to a piece of *writing* considered worthy of study and explication. Both biblical criticism and literary criticism work with this loose definition of text which limits itself to units of writing that have assumed special value within the tradition established by communities of readers. In the case of biblical criticism, these canonical texts make up the Bible. In the case of literary criticism, canonical texts are those that have received close textual study over a long period of time – for instance, Shakespeare's sonnets, Thomas Hardy's novels, or the plays of Sophocles. In linguistics, however, the definition of text is broader, encompassing both *speech* and writing, and here the term refers to any instance of language in action in a specific context without respect to its cultural or aesthetic value. From this perspective, any text is worthy of study for what it can reveal about how language works in context, simply as a meaningful unit of language in use or the verbal trace of a communicative act. With the growing interest in *communication* in all its modalities, partly as a result of advances in digital communication, there is an increasing tendency to include visual material – photography, film, video, painting, diagram – within an enlarged definition of text, especially when the different kinds of modality such as sound and image interact within the same communicative act. => COHESION, MULTI-MODALITY.

thought balloon => SPEECH BALLOON.

time-space compression/distantiation *np.* MEDIA & CULTURAL STUDIES, SOCIOLOGY. Two interrelated concepts that address questions of how the social world changes through alterations in our sense of time and space. When the movement of goods, people and symbols speeds up, our sense of distance changes as well, so that, as Karl Marx noted, we experience the "annihilation of space by time". Likewise, the economic geographer David Harvey observed that the 'speed up' of social life under capitalism means that "we have to learn how to cope with an overwhelming sense of *compression* of our spatial and temporal worlds" (Harvey 1990, 240). In a complementary fashion, the sociologist Anthony Giddens (1981) observes how different kinds of society extend themselves through space and time in different ways. Hunter-gatherer societies tend to operate over limited spatial territories, communicating between members of the *group* largely through face-to-face contact in 'real time'. The development of means of *communication* like *writing*, however, allows societies and their means of social *control* to spread out and 'stretch' over space and time, hence 'time-space distantiation'. Writing, for instance, allows for various kinds of codification – lists, laws, decrees, chronicles – that facilitate administration and the maintenance of social structure over wide expanses of territory. Now, in the digital era, both distantiation and compression come together in compelling ways, facilitated by the almost instantaneous flow of information on a global scale. => ASYNCHRONOUS COMMUNICATION, REAL-TIME COMMUNICATION, SYNCHRONOUS COMMUNICATION. *Further reading* Giddens, A. (1981); Harvey, D. (1990, 240);

transculturation *n.* COMMUNICATION AND CULTURAL STUDIES. The transformation of *culture* through processes of influx, merging, loss and alteration of cultural elements. In contrast to acculturation, which refers to the process of assimilating a different culture, or deculturation, which describes the phenomenon of losing a culture, transculturation involves the sense of producing a new culture or cultural elements from the fusion of previously discrete ones. => BRICOLAGE, CROSSING GENRE, ORALITY. *Further reading* Piller, I. (2017) (2nd Ed.) SJ

transformation *n.* LINGUISTICS. A particular kind of syntactic rule which takes one string of syntactic categories or symbols and converts it into another string by processes of addition, deletion or permutation. In transformational-generative *grammar* the relation between the deep structure and surface structure of a sentence is specified by a set of transformational rules. The notion, however, need not be restricted to syntactic rules for sentences. Some accounts of folktales and *myths* propose that their diverse heterogeneity is really the result of transformations being worked upon a small number of very simple underlying structures or formulae. => GENRE, MYTH, NARRATIVE. *Further reading* Barthes, R. (2012); Chomsky, N. (1965) (2008); Lévi-Strauss, C. (1963); Propp, V. (1971).

transgression *n.* SOCIOLOGY. The act of crossing a social, moral or legal boundary or infringing upon established standards or norms of behaviour. SJ

transitivity *n.* LINGUISTICS, STYLISTICS. Traditionally refers to a distinction between verbs which take a direct object and those that don't. In systemic functional linguistics the notion was developed to describe a linguistic system operating within the clause which encodes the relationship between actions (or processes) and those entities or participants associated with them – basically, 'who (or what) does what to whom (or what)'.

Transitivity relations and the roles of participants depend crucially upon the kind of process encoded by the main verb in the clause. For English, four fundamental types of process may be distinguished (for a more complete and complex treatment see Halliday, 2014):

(1) *Material* 'John broke the lock'.
(2) *Mental* 'She understood immediately'.
(3) *Verbal* 'Michael said he was hungry'.
(4) *Relational* 'The main course is excellent'.

(1) Material action processes (realised by verbs such as 'break', 'wipe', 'dig', 'unbolt') are associated with inherent roles such as an AGENT

TRANSITIVITY

(someone or something to perform the action) and AFFECTED (ENTITY) (someone or something on the receiving end of the action). Thus:

John	broke	the lock
AGENT	PROCESS	AFFECTED

There need, of course, be no necessary correspondence between the participant role AGENT and the syntactic element 'subject'. The passive makes possible one obvious kind of non-congruence, e.g.:

The lock	was broken	by John
AFFECTED	PROCESS	AGENT
Subject	Predicator	

The passive thereby allows the topicalisation or thematisation of the AFFECTED.
It also allows the deletion or non-statement of the AGENT, e.g.:

The lock	was broken
AFFECTED	PROCESS

(2) Mental processes (realised by verbs such as 'know', 'feel', 'think', 'believe') are associated with inherent roles such as SENSER (the one who performs the act of 'knowing', 'thinking' or 'feeling') and PHENOMENON – that which is experienced by the SENSER. Thus:

James	considered	the problem
SENSER	PROCESS	PHENOMENON
Mary	understood	the message
SENSER	PROCESS	PHENOMENON
The message	amazed	me
PHENOMENON	PROCESS	SENSER

Quite commonly, the PHENOMENON will not be realised in the surface structure of the clause, but there may be some reference to the CIRCUMSTANCES of the action:

The doctor	thought	hard
SENSER	PROCESS	CIRCUMSTANCE
Mary	understood	immediately
SENSER	PROCESS	CIRCUMSTANCE

(3) Verbal processes are processes of saying, though this comes in many forms – e.g. 'suggest', 'promise', 'enquire', 'tell', 'inform'. Typical participant roles are SAYER, VERBIAGE and RECIPIENT. Thus:

```
I       | said    | it was time to leave
SAYER   | PROCESS | VERBIAGE

I       | told    | him       | it was time to leave
SAYER   | PROCESS | RECIPIENT | VERBIAGE
```

(4) Relational processes in their simplest form involve some entity which is identified by reference to some attribute. The process may be realised by verbs such as 'become', 'seem', 'be' and 'have' and typical roles are IDENTIFIER and IDENTIFIED.

```
The sky    | is      | blue
IDENTIFIED | PROCESS | IDENTIFIER
```

Other important roles are those of POSSESSOR and POSSESSED, as in:

```
He        | had     | no money
POSSESSOR | PROCESS | POSSESSED
```

Any event or relationship in the 'real world' is filtered through, and given linguistic shape by means of, one or other of the types of process outlined above. Transitivity relations, therefore, go to the heart of the linguistic construction and *mediation* of experience. And the patterning of transitivity choices in any one *text* can reveal crucial predispositions to construct experience along certain lines rather than others. The analysis of transitivity, therefore, makes available an important tool for exploring the ideological dimensions of text. => IDEOLOGY, REPRESENTATION, SEMANTICS. *Further reading* Halliday, M.A.K. (2014)

troll *n.* **to troll, trolling** *v., prppl.* COMMUNICATION & INTERNET STUDIES. Slang expression for one who posts inflammatory, irrelevant or topically irrelevant comments on the *internet* in order to disrupt discussion and provoke an emotional response. Although the term originated as a slang expression (it may have roots in Scandinavian folklore and tales of dwarves or imps who live in caves and trouble travelers and by-passers), it has attracted the attention of scholars concerned about the aspects of the *communicative ethos* of the internet. The disembodied nature of internet *communication*, where it is possible to communicate anonymously under the guise of an assumed identity, may well encourage general degrees of belligerence, verbal aggression and harassment that are kept in check when communication takes place between persons who may more easily and directly be held accountable for their words. Trolling in this sense may be seen as part of a wider issue of the communicative ethos of dominant forms of communication such as the press, *broadcasting* and the internet. => COMMUNICATIVE ETHOS, *DISCOURSE ACT*, FISKING, SPEECH ACT.

truth *n*. MEDIA & JOURNALISM STUDIES. A statement or claim about reality which can survive empirical, logical, ethical or religious tests of its validity. Truth, especially in terms of objective truth, operates as a touchstone of value in criticisms of media *bias* or of the media as purveyors of *propaganda*. => BIAS, OBJECTIVITY, PROPAGANDA, SINCERITY, TRUTHINESS, VALIDITY CLAIMS.

truthiness *n*. CULTURAL AND INTERNET STUDIES, MEDIA, RHETORIC. The quality of a claim made without factual evidence, or in defiance of the facts, which is designed to advance a particular position and which is given credence because it feels right and lends support to a particular established or emerging world view. Applies particularly in areas of public debate such as the U.K. referendum on membership of the EU or U.S. presidential debates. The claim that the UK 'sends 350 million pounds a week to the EU' was demonstrably untrue but survived rebuttal because of its 'truthiness'. The Republican presidential candidate Donald Trump dispenses examples of truthiness to such an extent that Stephen Colbert, who has been credited with the initial coinage of 'truthiness', has now offered a further neologism, 'Trumpiness'. => SINCERITY, TRUTH, VALIDITY CLAIMS. *Further reading* Zelizer, B. (ed) (2009)

turn *n*. CONVERSATION ANALYSIS, SOCIAL INTERACTION. A contribution to a *conversation* by a speaker. Turns may be as short as a single word or may extend across several turn components. Where a turn seems to be complete, transition to the next speaker's turn may take place subject to the workings of the *turn-taking* system. => CONVERSATION ANALYSIS, TALK IN INTERACTION, TURN TAKING. *Further reading* Clift R. (2016)

turn-taking *n*. CONVERSATION ANALYSIS, SOCIAL INTERACTION. *Conversation*, and *talk-in-interaction* more generally, is composed of successive contributions by parties to the *talk*. Taking *turns* is managed by a basic 'machinery' or system of interactional rules, consisting fundamentally of: (1) one person speaks at a time and (2) speaker change recurs. The transition from one speaker to the next is accomplished by their attending to points where a speaker's turn may seem complete and managing the placement of the next turn to coincide with it. Ideally – if the turn-taking machinery is working smoothly – a conversation will proceed without *silences* and without overlaps. Where gaps or overlaps occur, conversationalists take steps to overcome them in accordance with the basic turn-taking machinery. => CONVERSATION ANALYSIS, TALK-IN-INTERACTION, TURN. *Further reading* Clift R. (2016); Hutchby, I. and Woofit, R. (2008) (2nd Ed.)

two-way *n. BROADCAST JOURNALISM.* Exchange between a news reporter in the field and the *news anchor*, usually in the studio, for the purpose of providing an update on an unfolding event. Typically, for a two-way the reporter or correspondent performs *live*, unscripted and on camera to provide a sense of *immediacy* and to dramatise proximity to the site of the news event. => NEWS. *Further reading* Montgomery, M. (2006)

★★

universality *n.* The notion that something is applicable to every case or individual in a class or category. For example, in linguistics, universality implies the existence of a grammatical rule or a linguistic feature that is found in all languages. The notion of universality informs schools of thought in the disciplines of philosophy, ethics, logic and mathematics. *SJ*

★★

validity claims *np. CRITICAL SOCIOLOGY, DISCOURSE ANALYSIS, RHETORIC.* The basis on which utterances may be considered valid, deriving from the work of the German sociologist and critical theorist, Jürgen Habermas. For Habermas (1979), interlocutors make routine assessments of the validity of each other's utterances in three main ways, judging them in terms of *truth*, appropriateness, or *sincerity*. Thus, in any *discourse act*, the speaker may claim truth for a stated propositional content, may claim appropriateness for the utterance in terms of the interpersonal norms governing the relation between speaker and hearer, and may claim sincerity for the utterance insofar as it authentically expresses his or her subjective state. For Habermas, the achievement of mutual understanding between the speaker and hearer depends upon the acknowledgement, vindication or redemption of these validity claims. In projecting a truth claim, for instance, the speaker accepts that obligations may be incurred to supply grounds to support the claim. Claims to appropriateness may need to be justified by reference to interpersonal norms. Claims to sincerity may need to be demonstrated by displays of trustworthiness. Thus, it is not merely that claims are projected by utterances. In order for understanding to be achieved, the claims must be capable of redemption or validation. But the three different kinds of claim – truth, sincerity and appropriateness – implicate different kinds of validation. The grounds for validating a truth claim are different in kind from those at risk in the projection of appropriateness. And these in turn are different from those at stake in the projection of sincerity. Indeed, claims to sincerity are perhaps the most difficult to guarantee since they implicate a match between the outward form of the utterance and the speaker's interior state. Put crudely, it is possible to have an argument about the truth of the claim that God exists but more difficult to validate the sincerity of a statement like 'I love you very much'. Indeed, Habermas comments that truth and appropriateness may be validated implicitly or explicitly by negotiation in the discourse but that sincerity may need to be taken on trust and vindicated or validated only by the subsequent behaviour of the speaker. It should be noted that Habermas is not advancing this framework in the first instance as an analytical model for investigating spontaneous, naturally occurring speech data. It is an abstract framework designed to advance an argument about the conduct of reason in social life – an argument in which the guarantee of rationality is grounded in the potential testability and criticisability of all validity claims. By outlining what he believes to be fundamental, universal features of any speech situation, Habermas hopes to set out the principles that will guarantee or underpin the search for truth, *consensus* and understanding in civil society. In this way, the emphasis on validity claims adds a hitherto neglected dimension to the systematic study of language and *communication*. It is not just that *speech*, among other things, is intentional, has a referential basis and a propositional content and is framed according to the grammatical and pragmatic *codes* of the surrounding *speech community*. It also achieves validity and is 'appropriated' within a normative framework of judgement about right or wrong, true or false, sincere or insincere. Such judgements inform our reactions and play an important role in the way we arrive at a response to what speakers have to say, or more generally to surrounding discourse. In short, the human significance of a *discourse act* lies not just in the way it means something propositionally in the here and now but also in the ways it can be deemed valid (or invalid). In the case of Donald Trump, for instance, it is clear that different kinds of validity are attributed to his utterances by different segments of the public. For some they are valid or invalid on the basis of their truth claims. For others their sincerity or insincerity (whether he means what he says) is more important. Indeed, the general framework of validity claims has proved especially useful for analyzing moments of discursive crisis or instability in the public domain. => AUTHENTICITY, COMMUNICATIVE ETHOS, PRAGMATICS, PUBLIC SPHERE, SINCERITY, TRUTH, TRUTHINESS. *Further reading* Montgomery, M. (1999), (2017); Simpson, P. (2003)

verbal devices *np.* CONVERSATION ANALYSIS, POLITICAL COMMUNICATION, RHETORIC. Ways of using language for rhetorical effect, especially in order to gain or facilitate applause. The occasions where applause occurs during public speeches have been linked to particular kinds of verbal pattern or device such as the use of pairs of propositions or lists where the third or subsequent item clearly culminates the pattern. These are sometimes referred to as 'clap-traps', following extensive studies of political speeches by the British sociologist J. Maxwell Atkinson. *Further reading* Atkinson, J.M.(1984)

viral *n.* MEDIA & INTERNET STUDIES. Adopted from the medical terminology that relates to the manner in which a virus spreads through patterns of contagion, the use of viral in social, cultural and commercial contexts refers to the ways in which a phenomenon, such as a video, a *marketing* campaign or a computer *virus*, can spread rapidly through virtual *social networks*. => ONLINE COMMUNITY, SOCIAL NETWORKS, VIRUS, WORLD WIDE WEB. *SJ*

virtual community *np.* MEDIA & INTERNET STUDIES. A *social network* of individuals who interact through specific *social media*, potentially crossing national and geographical boundaries in order to pursue mutual interests or goals. Virtual communities rely on digitally encoded telecommunications to transcend the physical constraints of *face-to-face communication*. => AMBIENT AFFILIATION, COMMUNITY, CYBERSPACE, ONLINE COMMUNITY, SOCIAL NETWORKS. *Further reading* Rheingold, H. (2000)

virtual reality *np.* MEDIA & INTERNET STUDIES, TECHNOLOGY. A computer-simulated environment, based on an imagined or real-world analogue, that allows the computer-user to interact with it in ways that resemble our bodily experience of the real world. The techniques of creating a virtual reality underlie the development of training simulators for a variety of specialised roles such as airline captain, oil-rig operator or surgeon. They can also be used to create large fully integrated immersive systems such as *Second Life*, perhaps better described as a virtual world.

virus *n.* MEDIA & INTERNET STUDIES. A software program that that can spread from one computer to another by serially replicating itself, making unauthorised changes to the computers' functions and thereby interfering with their operation. SJ

visual culture *np.* MEDIA & CULTURAL STUDIES. The everyday expression, shaping and circulation of frameworks of belief, meaning and value through images. Contemporary urban *culture* has multiplied the possibilities for the production, reproduction and dissemination of images, and the study of visual culture seeks to understand the ways in which meanings are encoded, distributed and interpreted in visual form in urban space. => MULTI-MODALITY, RESEMIOTISATION, SEMIOSIS. *Further reading* Mirzoeff, N. (ed.) (2012)

voice-over *n.* FILM AND MEDIA STUDIES. Use of a *voice* by someone out of shot to narrate or comment on the scene. The voice-over is usually added to film or footage in post-production: in other words it is not recorded or transmitted *live* as the scene unfolds but added later. The words of a reporter in recorded television news reports are often conveyed in voice-over, and the device is sometimes used in *documentary* and fiction film for an unseen narrator. => EXTRA-DI-EGETIC SOUND, FILM LANGUAGE, NARRATION.

vox pop (abb. from *L. vox populi*, 'voice of the people') *np.* BROADCAST NEWS. A technique used primarily in *news* and current affairs *broadcasting*, but also in reportage and *documentary*, in which ordinary people are interviewed for their responses to an event or issue, usually in chance encounters in public spaces, so that their views can be incorporated, usually in heavily edited form, into a news item or other forms of documentary footage, in such a way as to suggest a range of reactions and opinions. => ACTUALITY, DOCUMENTARY, REPORTAGE.

★★

white space *np.* PRINT. Portions of a page left unmarked or the space between words in a *text*. SJ

Wikipedia *n.* INTERNET AND MEDIA STUDIES, PUBLISHING. A collaborative, open-access and multilingual online knowledge and information resource launched in 2001 by Jimmy Wales and Larry Sanger, which provides reference articles that can be written by anyone with *access* to the *internet*. The etymology of its name implies its principles and methodology: a combination of 'wiki', from the Hawaiian word meaning 'quick', and 'encylopedia', from the Greek meaning 'general education' or 'complete knowledge'. SJ

wired society *np. INTERNET & MEDIA STUDIES.* A society connected by telecommunication and *mass communication networks*. The term was coined by the British *information technology* expert James Martin (b. 1933) and formed the title of his Pulitzer Prize–winning book *The Wired Society: A Challenge for Tomorrow* (1977), which anticipated many future developments such as the *internet* and the creation of the *World Wide Web*. With the advent of digitisation the term has been superseded by alternatives such as the *network society*.

wired world *INTERNET & MEDIA STUDIES.* => WIRED SOCIETY.

World Wide Web *np. INTERNET AND MEDIA STUDIES.* A system of interlinked hypertext documents that can be accessed through the *internet* by using a web-browser. The system was formally proposed by British scientist Tim Berners-Lee (b. 1955) with assistance from the Belgian scientist Robert Cailliau, (b. 1947) in 1990, and by 1994 a number of important websites were linked and active, including precursors of today's most popular services. => CYBERSPACE.

writing *n. COMMUNICATION STUDIES, LINGUISTICS.* The transformation of the sound signals that constitute *speech* into permanent or semi-permanent marks that may be used to communicate across time and space. The earliest known writing systems date from Mesopotamia around 3200 BC. The history of writing systems displays various solutions to the technical problem of turning the sounds of speech into marks. Some *cultures* adopted pictographic and ideographic means, relying – at least in part – on pictures for ideas. Others evolved alphabetic means of representing the sounds of a particular language by discrete marks (or letters). The choice of writing instead of speech as a medium of *communication* may entail particular grammatical, syntactic or lexical preferences over others. Indeed, some work suggests that certain kinds of linguistic patterning may be distinctive to particular media (e.g. Biber, D. 1988).

Thus, it is suggested that the written medium is associated with greater lexical density, a wider range of grammatical structures, a greater degree of embedding and more varied forms of connectivity between sentences than in speech. Conversely, the spoken medium is associated with lexical repetition, low lexical density, vague or indefinite expressions ('sort of', 'whatsit'), a higher incidence of coordinated clauses linked by common conjunctions ('and', 'but') and selection of the active rather than the passive *voice*. The character of these differences led the British linguist Michael Halliday (1925-2018) to characterise speech as a process and writing as a product

(Halliday, 2014). Certainly there is widespread agreement that the communicative *affordances* of writing and speech are very different. Speech typically takes place between interlocutors who are in some way co-present to each other, and this enables them to adjust their utterance in the light of the apparent reactions of the other. The process of composing and planning speech goes hand in hand with the act of speaking, and speaking, in turn, goes hand in hand with the process of interpretation that must keep pace with it. There is no time lag between production and reception. Instead, speech is temporally bound, transient and dynamic, rooted in an unfolding context, with paralinguistic behaviour providing an important supplementary layer to communication. Conversely, writing as a semi-permanent product opens up radically different affordances: it enables a gap across time and space to open up between participants. The process of composition may be lengthy, involving several stages and many revisions. And writing – especially in printed or other permanent forms – may be received in quite different contexts from those in which it was produced. The writer must anticipate how the effects of a displaced or unknown context might guide interpretation or lead to misinterpretation. And readers, of course, must typically rely on the written *text* alone in arriving at its sense. Writing, consequently, is forced to be less reliant on its immediate context for its meaning. These differences between the affordances of speech and writing as *media of communication* are undoubtedly bound up with variations in the technical and technological resources at stake in the realisation of these alternative modes of communication. The development of writing as a medium of communication is not, of course, the end of the story. Indeed, we may distinguish broadly between three overlapping phases in the technological development of alternatives to speech as media of communication: mechanical (writing, print); electrical (telegraphy and wireless telegraphy, radio, and television); and *digital* (*World Wide Web* and the *internet*, cellular phones, as well as the convergence or *interaction* between these and previous media of communication). => COMMUNICATION TECHNOLOGY, SPEECH. *Further reading* Rogers, H. (2004)

★★

youth culture *np.* CULTURAL STUDIES. Symbolic framework of norms, values and beliefs that underpin a distinctive set of social practices and identities associated with adolescents or young people. Since these reflect a particular stage of life, youth culture is commonly understood to be focused around social practices that feature dress, sport, music, *styles* of speaking and sex. Not all societies will feature distinctive youth cultures, and the concept is peculiar to particular stages of societal change and development. Academic interest in them has accelerated since the latter half of the 20th century by the apparent overlap between youth cultures, social change and youth-led revolutions. =>COUNTER CULTURE, CULTURE, SUB-CULTURE *Further reading* Buckingham, D. et.al. (eds.) (2014)

★★

zoetrope *n. MEDIA*. From the Greek '*zoē*' (alive, active), and '*tropē*' (turn), a device that creates the illusion of motion by means of the quick revolution of static images achieved through the use of a rotating cylinder which has slits cut vertically in the sides at equal intervals so that while it spins an observer outside may see opposite a sequenced set of images arranged in order on the inside. The zoetrope can be seen as a forerunner of the cinema, although the first recorded example of one dates from around AD 180 in China. => MONTAGE, PERSISTENCE OF VISION.

BIBLIOGRAPHY

Abercrombie, N., and Turner, Bryan S. (1978) The dominant ideology thesis. *The British Journal of Sociology* 29(2) (June), 149–170.
Allan, S. (Ed.) (2011) *The Routledge Companion to News and Journalism*. London: Routledge.
Allan, S., and Thorsen, E. (Eds.) (2009) *Citizen Journalism: Global Perspectives – Vols. 1 & 2*. New York: Peter Lang Publishing Inc.
Allen, R.C. (Ed.) (1994) *To Be Continued: Soap Operas Around the World*. London: Routledge.
Althusser, L. (1971) Ideology and Ideological State Apparatuses (Notes towards an Investigation). In *Lenin and Philosophy, and Other Essays*. Harmondsworth: Penguin.
Anderson, B. (2006) *Imagined Communities: Reflections on the Origin and Spread of Nationalism*. London: Verso.
Anderson, D. and Sharrock, W. (1979) Biassing the news: Technical issues in 'Media Studies'. *Sociology* 13(3), 367–385
Ardehali, P. (1990) Pronoun exchange as a barometer of social change. *Dialectical Anthropology*, 15(1), 81–98.
Atkinson, J.M. (1984) *Our Masters' Voices: The Language and Body Language of Politics*. London: Routledge.
Baker, P., and Ellece, S. (2011) *Key Terms in Discourse Analysis*. London: A&C Black.
Bal, M. (2009) *Narratology: Introduction to the Theory of Narrative*. Toronto: University of Toronto Press.
Barthes, R. (1977) The death of the author. In *Image-Music-Text* London: Fontana, pp. 142–149.
Barthes, R. (1990) *S/Z*. Oxford: Basil Blackwell.
Barthes, R. (2012) *Mythologies: The Complete Edition*. New York: Hill & Wang.
Baumann, Z. (2000) *Liquid Modernity*. Oxford: Polity.
Bednarek, M., and Caple, H. (2012) *News Discourse*. London: Palgrave Macmillan.
Bednarek, M., and Caple, H. (2017) *The Discourse of News Values: How News Organisations Create Newsworthiness*. Oxford: OUP scholarship online.
Bell, A. (2011) Re-constructing Babel: Discourse analysis, hermeneutics and the Interpretive Arc. *Discourse Studies* 13(5), Special Issue on Hermeneutics and Discourse Analysis (October 2011), 519–568.

Belsey, C. (2002) *Poststructuralism: A Very Short Introduction*. Oxford: Oxford University Press.
Benjamin, W. (2008) *The Work of Art in the Age of Mechanical Reproduction*. Harmondsworth: Penguin.
Bergmann, J. (1993) *Discreet Indiscretions: The Social Organisation of Gossip*. Piscataway, NJ: Aldine Transaction.
Besnier, N. (2009) *Gossip and the Everyday Production of Politics*. Honolulu: University of Hawaii Press.
Bettie, J. (2014) *Women Without Class: Girls, Race and Identity*. Oakland, CA: University of California Press.
Biber, D., and Conrad, S. (2009) *Register, Genre, and Style*. Cambridge: CUP.
Biber, D., and Finegan, E. (1988) Adverbial stance types in English. *Discourse Processes* 11(1), 1–34.
Billiani, F. (Ed.) (2007) *Modes of Censorship and Translation: National Contexts and Diverse Media*. London: Routledge.
Biressi, A., and Nunn, H. (2005) *Reality TV: Realism and Revelation* New York: Columbia University Press.
Bordwell, D. and Thompson, K. (2004) *Film Art: An introduction* New York: McGraw-Hill.
Bourdieu, P. (1977) *Outline of a Theory of Practice*. Cambridge: CUP.
Bourdieu, P. (1984/2010) *Distinction: A Social Critique of the Judgment of Taste*. London: Routledge.
Boxer, D. (2002) *Applying Sociolinguistics: Domains and Face-to-Face Interaction*. Philadelphia and Amsterdam: John Benjamins.
Brown, P., and Levinson, S.C. (1987) *Politeness: Some Universals in Language Usage*. Cambridge: CUP.
Brown, R., and Gilman, A. (1972) The pronouns of power and solidarity. In P.P. Giglioli (ed.), *Language and Social Context*. New York: Penguin Books, pp. 252–282.
Buckingham, D. et al. (Eds.) (2014) *Youth Cultures in the Age of Global Media*. London: Palgrave Macmillan.
Butler, C. (2010) *Modernism: A Very Short Introduction*. Oxford: OUP.
Calhoun, C. (Ed.) (1992) *Habermas and the Public Sphere*. Cambridge, MA: MIT Press.
Cameron, D. (1995) *Verbal Hygiene* London: Routledge.
Castells, M. (2009) *The Rise of the Network Society* (2nd Ed.). Oxford: Wiley Blackwell.
Caughie, J. (Ed.) (1981) *Theories of Authorship*. London: BFI/Routledge.
Charteris-Black, J. (2013) *Analysing Political Speeches: Rhetoric, Discourse and Metaphor*. London: Palgrave Macmillan.
Chatman, S. (1980) *Story and Discourse: Narrative Structure in Fiction and Film*. Ithaca: Cornell University Press.
Cherry, C. (1978) *On Human Communication*. Cambridge, MA: MIT Press.
Chomsky, N. (1965) *Aspects of the Theory of Syntax*. Cambridge, MA: The MIT Press.
Chomsky, N. (2008) *The Essential Chomsky*. London: The Bodley Head.
Clift, R. (2016) *Conversation Analysis*. Cambridge: CUP.

BIBLIOGRAPHY

Cobley, P. (Ed.) (2010) *The Routledge Companion to Semiotics*. London: Routledge.
Cohen, S. (1972) *Folk Devils and Moral Panics: The Creation of the Mods and Rockers*. London: McGibbon and Kee.
Clayman, S., and Heritage, J. (2002) *The News Interview: Journalists and Public Figures on the Air*. Cambridge: Cambridge University Press.
Coates, J., and Pichler, P. (Eds.) (2011) *Language and Gender: A Reader*. Oxford: Wiley-Blackwell.
Cohn, N. (2013) *The Visual Language of Comics: Introduction to the Structure and Cognition of Sequential Images*. London: Bloomsbury Academic.
Compaine, B.M. (2001) *The Digital Divide: Facing a Crisis or Creating a Myth?* Cambridge, MA: MIT Press.
Conboy, M. (2004) *Journalism: A Critical History*. London: Sage.
Conboy, M. (2005) *Tabloid Britain*. London: Routledge.
Cornbleet, S., and Carter, R. (2001) *The Language and Speech and Writing*. London: Routledge.
Cotter, C. (2010) *News Talk: Investigating the Language of Journalism*. Cambridge: CUP.
Couldry, N. (2008a) Digital storytelling, media research and democracy: conceptual choices and alternative futures. In Knut Lundby (ed.), *Digital Storytelling, Mediatized Stories: Self-Representations in New Media. Digital Formations* (52). New York: Peter Lang Publishing, Inc., pp. 41–60.
Couldry, N. (2008b) Mediatization or mediation? Alternative understandings of the emergent space of digital storytelling. *New Media and Society* 10(3), 373–391.
Crisell, A. (2002) *An Introductory History of British Broadcasting*. London: Routledge.
Critcher, C (2003) *Moral Panics and the Media*. Buckingham: Open University Press.
Critcher, C. et al. (2013) *Moral Panics in the Contemporary World*. London: Bloomsbury.
Culler, J.D. (1977) *Ferdinand de Saussure*. Harmondsworth: Penguin.
Dayan, D., and Katz, E. (1994) *Media Events*. Harvard: Harvard University Press.
De Lauretis, T., and Heath, S. (Eds.) (1985) *The Cinematic Apparatus*. London: Palgrave Macmillan.
De Saussure, F. (1974) *Course in General Linguistics*. London: Fontana.
Drew, P. et al. (2006) *Talk and Interaction in Social Research Methods*. London: Sage.
Dutton, W. H. (2012) The Fifth Estate: A New Governance Challenge. In D. Levi-Faur (ed.), *The Oxford Handbook of Governance* Print Publication Date: Mar 2012.
Dyer, R. (2006) *Pastiche*. London: Routledge.
Dynel, M. (2016) New Theoretical Insights Into Untruthfulness. *Special Issue of Pragmatics & Cognition* 23(1).
Dynel, M., and Chovanec, J. (2015) *Participation in Public and Social Media Interactions*. Amsterdam: John Benjamins.
Eagleton, T. (2000) *The Idea of Culture*. Oxford: Wiley.

Eagleton, T. (2007) *Ideology: An Introduction*. London: Verso
Eagleton, T. (Ed.) (2013) *Ideology*. London: Routledge.
Eco, U. (1981) *The Role of the Reader*. London: Hutchinson.
Eco, U. (2010) *On Beauty: A History of a Western Idea*. London: MacLehose Press.
Eggins, S., and Slade, D. (1997) *Analysing Casual Conversation*. London: Cassell Academic.
Eggins, S., and J.R. Martin. (1997) Genres and register of discourse. In Teun A. van Dijk (ed.) *Discourse as Structure and Process (Discourse Studies – A Multidisciplinary Introduction)*. Vol. 1. London: Sage; 230–256.
Elias, N. (2000) *The Civilizing Process*. Oxford: Blackwell.
Elias, N., Schröter, M., and Dunning, E. (1996) *The Germans: Power Struggles and the Development of Habitus in the Nineteenth and Twentieth Centuries*. Columbia: Columbia University Press.
Elsaesser, T. (2015) *Film Theory: An Introduction Through the Senses*. London: Routledge.
Fabian, J. (2014) *Time and the Other: How Anthropology Makes Its Object*. New York: Columbia University Press.
Fairclough, N. (1992) *Discourse and Social Change*. Cambridge: Polity Press.
Fairclough, N. (1994) Conversationalization of public discourse and the authority of the consumer. In Russell Keat, Nigel Whiteley, and Nicholas Abercrombie (eds.), *The Authority of the Consumer*. London Routledge.
Fairclough, N. (2015) *Language and Power* (3rd Ed.). London: Routledge.
Ferguson, C.A. (1959) Diglossia. *WORD* 15(2), 325–340.
Firth, J. (1957) *A Synopsis of Linguistic Theory 1930–1955*. London: Longman.
Fischer, O., and Nanny, M. (Eds.) (2001) *The Motivated Sign: Iconicity in language and literature*. Amsterdam: John Benjamins.
Fish, S. (1990) *Is There a Text in This Class: The Authority of Interpretive Communities*. Boston: Harvard University Press.
Fiske, J. (1987) *Television Culture*. London: Methuen.
Fitzgerald, R., and Housley, W. (Eds.) (2015) *Advances in Membership Categorisation Analysis*. London: Sage.
Flew, T. (2014) *New Media* (4th Ed.). Oxford: Oxford University Press ANZ.
Frawley, W.J., Piatetsky-shapiro, G., and Matheus, C.J. (1992) Knowledge discovery in databases: An overview. *AI Magazine* 13(3), 57–70.
Friedrich, P. (1972) Social context and semantic feature: The Russian pronominal usage. In Gumperz, J. & Hymes, D. (Eds.) *Directions in Sociolinguistics* New York: Holt, Rinehart & Winston, pp. 270–300.
Frosh, P. (2009) The Face of Television. *Annals of the American Academy of Political and Social Science* 625, 87–102.
Fuchs, C. (2017) *Social Media: A Critical Introduction*. London: Sage.
Galtung, J., and Ruge, M.H. (1965) The structure of foreign news: The presentation of the Congo, Cuba and Cyprus crises in four Norwegian newspapers. *Journal of Peace Research* 2(1), 64–90.
Gans, H.J. (1999) *Popular Culture and High Culture: An Analysis*. New York: Basic Books.
Gardner, R. (2001) *When Listeners Talk: Response Tokens and Listener Stance*. Amsterdam: John Benjamins.

Gee, J.P. (2014) *An Introduction to Discourse Analysis* (3rd Ed.). London: Routledge.
Gelder, K. (Ed.) (2005) *The Subcultures Reader*. (2nd Ed.) London: Routledge.
Genette, G. ([1972] 1980). *Narrative Discourse. An Essay in Method*. Oxford: Blackwell.
Gerbner, G. (2002) *Against the Mainstream: The Selected Works of George Gerbner* (Ed. Morgan). New York: Peter Lang.
Gibson, J.J. (1979) *The Ecological Approach to Visual Perception*. Boston: Houghton Mifflin.
Giddens, A. (1981) *The Critique of Historical Materialism*. London: Macmillan.
Glynn, C.J. et al. (2016) *Public Opinion* (3rd Ed.). Boulder, Co: Westview Press.
Goffman, E. (1959) *The Presentation of Self in Everyday Life*. New York: Doubleday Anchor Books.
Goffman, E. (1981) *Forms of Talk*. Philadelphia: University of Pennsylvania Press.
Goffman, E. (2005) *Interaction Ritual: Essays in Face to Face Behaviour*. Aldine: Transaction.
Gramsci, A. (1971) *Selections From the Prison Notebooks*. London: Lawrence and Wishart.
Gray, J. (2006) *Watching With the Simpsons: Television, Parody, and Intertextuality*. New York: Routledge.
Gray, J. et al. (Eds.) (2009) *Satire TV: Politics and Comedy in the Post-Network Era*. New York: NYU Press.
Gregory, M., and Carroll, S. (1978) *Language and Situation: Language Varieties and Their Social Contexts*. Abingdon, UK: Routledge.
Grice, H.P. (1975) Logic and conversation. In P. Cole and J.L. Morgan (eds.), *Syntax and Semantics Volume 3: Speech Acts*. New York: Academic Press, pp. 41–58.
Habermas, J. (1979) Historical materialism and the development of normative structures. *Communication and the Evolution of Society*, 95–129.
Habermas, J. (1979) Universal pragmatics. In Habermas, J. *Communication and the Evolution of Society* Boston MA: Beacon Press, pp. 1–6.
Habermas, J. (1988) *Legitimation Crisis*. Cambridge: Polity.
Habermas, J. (1989) *The Structural Transformation of the Public Sphere: An Inquiry Into a Category of Bourgeois Society*. Cambridge: Polity.
Hafez, K. (2007) *The Myth of Media Globalization*. Cambridge: Polity.
Hall, S. (2007) Encoding, Decoding. In S. During (ed.) *The Cultural Studies Reader* (3rd Ed.). London: Routledge, pp. 477–487.
Hall, S., and Jefferson, T. (1993) *Resistance Through Rituals: Youth Subcultures in Post-War Britain*. London: Psychology Press.
Halliday, M.A.K. (1973) *Explorations in the Functions of Language*. London: Edward Arnold.
Halliday, M.A.K. (1978) *Language as Social Semiotic*. London: Edward Arnold.
Halliday, M.A.K. (2014) *Halliday's Introduction to Functional Grammar* (4th Ed.). (revised by Christian Mathiesson) London: Routledge.
Halliday, M.A.K., and Hasan, R. (1976) *Cohesion in English*. London: Longman.
Hallin, D. (1986) *The Uncensored War: The Media and Vietnam*. New York: Oxford University Press.

Hartley, J. (Ed.) (2005) *Creative Industries*. Oxford: Wiley Blackwell.
Hartley, J., and McWilliam, K. (Eds.) (2009) *Story Circle: Digital Storytelling Around the World*. John Wiley & Sons.
Harris, R. (2003) *Saussure and His Interpreters*. Edinburgh: Edinburgh UP.
Hartley, P. (1999) *Interpersonal Communication*. New York: Routledge.
Harvey, D. (1990) *The Condition of Postmodernity: An Enquiry Into the Origins of Social Change*. Malden, MA: Blackwell.
Hawkes, T. (2003) *Structuralism and Semiotics*. London: Routledge.
Hayes, A.F. (2015) *Statistical Methods for Communication Science*. London: Routledge.
Hebdige, D. (1979) *Subculture: The Meaning of Style*. London: Methuen.
Herman, E.S., and Chomsky, N. (1988) *Manufacturing Consent*. New York: Pantheon.
Hesmondhalgh, D. (2013) *The Cultural Industries*. London: Sage.
Higgins, M., and Smith, A. (2017) *Belligerent Broadcasting: Synthetic Argument in Broadcast Talk*. London: Routledge.
Hill, A. (2005) *Reality TV: Audiences and Popular Factual Television*. London: Routledge.
Hine, C. (2015) *Ethnography for the Internet*. London: Bloomsbury.
Hodson, J. (2014) *Dialect in Film and Literature*. London: Palgrave Macmillan.
Hooks, bell (2000) *Feminism is for Everybody*. London: Pluto Press
Hoey, M. (1991) *Patterns of Lexis in Texts*. Oxford: OUP.
Horton, D. and R. Richard Wohl (1956) Mass communication and para-social interaction. *Psychiatry* 19(3).
Hunston, S. (2007) Semantic prosody revisited. *International Journal of Corpus Linguistics* – special issue, Moon, R. (Ed.) (2007) *Words, Grammar, Text* 12(2), 249–268.
Hutchby, I. (2000) *Conversation and Technology: From the Telephone to the Internet*. Oxford: Polity.
Hutchby, I. (2001) Technologies, texts and affordances. *Sociology* 35(2), 441–456.
Hutchby, I. (2006) *Media Talk: Conversation Analysis and the Study of Broadcasting*. Maidenhead: Open UP.
Hutchby, I., and Woofit, R. (2008) *Conversation Analysis* (2nd Ed.). Oxford: Wiley.
Hutcheon, L. (1994) *Irony's Edge: The Theory and Politics of Irony*. London: Routledge.
Hutcheon, L. (with S. O'Flynn) (2012) *A Theory of Adaptation* (2nd Ed.). London: Routledge.
Hyland, K. (2007) *Metadiscourse: Exploring Interaction in Writing*. London: Continuum.
Iedema, R. (2001) Resemiotization. *Semiotica* 137–1/4(2001), 23–39.
Iedema, R. (2003) Multimodality, resemiotization: Extending the analysis of discourse as multi-semiotic practice. *Visual Communication* 2(1)
Jakobson, R. (1960) Closing statement: linguistics and poetics. In T. Sebeok (eds.), *Style in Language*. Cambridge, MA: MIT Press.
Jameson, F. (1991), *Postmodernism, or, the Cultural Logic of Late Capitalism*. Durham: Duke University Press.
Jeong, Seung-hoon, and Szaniawski, J. (Eds.) (2017) *The Global Auteur: The Politics of Authorship in 21st Century Cinema*. London: Bloomsbury Academic.

Jewitt, C. (Ed.) (2014) *The Routledge Handbook of Multi-Modal Analysis* London: Routledge

Jones, R.H. et al. (Eds.) (2015) *Discourse and Digital Practices: Doing Discourse Analysis in the Digital Age.* London: Routledge.

Juris, J.S. (2012) Reflections on #Occupy Everywhere: Social media, public space, and emerging logics of aggregation. *American Ethnologist* 39(2) (May 2012), 259–279.

Katz, E. (1980) Media events: The sense of occasion. *Studies in Visual Anthropology* 6, 84–89.

Katz, E., and Lazarsfeld, P.F. (1955) *Personal Influence: The Part Played By People in the Flow of Mass Communications.* Glencoe, IL: Free Press & Columbia University.

Kennedy, B.M., and Bell, D. (Eds.) (2007) *The Cybercultures Reader.* London: Routledge.

Kraidy, M. (2005) *Hybridity: The Cultural Logic of Globalization.* Philadelphia: Templeton University.

Labov, W. (1972) *Sociolinguistic Patterns.* Philadelphia: University of Pennsylvania Press.

Labov, W., and Fanshel, D. (1977) *Therapeutic Discourse: Psychotherapy as Conversation.* New York: Academic Press.

Laclau, N., and Mouffe, C. (2014) *Hegemony and Socialist Strategy* (2nd Ed.). London: Verso.

Lambert, J. (2013) *Digital Storytelling: Capturing Lives, Creating Community.* London: Routledge.

Landert, D. (2014) *Personalisation in Mass Media Communication: British Online News Between Public and Private.* Amsterdam; Philadelphia, PA: John Benjamins.

Leech, G. (1983) *Principles of Pragmatics.* London: Longman.

Levi-Strauss, C. (1963) *Structural Anthropology.* New York: Basic Books.

Levinas, E. (1987) *Time and the Other.* Duquesne University Press.

Levinson, S. (1983) *Pragmatics.* Cambridge: Cambridge University Press.

Lin, C., and Atkin, D. (Eds.) (2009) *Communication Technology and Social Change: Theory and Implications.* London: Routledge.

Lippmann, W. (2004/1922) *Public Opinion.* New York: Dover Publications.

Lister, M. et al. (2008) *New Media: A Critical Introduction* (2nd. Ed.). London: Routledge.

Lorenzo-Dus, N., and Blitvich, P. (2013) (Eds.) *Real Talk: Reality TV and Discourse Analysis in Action.* London: Palgrave Macmillan.

Lucy, J.A. (1992) *Language Diversity and Thought: A Reformulation of the Linguistic Relativity Hypothesis.* Cambridge: Cambridge University Press.

Lundby, K. (Ed.) (2008) *Digital Storytelling, Mediatized Stories: Self-Representations in New Media.* Digital Formations (52). New York: Peter Lang Publishing, Inc.

Lyons, J. (1981) *Language and Linguistics.* Cambridge: Cambridge University Press.

Lyotard, J.-F. (1984) *The Postmodern Condition: A Report on Knowledge.* Manchester: Manchester University Press.

Marriott, S. (1996) Time and time again: 'Live' television commentary and the construction of replay talk. *Media, Culture & Society* 18(1), 69.
Marriott, S. (2007) *Live Television: Time, Space and the Broadcast Event.* London: Sage.
Marshall, P.D. (2006) *The Celebrity Culture Reader.* London: Routledge.
McCombs, M. (2005) A look at agenda-setting: Past, present and future. *Journalism Studies* 6 (4), 543–557.
Mcleod, D. (2014) *News Frames and National Security.* Cambridge: CUP.
McLuhan, M. (1962) *The Gutenberg Galaxy: The Making of Typographic Man.* Toronto: University of Toronto Press.
McLuhan, M. (2001) *Understanding Media.* London: Routledge Classics.
McNair, B. (2009) (5th Ed.) *News and Journalism in the UK.* London: Routledge.
Mercer, J., and Shingler, M. (2004) *Melodrama: Genre, Style, Sensibility.* New York: Columbia University Press.
Miller, D. (Ed.) (2004) *Tell Me Lies: Propaganda and Media Distortion in the Attack on Iraq.* London: Pluto Press.
Miller, T., and Kraidy, M. (2016) *Global Media Studies.* Cambridge: Polity.
Mills, S. (2004) *Discourse.* London: Routledge.
Milroy, J., and Milroy, L. (2012) *Authority in Language.* London: Routledge Classics.
Mirzoeff, N. (Ed.) (2012) *The Visual Culture Reader.* London: Routledge.
Monaco, J. (2009) *How to Read a Film: Movies, Media and Beyond.* Oxford: OUP.
Montgomery, M. (1986) DJ Talk. *Media, Culture & Society* 8(4), 421–440.
Montgomery, M. (1999) Speaking sincerely: Public reactions to the death of Diana. *Language and Literature* 8(1), 5–33.
Montgomery, M. (2001) Defining authentic talk. *Discourse Studies* 3(4), 397–405.
Montgomery, M. (2006) Broadcast news, the live two-way and the case of Andrew Gilligan. *Media, Culture and Society* 28(2).
Montgomery, M. (2007) *The Discourse of Broadcast News: A Linguistic Approach.* London: Routledge.
Montgomery, M. (2008a) *An Introduction to Language and Society* (3rd Ed.). London: Routledge.
Montgomery, M. (2008b) The discourse of the broadcast news interview: A typology. *Journalism Studies* 9(2), 260–277.
Montgomery, M. (2017) Post-truth politics? Authenticity, populism and the electoral discourses of Donald Trump. *Journal of Language and Politics* 16(4), 619–639.
Montgomery, M., and Shen, J. (2017) Direct address and television newsreading: Discourse, technology and changing cultural form in Chinese and Western TV news. *Discourse, Context & Media* 17, 30–41.
Moores, S. (2007) *Media/Theory: Thinking About Media and Communications.* London: Routledge.
Morgan, M. (2014) *Speech Communities.* Cambridge: CUP.
Morley, D. (2004) Broadcasting and the construction of the national family. In R.C. Allen and A. Hill (eds.), *The Television Studies Reader.* London and New York: Routledge, pp. 418–441.
Morley, D. (1992) *Television Audiences and Cultural Studies.* London: Routledge.
Morris, M. (2007) *An Introduction to the Philosophy of Language.* Cambridge: CUP.

Mortensen, J., and Coupland, N. (Eds.) (2017) *Style, Mediation and Change.* Oxford: OUP.

Mulvey, L. (1990) Visual pleasure and narrative cinema. In P. Erens (ed.), *Issues in Feminist Film Criticism.* Bloomington: Indiana University Press, pp. 28–40.

Nichols, B. (2010) *Introduction to Documentary.* Indiana: Indiana University Press.

Norris, C. (2002) *Deconstruction: Theory and Practice* (3rd Ed.). London: Routledge.

Ong, W.J. (2012) *Orality and Literacy: The Technologizing of the Word* (2nd Ed.). London: Routledge.

Örnebring, H., and Jönsson, A.M. (2004) Tabloid journalism and the public sphere: A historical perspective on tabloid journalism. *Journalism Studies* 5(3).

Orr, M. (2003) *Intertextuality: Debates and Contexts.* Cambridge: Polity.

Page, R.E. (2013) *Stories and Social Media* London: Routledge.

Page, R.E. (2018) *Narratives Online: Shared Stories and Social Media Controversies.* Cambridge: CUP.

Pettey, G. et al (2018) *Communication Research Methodology: A Strategic Approach to Applied Research.* London: Routledge.

Piller, I. (2017) *Intercultural Communication: A Critical Introduction* (2nd Ed.). Edinburgh: EUP.

Pinker, S. (2015) *The Language Instinct.* London: Penguin.

Propp, V. (1971) *Morphology of the Folktale.* Austin: University of Texas Press.

Quaglio, P. (2009) *Television Dialogue: the sitcom Friends vs. natural conversation* Amsterdam: John Benjamins.

Radway, J. (1992) *Reading the Romance.* Chapel Hill: University North Carolina Press.

Rampton, B. (2017) *Crossing: Language and Ethnicity Among Adolescents.* London: Routledge Classics.

Rasmussen, T. (2014) *Personal Media and Everyday Life: A Networked Lifeworld.* London: Palgrave Macmillan.

Rheingold, H. (2000) *The Virtual Community: Homesteading on the Electronic Frontier.* Cambridge, MA: MIT Press.

Richardson, K. (2010) *Television Dramatic Dialogue: a sociolinguistic study* Oxford: OUP.

Rimmon-Kenan, S. (2002) *Narrative Fiction: Contemporary poetics* London: Routledge.

Rogers, H. (2004) *Writing Systems: A Linguistic Approach.* Oxford: Blackwell.

Roszak, T. (1969/1995) *The Making of a Counter Culture: Reflexions on the Technocratic Society and Its Youthful Opposition.* Berkeley: University of California Press.

Sacks, H. (1992) *Lectures on Conversation (Vol. 1).* Oxford: Blackwell.

Saeed, J.I. (2016) *Semantics* (4th Ed.). Oxford: Wiley Blackwell.

Sampson, A. (2005) *Who Runs This Place?: An Anatomy of Britain in the 21st Century.* London: John Murray.

Saville-Troike, M. (2008) *Ethnography of Communication: an Introduction.* Oxford: Wiley.

Scannell, P. (1989) Public service broadcasting and modern public life. *Media, Culture & Society* 11(2), 135–166.
Scannell, P. (1996) *Radio, Television, and Modern Life: A Phenomenological Approach.* Oxford: Blackwell.
Scannell, P. (1998) Media – language – world. In A. Bell and P. Garrett (eds.), *Approaches to Media Discourse.* Oxford: Blackwell.
Scannell, P. (2000) For-anyone-as-someone structures. *Media Culture and Society* 22(1), 5–24.
Scannell, P. (2007) *Media and Communication.* London: Sage.
Scannell, P. (2014) *Television and the Meaning of 'Live': An Inquiry into the Human Condition.* Cambridge: Polity.
Scannell, P., and Cardiff, D. (1991) *A Social History of British Broadcasting: Volume 1–1922–1939, Serving the Nation.* Oxford: Wiley-Blackwell.
Schegloff, E. (2007) *Sequence Organization in Interaction.* Cambridge: CUP.
Scholes, R. (2009) *Semiotics and Interpretation.* New Haven: Yale University Press.
Schudson, M. (1981) *Discovering the News: A Social History of American Newspapers.* New York: Basic Books.
Schudson, M. (2011) *The Sociology of News* (2nd Ed.). New York: W.W. Norton & Co.
Schulz, W. (2004) Reconstructing mediatization as an analytical concept. *European Journal of Communication* 19(1), 87–101.
Schutz, A. (with Thomas Luckmann) (1973) *The Structures of the Life World.* Evanston, IL: Northwestern University Press.
Silver, A. (Ed.) (2004) *Film Noir Reader.* Limelight Ed.
Silverstone, R. (1999) *Why Study the Media.* London: Sage.
Simon, J. (2014) *The New Censorship: Inside the Global Battle for Media Freedom.* New York: Columbia University Press.
Simpson, P. (2003) *On the Discourse of Satire: Towards a Stylistic Model of Satirical Humour.* Amsterdam: John Benjamins.
Sinclair, J. (1991) *Corpus, Concordance, Collocation.* Oxford: OUP.
Sinclair, J. (2004) *Trust the Text: Language, Corpus and Discourse.* London: Routledge.
Smith, A., and Higgins, M. (2013) *The Language of Journalism.* London: Bloomsbury.
Standop, E. (1988) Collins COBUILD English language dictionary. *System*, 16.
Stehr, N., and Meja, V. (2017) *Society and Knowledge: Contemporary Perspectives in the Sociology of Knowledge and Science.* London: Routledge.
Storey, J. (2015) *Cultural Theory and Popular Culture* (7th Ed.). London: Routledge.
Storr, W. (2017) *Selfie.* London: Picador.
Swift, J. (2015/1729) *A Modest Proposal for preventing the Children of Poor People From being a Burthen to Their Parents or Country, and For making them Beneficial to the Publick.* Harmondsworth: Penguin.
Tannen, D. (1992) *You Just Don't Understand: Women and Men in Conversation.* London: Virago Press.
Tannen, D. (2002) Agonism in the academy: Surviving higher learning's argument culture. *Journal of Pragmatics* 34(10), 1651–1669.

Thøgersen et al. (Eds.) (2016) *Style, Media and Language Ideologies*. Copenhagen: Novus Forlag.
Thompson, J.B. (1990) *Ideology and Modern Culture*. Cambridge: Polity.
Thornborrow, J. (2002) *Power Talk*. London: Routledge.
Thornborrow, J. (2015) *The Discourse of Public Participation Media*. London: Routledge.
Thornborrow, J.T., and Morris (2004) Gossip as strategy: The management of talk about others on reality TV show *Big Brother. Journal of Sociolinguistics* 8(2) (May 2004), 246–271.
Titunik, I.R. (1973) Formal method and the sociological method. In V. Volosinov (ed.), *Marxism and the Philosophy of Language*. London: Academic Press.
Toolan, M. (2001) *Narrative: A Critical Linguistic Introduction*. London: Routledge.
Tolson, A. (1991) Televised chat and the synthetic personality. In Scannell (ed.), *Broadcast Talk*. London: Sage, pp. 179–187.
Tolson, A. (Ed.) (2001a) *Television Talk Shows: Discourse, Performance, Spectacle*. London and Mahwah, NJ: Lawrence Erlbaum Associates.
Tolson, A. (2001b) 'Being yourself': The pursuit of authentic celebrity. *Discourse Studies* 3(4), 443–457.
Tolson, A. (2005) *Media Talk: Spoken Discourse on TV and Radio*. Edinburgh: EUP.
Trilling, L. (1973) *Sincerity and Authenticity*. Boston: Harvard University Press.
Tuchman, G. (1980) *Making News: A Study in the Construction of Reality*. Glencoe: The Free Press.
Turkle, S. (2011) *The Inner History of Devices*. Cambridge, MA: MIT Press.
Turkle, S. (2015) *Reclaiming Conversation: The Power of Talk in the Digital Age*. Harmondsworth: Penguin.
Van Dijk, T.A. (2008) *Discourse and Power*. London: Palgrave Macmillan.
Van Dijk, T.A. (1998) *Ideology: A Multidisciplinary Approach*. London: Sage.
Van Dijk, Jan A.G.M. (2012) (3rd Ed.) *The Network Society*. London: Sage.
Volosinov, V. (1973) *Marxism and the Philosophy of Language*. London and New York: Academic Press.
Wahl-Jorgensen, K. et.al. (2017) Rethinking balance and impartiality in journalism? How the BBC attempted and failed to change the paradigm. *Journalism* 18(7), 781–800.
Watt, I. (2015) *The Rise of the Novel* (2nd Ed.). London: Bodley Head.
Webster, F. (2014) *Theories of the Information Society* (4th Ed.). London: Routledge.
Wichmann, A. (2000) *Intonation in Text and Discourse*. London: Routledge.
Williams, K. (2010) *Read All About It: A History of the British Newspaper*. London: Routledge.
Williams, R. (1962/2016) *Communications*. London: Chatto and Windus.
Williams, R. (1963a) The idea of community. In R. Williams (ed.), *Culture and Society*, 314–318.
Williams, R. (1963b) *Culture and Society 1780–1950*. Harmondsworth: Penguin.
Williams, R. (1983) *Keywords: A Vocabulary of Culture and Society*. London/New York: Fontana.
Williams, R. (1986) *Culture*. London: Fontana.

Williams, R. (2003) *Marxism and Literature*. Oxford: OUP.
Wittgenstein, L. (1967) Philosophical investigations. *The Philosophical Quarterly*, 17.
Whorf, B.L. (1956) Science and Linguistics. In B.L. Whorf and J.B. Carroll (eds.), (1956), pp. 207–219.
Whorf, B.L., and Carroll, J.B. (Ed.) (1956) *Language, Thought and Reality: Selected Writings of Benjamin Lee Whorf*. Cambridge, MA: MIT Press.
Widdowson, H.G. (2004) *Text, Context, Pretext: Critical Issues in Discourse Analysis*. Oxford: Blackwell.
Williams, R. (1976) *Keywords*. London: Harper Collins.
Wodak, R. (2015) Critical Discourse Analysis, Discourse-Historical Approach. *The International Encyclopedia of Language and Social Interaction*. Oxford: Wiley Blackwell, pp. 1–14.
Wodak, R., and Meyer, M. (2009) *Methods of Critical Discourse Analysis*. London: Sage.
Yule, G. (2016) *The Study of Language* (6th Ed.). Cambridge: CUP.
Zappavigna, M. (2011) Ambient affiliation: A linguistic perspective on Twitter. *New Media & Society* 13(5).
Zappavigna, M. (2013) *Discourse of Twitter and Social Media: How We Use Language to Create Affiliation on the Web*. London: Bloomsbury.
Zelizer, B. (Ed.) (2009) *The Changing Faces of Journalism: Tabloidization, Technology and Truthiness*. London: Routledge.

INDEX

Note: main entries are designated by numbers given in **bold**.

Abercrombie, N. 40
accent **3**, 33
access **4**, 14, 27, 41, 49, 53, 62, 101, 138
accessed voices **4**
accountability/accountability interview **4**, 46
active audience **5**, 9, 30
actuality **5**, 88, 103
adaptation **5**
address **5**, 11, 61, 86, 93–4
addressee 67
addresser 67
adjacency pair **5**
advertising 24
aesthetics **5–6**
affiliation **6**
affordance/affordances **6–7**, 81, 106, 117, 120, 140
agenda setting **7**
agent **8**
Allan, S. 68, 85
Allen, R. 116
Althusser, L. 58, 64–65
ambient affiliation **8**, 117
ambient sound **8**
analogue signals 35
anchor **8**
Anderson, B. 20, 58
Anderson, D. 12
animator **8**, 92
anti-language **8**
antonymy 112
appraisal 75
Ardehali, P. 61
Arnold, M. 28

Article 19 **9**
asynchronous communication **9**, 102, 126
Atkin, D. 129
Atkinson, J.M. 137
audience(s) 5, 8, **9**, 10, 11, 12, 16, 25, 30, 31, 38, 34, 39, 42, 47, 51, 52, 71, 73–74, 78, 79, 86, 90, 92, 93, 98, 102, 116, 126
Austin, J.L. 120–121
Auteur Theory **10**
authentic, authenticity 8, **10–11**, 116
authentic talk 11
author 8, 11, 71, 92
autocue **11**, 25, 79, 86

back channel behaviour **11–12**
Bakhtin, M. 50
Bal, M. 48
Barthes, R. 67–68, 83, 84, 88, 131
Baumann, Z. 95
BBC 3, 59
beauty 5–6
Becker, H. 69
Bednarek, M. 88
Bell, A. 56
bell hooks 45
Belsey, C. 96
Benjamin, W. 101
Bergmann, J. 107
Berners-Lee, T. 139
Besnier, N. 54
Bettie, J. 69
bias **12**, 15, 59
Biber, D. 120, 139
Billiani, F. 14

binary oppositions 30, 96
Biressi, A. 104
Blitvich, P. 104
blogosphere 47
Bourdieu, P. 27, 55
Boxer, D. 45
bricolage **12**, 81, 93, 95
broadcasters 12, 29
broadcasting **12–13**, 14, 31, 36, 39, 46, 51, 72, 73, 75, 76, 85, 91, 116, 118, 119, 127, 134, 138
broadcasting and accents 33
broadcast media 6
broadcast news **12–13**
broadcast talk 11, 44, 117
broadsheet **13**, 126
Brown, Penelope 44
Brown, R. 61
Burke, E. 49
Butler, C. 79

Cailliau, R. 139
Calhoun, C. 101
Cameron, D. 69
Caple, H. 88
Cardiff, D. 13, 101
Carlyle, T. 49
Carter, R. 120
Castells, M. 85, 118
Caughie, J. 10
celebrity **14**, 91
censorship **14**, 15, 45
channel 67
Charteris-Black, J. 31
Chatman, S. 83
chat room **14**, 126
chat show **14**, 127
Cherry, C. 19, 104
Chomsky, N. 20–21, 69, 73, 98, 131
Chomskyan 54
Chovanec, J. 92
cinematic apparatus **15**
citizen journalism **15**
Clayman, S. 4, 85
Clift, R. 134–135
closed text **15**
closure **15**
Coates, J. 50
Cobley, P. 115

code(s) **16**, 22, 29, 42, 67, 68, 84, 88, 92, 106, 124, 136
Cohen, S. 81
coherence **16**, 37
cohesion **16–17**
Cohn, N. 122
cold media **17–18**
collocation 17, **18**, 113
colloquial 69
commissioning editor **18**
communication **18–19**, 64, 67, 71–72, 76, 79, 91–92, 94, 95, 97–99, 101, 102, 104, 107, 109, 119, 121, 126, 130, 134, 136, 139
communication science **19**, 67
communicative ethos **19**, 47, 91, 116, 134
communicative functions **18**
community 19, **20**, 48, 50, 54, 58, 65, 74, 118, 121
competence **20–21**
conative 67
Conboy, M. 13, 49, 88, 126
concordance **21**
congruence theory **22**
consensus 22, 72–**73**, 99–100, 136
consent **22**
content analysis **22**
context of culture 23, 75
context (of situation) 16, **22–23**, 30, 38, 75, 96, 104–105, 114
continuity (editing) **23**, 86, 103, 126
control **23–24**, 26, 40, 96, 100, 101, 104, 130
conversation 5, 9, 23, **24**, 36, 59, 60, 65, 102, 105, 117, 126, 134
conversationalisation **25**
conversational styles **24**, 103
conversation analysis (CA) 21, **24**, 56, 121
cooperative principle 60
copy editor **25**
copyright 63
copywriter **25**
Cornbleet, S. 120
corpus linguistics 21, **25**, 54, 110
Couldry, N. 36, 76, 78
counter culture **25**
creative/creativity **26**, 57, 63
creative and cultural industries **25–26**

Crissell, A. 13
Critcher, C. 48
critical discourse analysis (CDA) **26**
crossing **27**
Culler, J. 32, 70, 92
cultivation theory **27**
cultural capital 13, **27**, 95
cultural code 84
cultural imperialism **28**
cultural industries **28**, 31
culture(s) **28**, 35, 48, 56–57, 64, 66, 72, 89, 91, 94–95, 124, 138, 139
current affairs 4, 6, 15, 59, 66, 91, 127, 138
cyberculture **28–29**
cyberspace 14, **29**

data mining **29**
Davidson, R.J. 43
Dayan, D. 76
dead air **29**
decode **29**
decoding **29–30**, 42
deconstruction **30**
defamation **30**
deictic(s) 96, 105
deixis **30–31**, 97
De Lauretis 15
demographics **31**
Derrida, J. 96
deviance/deviant/deviancy **31**, 48, 68, 81
diachronic **31–32**, 96
dialect 8–9, **32–33**, 50, 123
dialogue/dialogic **34**, 34, 66, 82, 108, 124
diegesis **34**
diegetic sound **34**
diffusion **35**, 107
digital/digitalisation/digitisation 13, **35**, 44–45, 85, 100, 140
digital divide **35**
digital media **35–36**, 15, 119, 129
digital platform 13, **36**, 117
digital storytelling **36**
digital technologies 46
diglossia **36–37**
discourse 16, 25, **37–38**, 50, 51, 61, 72, 76, 79, 85, 93, 101, 114, 120, 126

discourse act 16, **38**, 75, 80, 134–136
discourse analysis 26, 121
discourse historical approach 26, 38
discursive amplification **39**
discursive gap **38–40**
discursive practice 73, 79
disinformation **40**
documentary 5, **40**, 103, 138
dominant ideology 15, **40**
domination **40**, 56
doxing **40**
Drew, P. 127
dumbing down **40–41**
Durkheim, E. 68
Dutton, W. 46
Dynel, M. 11, 92

Eagleton, T. 28, 40, 57, 58
Eco, U. 6, 15, 88
editorial(s) 36, **41**, 74, 88
Eggins, S. 16
Ekman, P. 43
electronic commons **41**
electronic democracy **41**
electronic publishing **41**
Elias, N. 55, 61–62
Elsaesser, T. 47
emergent culture **41–42**
emotive 67
encoding **42**, 119
entailment 113, 114
establishment **42–43**
ethnography (of communication) **43**, 121
ethnomethodology 24

Fabian, J. 90
face **44**
face-threatening act (FTA) **44**
face-to-face communication 9, **44–45**, 54, 105, 137
facework **44**
Facial Action Coding System (FACS) **43**
Facial Affect Scoring Technique (FAST) **43–44**
fact-checking 85
Fairclough, N. 24, 25, 26, 62, 73, 126
fake news **45**
Fanshel, D. 16

FAST **44**
feedback 11
feminism **45**, 82
field (register) 105
Fifth Estate **45–46**
film 5, 23, 55
film criticism 10
film language **46**, 92
film noir **46–47**
film theory 15, 34, 94
Firth, J.R. 18, 23, 43
Fischer, O. 57
Fish, S. 65
fisking **47**, 117
Fitzgerald, R. 79
flaming **47**, 117
flashback **47–48**, 83
Flew, T. 85
focalisation **48**
folk culture **48**, 57
folk devils **48**
footing **48**, 92
formality 61–62
Foucault, M. 38, 96
Fourth Estate 4, 45–46, **49**
frame/framing **49**, 76, 87, 92
freedom of information **49–50**
Freedom of Information Act **49**
free press **49**
Friedrich, P. 61
Friesen, W.V. 43
Fuchs, C. 118

Galtung, J. and Ruge, M.H. 87
Gans, H.J. 57
gatekeeper **50**
Gee, J.P. 38
Geertz, C.J. 28
genderlects **50**
Genette, G. 48
genre 4, 14, 17, 24, 25, 40, 41, **50–51**, 53, 57, 66, 73, 78, 88, 91, 95, 105, 107, 124, 127
geodemographics **51–52**
Gerbner, G. 27
gesture 52, 90, 119
ghost writer **52**
Gibson, J.J. 7
Gibson, W. 29
Giddens, A. 130

Gilman, A. 61
Gitlin, T. 49
glasnost **52**
globalisation **53**
global media **52**
global village **52–53**
Glynn, C.J. 100
Goffman, E. 43, 44, 49, 92, 110
gossip 50, **53–54**, **107**
grammar 16, 21, 37, 46, **54–55**, 71, 104, 121, 123, 131
grammatical 20
Gramsci, A. 22, 56
Gray, J. 91, 108
Grice, H.P. 59, 61
Grierson, J. 40
group(s) 4, 12, 16, 20, 22, 40, 42, 48, **55**, 56, 58, 61, 63, 64, 65, 76, 78, 81, 82, 89, 94, 97, 118, 123, 130

Habermas, J. 70, 101, 116, 135–136
habitus **55**
Hafez, K. 53
Hager, J.C. 43
Hall, S. 29–30, 42, 98
Halliday, M.A.K. 22–23, 69, 75, 120, 131, 133, 139, 140
Hallin, D.C. 122, 123
hard news **55**
harijans **56**
Harris, R. 70, 92, 124
Hartley, J. 26
Hartley, P. 65
Harvey, D. 95, 130
Hawkes, T. 70, 92, 124
Hayes, A.F. 19
headlines 78
Heath, S. 15
Hegemony 22, **56–58**
Heritage, J. 4, 85
Herman, E. 73, 98
hermeneutic code 84
hermeneutics **56**
Hesmondhalgh, D. 26
Higgins, M. 47
high culture 28, **56–57**, 95
Hine, C. 64
Hollywood (cinema) 5, 23, 46, 78
Horton, D. 90
hot media 17–18, **57**

Housley, W. 79
Hutchby, I. 5, 6, 7, 24, 127, 135
Hutcheon, L. 5
hybridity **57**, 103
hyponomy 112

iconic **57**
identification (process) **57**, 58, 87
identity **57**
ideological state apparatus (ISA) **58**, 64
ideology 19, **58**, 65
Iedema, R. 106
imagined community 20, **58**, 118
immediacy **58–59**, 72, 135
impartiality 12, **59**, 99, 122
implicature 16, 37, **59–61**, 97
improvisation **61**
indexical 96
individualisation **61**
influence 38, 42, 46, 49, **61**, 101
informalisation **61–62**
information commons **62**
information and communications technology (ICT) 35, **62**, 139
information rich **62**
information society **62**
information technology **62**
infotainment 41, **62**
inoculation effect **62–63**
instant messaging 9, **63**, 64, 84, 94, 126
institutional voice 86
integration **63**
intellectual property 26, **63**, 101, 107
interaction (social) 38, 44, 47, 48, **63**, 65, 82, 90–91, 99, 102, 110, 117, 120, 127
interactive media **63**
interactivity 85
intercultural communication **64**
internet 14, 28, 41, 45, 46, 53, 62, **64**, 76, 77, 84, 85, 107, 129, 133, 134, 137, 138–140
interpellation **64–65**
interpersonal communication 19, **65**
interpretation 115
interpretive community 20, **65**
intersubjectivity **66**
intertextuality **66**
interview 12, 51, **66**, 105, 118, 127
interviewee 12

interviewer 12
intonation **66–67**, 104
intrapersonal communication **67**
irony 66, **67**, 95, 107

Jakobson, R. 19, 67
Jakobson's model of communication **67**
Jameson, F. 95
Jones, R.H. 35–36
jouissance **67–68**
journalese **68**
journalism 15, 47, 51, **68**, 85, 88, 101, 119, 122
journalists 85
Juris, J.S. 6, 7

Katz, E. 19, 61, 75, 76, 94
kernel (of narrative) **68**
knowledge society **68**
Kraidy, M. 52–53, 57
Kristeva, J. 66

labeling process 31, **68–69**
Labov, W. 16, 37
Lacan, J. 67, 90
Laclau, E. 38, 56
Lambert, J. 36
Landert, D. 94
language **69–70**
language variety 50
langue **69–70**, 91–92, 124
Lazarsfeld, P. 19, 61, 94
leak **70**
Leech, G.N. 98
legitimation 19, **70**
Levinas, E. 90
Levinson, S.C. 16, 31, 44, 98
Levi-Strauss, C. 83, 131
lexis/lexical 16, 17, 61
libel 30, **70**
Lin, C. 129
linguistic determinism **70**
linguistic relativity **70–71**
linguistic variation/varieties 33, 36, 54, 68
Lippman, W. 73
Lister, M. 85
literary agent **71**
live/liveness **71–72**, 74, 75, 116, 135, 138
localisation **72**
Lorenzo-Dus, N. 104

INDEX

Lucy, J. 70, 71
Lyons, J. 114
Lyotard, J.-F. 95

magazine 54, **72**, 74, 102, 105, 107
mainstream media 15, 46, **72–73**
Malinowski, B. 23, 43
manner (maxim of) 60
manufacture of consent **73**
marketing 24, 31, **73**, 118, 137
marketisation of discourse **73**
market research **73**
Marriott, S. 7, 72
Martin, J. 139
Marx, K. 56, 129
mass audience 40, **73–74**, 75, 126
mass communication 4, 19, **74**, 76, 108, 126, 139
mass media 19, **74**
mass production **74**
maxims 60
McGuire, W.J. 62
Mcleod, D. 49
McLuhan, M. 17–18, 52–53, 74, 76, 128, 129
McLuhanism **74**
McNair, B. 12
Mead, G.H. 89
meaning(s) 5, 30–31, 59, 65, 66, 68, **75**, 77, 96, 106, 110, 111–114
meaning potential **75**
media of communication **76**, 77, 140
media events **75–76**
mediasphere **76**
mediated communication 22, 44, 72, 73, **76–77**, 115
mediate/mediated 71, **76–77**, 112, 115, 121
mediation 10, **76–77**
mediatisation 10, **77–78**
medium 17–18, 22
Medvedev, P.N. 50
Meja, V. 68
melodrama **78**
membership categorisation device **78–79**
Mercer, J. 78
message(s) 5, 8, 12, 29, 35, 63, 65, 67, 76, 77, **79**, 81, 85, 94, 98, 104, 106, 115, 119, 126

messaging 7
meta-communication **79**
metadiscourse **79**
metalingual (function) 67
Metz, C. 46
Meyer, M. 26
micro-blogging 8
Miller, T. 52
Mills, S. 38
Milroy, J. 123
Milroy, L. 123
Mirzoeff, N. 138
modality 130
mode (register) 105
modernism **79**, 93, 95
modes of address 11, 25, 73, **79–80**
Monaco, J. 46, 126
montage **80–81**
Montgomery, M. 4, 11, 23, 66, 86, 116, 135, 137
moral panic **81**
Morgan, M. 122
Morley, D. 98
Morris, M. 121
Mouffe, C. 38, 56
multi-accentuality **81–82**
multi-modality 82
Mulvey, L. 108
myth **82–83**, 95, 124, 131

Nanny, M. 57
narration 34, **83**, 84, 103
narrative 23, 34, 47, 48, 57, 79, 80, 83, **83**, 95, 102, 103, 107
narrative codes **84**
narrative kernel **84**
narrative satellite **84**
narrator 34, 83, 94
native speaker 20–21
negotiated reading 42, **84**
Nelson, M. 57
neo-Firthian 54
netizen (digital native) **84**
network 27, 29, 42, 64, **84**, 139
network society **84–85**, 139
neutralism **85**
new media 13, 35, 73, **85**, 117
news 6, 7, 11–12, 15, 22, 45, 49–51, 55, 72, 74, 79, 84, **85**, 91, 93, 98, 108, 123, 126, 138

news anchor **85–86**, 135
newscaster/newsreader 11, 38, **86**, 86
news interview 85
newspaper(s) 12, 13, 14, 41, 52–54, 59, 62, 74, 81, **88**, 88, 99, 101, 108, 118, 126
news presentation 11, **86**
news value(s) 13, 39, 85, **86–88**, 126; compositional fit 87; conflict 87; intensity/discontinuity 86–87; meaningfulness/unambiguity 87; negativity 87; personalization 87; power 87; proximity/cultural relevance 87; scale/scope 87; unexpectedness 87
Nichols, B. 40
Nietzsche, F. 56
Nordic Noir 47
Norris, C. 30
Nunn, H. 104

objective/objectivity 59, 66, 71, **88**, 122
Ong, W. J. 20, 89
online community 20, 84
op-ed 41, **88**
open text **88–89**
opinion poll **89**, 99–100
oppositional reading 42, **89**
oral culture(s) 20, 83, **89**
orality **89**
Orr, M. 66
other/othering **89–90**
over-lexicalisation 9

Page, R. 36
paralinguistic(s) 79
para-social interaction **90–91**, 115
parody 66, **91**, 93, 107
parole **91–92**, 124
participation framework **92**
pastiche **92–93**, 95
perestroika 52
performance 21
persistence of vision **93**
persona **93**
personal influence **94**
personalisation 10, 13, 78, **93–94**, 126
personality 57, 76, 90, **93**
personal media 13, 85, **94**, 117

personal space **94**
persuasion 62, 94, 107
Pettey, G. 22
phatic (function) 67
philosophy 5
phonology 37, 66
Piatetsky-Shapiro, G. 29
Pichler, P. 50
Pierce, C.S. 114
Piller, I. 64, 131
Pinker, S. 21
platform 41, 63, **94**
pleasure 67–68
poetic 67
point of view 83, **94**
politeness 44
popular culture 13–14, 22, 28, 56, 57, 83, **94–95**, 124, 126
postmodernism 93, **95**
post-structuralism 71, **94–96**
power 27, 42, 52, 56, 61, 64, 82, **96**, 101
pragmatics 16, 44, 61, **96–98**, 114
preferred reading 42, **98**, 114
press officer **98**, 123
presupposition 16, 113
primary orality **98**
principal 92
proairetic code 84
projection 93, **98**
pronoun(s) 17, 96
pronunciation 32–33, 37
propaganda 24, 73, 94, **98**, 100, 123, 134
Propp, V. 131
protocols of use **98–99**
proxemics **99**
public opinion 7, 19, 73, **99–100**, 101, 122, 123
public relations (PR) 24, 76, 94, **100**, 110, 123
public service broadcasting **100–101**
public sphere 4, 10–11, 39–40, 39, 45, 76, **101**, 116, 126
publishing industry 18, **101–102**

Quaglio, P. 34
quality 60
quantity 60
questionnaire **102**

Rampton, B. 27
rapport-talk **102**, 105, 106
readership 13, 38, **102**, 116, 126
reading public **102**
reality television 40, 54, 57, **102–103**, 117
real-time communication 9, 44, 91, **102**, 130
reciprocity of perspectives 44, 66, **104**
redundancy 102, **104**, 115
reference 16, 17, 111
referential (function) 67
reflexivity **104**
regional variation in pronunciation 3
register 75, 91, 92, **104–105**
reinforcement **105**
relevance 60
re-lexicalisation 9
reported speech 66
report-talk **105–106**
representation 15, 16, 19, 38, 42, **106**, 111, 123
resemiotisation **106**
residual culture 42, **106**
resistive reading **106**
response token **107**
rhetoric **107**
Richardson, K. 34
Ricouer, P. 56
Rimmon-Kenan, S. 34
Rogers, H. 140
Roszak, T. 25
royalties **107**
RP (accent) 3
rumour **107**

Sacks, H. 24
Saeed, J.L. 114
salience 87, **107**
salutation display **107**
Sampson, A. 43
Sapir, E. 71
sarcasm 67
satellite (of narrative) **107**
satire 91, **107–108**
Saussure, Ferdinand de 32, 46, 69, 70, 91, 92, 115, 124
Scandi Noir 46
Scannell, P. 11, 13, 19, 20, 56, 59, 72, 76, 101, 116, 127

Schegloff, E. 24
Scholes, R. 94
Schudson, M. 88
Schulz, W. 78
scopophilia **108**
script 61, 103, 106, **108**
secondary orality 89, **108**
self-concept **108–109**
self-disclosure **109**
self-identity 68, **109**
selfie **109**
self-image **109**
self-monitoring **109–110**
self-presentation 109, **110**
semantic prosody **110–111**
semantics 54, **111–114**
semic code 84
semiosis **114–115**
semiotics 57
sense 111
sense relations 112, 113
sentence 113, 114
sexism **115**
Shannon and Weaver's model of communication **115**
Sharrock, W. 12
Shen Jin 86
Shingler, M. 78
sign(s) 57, 69, 70, 81, 106, **115**
signification 19, 92, **115**
signifying practice **115**
silence **115**, 135
Silver, A. 47
Silverstone, R. 77, 78
Simon, J. 14
Simpson, P. 108, 137
sincerity 10, **115–116**, 135
Sinclair, J. 18, 21, 25, 111
Slade, D. 16
slander 30, **116**
Smith, A. 47
soap opera 36, 54, **116**
sociability 91, **116–117**, 117
social control 23
socialisation 23, 89, **118**
social media 13, 20, 29, 31, 36, 45, 63, 74, 76, 84, 109, 116, **117–118**, 129, 137
social network **118**, 137
social relationship 22, 25

social role 27
soft news 55, **119**
sound 8
sound bite **118–119**
source **119**
speaker 20–21, 134
speaking 69, 91, 92
speech 7, 25, 61, 91, 96, 97, 102, 108, 118, **119–120**, 122, 130, 136, 136, 139, 140
speech (/language) community 36, 50, 105, **121**, 123, 136
speech act 19, 97, 116, **120–121**
speech balloon **122**
sphere of consensus **122–123**
spin **123**
spin-doctor **123**
standard dialect 33
standard language **69**, **123**
Stehr, N. 68
stereotype/stereotypical 78–79
Storr, W. 109
strategic silence **123**
striptitle **123–124**
structuralism 71, 96, **124**
structures of feeling **124–125**
studio audience 127
style 8, 12, 17, 24, 25, 50, 68, 79, 91, 92, 93, 95, **125**, 126, 141
sub-culture **125**
subjectivity/subjective 65, 66, 71, 124, **125**
subliminal **125–126**
substitution 17
suture **126**
symbolic code 84
synchronous 14
synchronous communication **126**
synonymy 112
syntax 16, 37
synthetic personalisation **126**
systemic functional linguistics 131

tabloid 13, 38, **126**
tabloidisation 41, **126–127**
talk 14, 24, 105, **127**
talk-in-interaction 5, 11–12, 102, **127**, 134
talk show 14, 117, **127**
Tannen, D. 20, 105–106

taste 6, 27, 55, **128**
technological determinism 129
technologies of communication 6–7, 9, 98
technology/technologies 35, 98, **128**
teleprompter 11
telex **129**
tenor (register) 105
tense 71
terrestrial broadcasting 20, 100
text 5, 15, 16, 17, 30, 36, 56, 63, 65, 66, 68, 79, 84, 88, 89, 91, 97, 102, 104, 105, 106, 114, 124, **129–130**, 133, 138
texting 7
Thompson, J.B. 40, 58
Thornborrow, J.T. 6, 24, 54, 96
thought balloon 122, **130**
time-space compression/distantiation 7, **130**
Titunik, I.R. 50
Tolson, A. 14, 93, 127
Toolan, M. 83
transculturation **131**
transformation **131**
transgression **131**
transitivity **131–133**
translation 71
Trilling, L. 116
troll, to troll, trolling 47, 117, **133–134**
true 10
Trump 45
truth 10, 40, 66, 82, 88, 95, 116, 121, **134**, 135
truthful 10
truthiness **134**
Tuchman, G. 88
Tunick, S. 57
Turkle, S. 129
turn 12, 24, **134**
Turner, B.S. 40
turn-taking 24, **134–135**
two step flow 19, 61
two-way **135**

universality 98, **135**
user-generated content 50

validity claims 10–11, 116, **135–137**
Van Dijk, Jan A. 85, 118

Van Dijk, T. 40, 96
verbal devices **137**
viral **137**
virtual community 20, 118, **137**
virtual reality 63, **137–138**
virus **138**
visual culture **138**
vocabulary 105
voice 36, 65
voice (active/passive) 61, 120, 139
voice-over 34, 103, **138**
Voloshinov, V.N. 82
vox pop 93, **138**

Webster, F. 62
white space **138**
Whorf, B.L. 71
Widdowson, H.G. 16
Wikipedia **138–139**
Williams, K. 13, 88

Williams, R. 19, 20, 28, 41–42, 77, 78, 106, 125
wired society **139**
wired world **139**
Wodak, R. 26
Wohl, R. 90–91
Woofit, R. 5, 24, 135
World Wide Web 35, 36, 53, 64, 85, 137, **139**
writing 7, 25, 41, 61, 68, 77, 81, 88, 89, 96, 98, 119, 129, 130, **139–140**
written communication 33

youth culture **140–141**
Yule, G. 55

Zappavigna, M. 8
Zelizer, B. 127, 134
zoetrope **141**

For Product Safety Concerns and Information please contact our EU representative GPSR@taylorandfrancis.com
Taylor & Francis Verlag GmbH, Kaufingerstraße 24, 80331 München, Germany

www.ingramcontent.com/pod-product-compliance
Lightning Source LLC
Chambersburg PA
CBHW070616300426
44113CB00010B/1548